THE PAGAN
BACKGROUND OF EARLY
CHRISTIANITY

THE PAGAN
BACKGROUND OF EARLY
CHRISTIANITY

BY

W. R. HALLIDAY, B.A., B.Litt.,

Rathbone Professor of Ancient History
in the University of Liverpool

πάντες δὲ θεῶν χατέουσ' ἄνθρωποι

COOPER SQUARE PUBLISHERS, INC.
NEW YORK
1970

Originally Published 1925
Published by Cooper Square Publishers, Inc.
59 Fourth Avenue, New York, N. Y. 10003
Standard Book No. 8154-0331-3
Library of Congress Catalog Card No. 70-118640

Printed in the United States of America

TO
RICHARD CATON

TABLE OF CONTENTS

PREFACE

"But although, gentle reader, I might well defend the
edition of it with good reasons and many, yet had I
rather excuse it. By this means I hope I shall best
satisfie all, and least offend those whom I most desire
to please, those, I meane, whose judgments are soundest,
and farthest from corruption. Fare well: and God
grant that my labour be profitable to all."

Thomas Underdowne, Preface to
An Aethiopian Historie of Heliodorus.

THE lectures here printed were originally
composed for an audience of a particular kind,
and were delivered on behalf of the Liverpool
Board of Biblical Studies. The task was
somewhat reluctantly undertaken, and it has,
in fact, involved the postponement of other
work at which I was eager to make progress.
But I have learned much by doing it, which,
I hope, may be a good augury of usefulness to
others.

To my taskmaster-in-chief, Dr. Richard Caton,
C.B.E., M.D., F.R.C.P., LL.D., I have ventured
to dedicate the result. In science, in letters
and in civic life he has attained an equal
eminence. One of the founders and first teachers
in our University, and still active as its Pro-
Chancellor, physician, classical scholar and
humanist, formerly Lord Mayor of Liverpool,
he has indeed an enviable tale of distinctions.

But it is not to these dignities so richly deserved but so lightly worn, to which I would like to pay my inadequate tribute, but rather to that good traveller, best of Grecians, kindest of friends and most genial of hosts, " the Doctor."

Since they were delivered, the lectures have been considerably modified in substance and in arrangement, though from motives of personal convenience, I have retained the lecture form. What I have tried to do, is to give a picture, necessarily impressionistic, of the general character of pagan society and pagan thought during the early centuries of the Christian era. Had my choice been entirely free, I should probably have devoted the whole series to the topics of the last six lectures, in which my personal interest is keenest and the subject of which it is particularly difficult to handle clearly and concisely, partly because of the character of the data upon which the conclusions of scholars are based, partly because it is obviously not easy to describe in a lucid and yet not misleading form, matter which is itself essentially incoherent. But though the earlier lectures are somewhat more elementary, they appeared to the lecturer to serve a useful purpose in practice, and I have, consequently, allowed them to stand in print.

The audience, which I have had in mind, has been, primarily, the educated clerical or general reader, probably better informed than I about the history of early Christianity, but perhaps not very well posted either in the secular, social and political history of the first two centuries, or in the contemporary movements of pagan

philosophical and religious thought. It was to
this possible gap, as it seemed to me, that
attention might most profitably be directed.

It will, of course, be quite clear that paganism,
not Christianity, is my theme. Except at the
end of the course, where honesty seemed to make
it a duty " to follow where the argument led,"
I have carefully avoided touching upon any topic
which can in any sense be called theological.
For obvious reasons I have attempted to give
value to the best elements in pagan life, that is
to say, to represent paganism at its best, not
paganism at its worst; but I have not otherwise
consciously loaded the dice. ἱκανὰ γὰρ τὰ κατ'
ἄγνοιαν γιγνόμενα τοῖς γράφουσιν, ἃ διαφυγεῖν ἄνθρωπον
δυσχερές· ἐὰν δὲ κατὰ προαίρεσιν ψευδογραφῶμεν ἢ πατρίδος
ἕνεκεν ἢ φίλων ἢ χάριτος, τί διοίσομεν τῶν ἀπὸ τούτου τὸν
βίον ποριζομένων ;

We should probably all agree that a book of
this kind, if undocumented, is an unmitigated
nuisance. A particular example of a valuable
work, the usefulness of which has been diminished
by more than half through lack of documentation,
will indeed at once suggest itself to any student
of this period. But the extent and character of
documentation to be adopted is not as easy to
decide as it might appear. My references are
not, and do not pretend to be, exhaustive. In
many cases indeed I could have referred the reader
more shortly to Dill or Friedländer for a fuller
list of passages. But such a course would have
made certain, what a writer has always reason to
fear, that the references would not, in fact, be
referred to. Now I am quite sure that the

proper first approach to the understanding of a period is the reading, not of books about it, but of the books it produced. For those whose Latin or Greek has become rusty, there are translations of most of the Latin and Greek authors of which I have made any considerable use. I have placed at the end of the book a list of some of them, and these I have used largely in the course of the lectures, though I have sometimes modified the renderings in small points. For Seneca's thought I have usually, though not quite invariably, turned to the *Letters* for illustration rather than to his other works. Only one more volume has yet to appear in the Loeb series, and perhaps even some reader whose Latin has suffered from disuse, may be induced by the indication of their contents as revealed in my notes, to study them again as a whole. For, in general, in spite of the obvious and specious arguments for casting a broad net, I am myself convinced that there is more to be learned from reading a considerable portion of a single author than from " source-books " or anthologies of snippets.

In the text the reader who knows no Latin or Greek will not find any serious obstacle. In the notes I have allowed myself some use of the original tongues and some references which may be of use to those who are a little more professionally interested than the general reader. For the latter I have appended at the end a list of books, which is not in any strict sense a bibliography but rather a series of suggestions as to where particular topics are best to be followed up in greater detail. It enables me also to mention works like that of Wendland, to which my debt is by no means adequately indicated in the notes. From books like this one learns so much, that even to attempt to trace the account in detail would be almost a matter of research.

Some mistakes have been corrected by the kindness of my friends, Mr. Cyril Bailey, Professor Ormerod and Professor Buckland; others, no doubt, remain. It is inevitable, too, that half-shades and the subtle nuances which the whole truth would exhibit, have sometimes been sacrificed to the necessities of lucidity and brevity. I may hope, perhaps, that the kind critic who, quite reasonably, considered to be unfair the brief reference to Stoicism, which alone I could allow myself in my *Lectures on Roman Religion*, will feel that I have now made some amends to that great system of noble thought.

The inevitably dreary task of preparing the lectures for the printer has been lightened by fortunate circumstance. The Widener Library of Harvard University can hardly have a rival, in the Old World or the New, as a model of convenient organisation; it is the perfect library in which to work. Nor can a visiting professor to Harvard easily forget the unwearied kindness, warm friendliness, and amazing hospitality of New England and her men of learning.

I am writing in the Schofield Memorial Rooms, the " College Rooms," as we should call them, of a lover of letters and a friend of many countries, which upon his death were endowed by him for the hospitable uses of his great University. Only those other visitors from foreign lands who have similarly been privileged to live for a space with his books and furniture, and under the shadow of his gracious personality, will fully appreciate the supreme fitness of a commemoration so evidently characteristic of the man.

W. R. HALLIDAY.

19, GRAYS HALL, CAMBRIDGE, MASS.
March 14th, 1925.

LECTURE I

" Christians are not distinct from the rest of mankind in land or language or customs. For they nowhere inhabit cities of their own, nor do they use any different form of speech, nor do they practise any peculiar mode of living. . . . They inhabit cities, Greek or Barbarian, wherever the lot of each has cast him, and they follow local custom in their clothes, food, and general way of living."

Anonymus *ad Diognetum*, 5 (Migne, *Patr. Graec.*, ii, p. 1174).

·There are two perfectly legitimate ways of approaching the topic of early Christianity in its relation to the later Paganism. One is to contrast Christianity with the civilisation which was contemporary with it, and to emphasise the points of difference. For this, the more usual approach, there is indeed ample justification. It is perfectly true that Christianity was revolutionary in character. It was intransigent and uncompromising in its hostility both towards the external foe and also towards the more insidious but not less dangerous enemy within. For despite the spiritual cost, its characteristically determined definition of orthodoxy and stern repression of internal schism was a practical necessity, the adequate recognition of which alone enabled it to win a struggle which it perceived to be for life or death. There was, indeed, a conflict of religions, in which Christianity, consistently refusing to give quarter, was finally victorious, and a struggle between the Church and the secular power, in which the State was forced eventually to make terms.

All this is true enough, but there is also another angle from which the matter may be viewed. Christianity came into being within the Roman Empire and formed a constituent element in the life of a great civilisation which it gradually permeated. Though the early Christian might be at war with society, he was yet inevitably a part of it. It is, therefore, equally permissible to regard early Christianity against the background of its temporal and spatial setting, emphasising, not the points of difference and conflict, but the no less essential bonds which linked it with the life and thought of contemporary paganism. From this angle of vision, something also is perhaps to be learned.

Any religion can only find its outward and temporal expression in the thoughts and actions of the individuals who profess it, and these, in turn, are necessarily conditioned by the social environment into which they are born. However absolute the truth of Christianity may be in itself, the expression of it at any given time must surely, in the nature of things, be but relative and partial. It must continually be undergoing reinterpretation at the hands of its human adherents. No single interpretation doubtless can be the whole truth, for each, in turn, is equally conditioned by human imperfection, nor can even the mystic convey to others the temporary experience of the Absolute, unconditioned by Time and Space, which he may sometimes claim to have enjoyed.

If that is true, it is obviously impossible to understand the Christian thought of any particular period without reference to the intellectual and social environment of the thinkers. For from that bondage not the greatest of human kind can escape. Not one of us can think away, I doubt indeed if he can justly analyse, the various influences of his education, his social surroundings, the thoughts, the amusements or the scientific opinions of the society to which he belongs. St. Basil, apart from Christianity, has more in common with Julian the Apostate than with any Christian of to-day, from whom he is widely separated by the mental outlook of a different and distant century. Without a considerable imaginative effort and without some understanding of their common ground we shall not fairly appreciate either of these great antagonists, nor even perhaps understand why their opposition was fatally irreconcilable. I would even go so far as to believe that no one who is devoid of any sympathetic understanding of pagan thought and literature, can have anything of essential value to tell us about the contemporary Christians.[1]

Further, it must surely be true that any particular human interpretation of religious truth, if it is to serve its end, must provide for the

---

1. A recent example of a book, which for this reason appears to me quite worthless, is Professor Sihler's, *From Augustus to Augustine.*

spiritual needs of which its peculiar generation is sensible. This necessarily holds good of all religions, true or false. As any student of comparative religions will know, a religious system which cannot adapt itself so as to meet the needs of a society which undergoes radical secular change, is doomed to extinction, even though it may for a time continue to drag out a formal but lifeless existence. Of this, the old Roman state religion provides a good example.

Now, to touch the spiritual needs of its day, a religion or a preacher must necessarily employ a language, vocabulary and imagery which the hearers can understand. Thus, as Reitzenstein has emphasised, St. Paul frequently employs for his purposes the imagery and technical vocabulary of the Hellenistic mystery religions. That he should do so is, if you think of it thus, not merely natural but almost inevitable. A little further reflection may suggest that here is the true explanation of the phenomenon of the " borrowing " of ideas and rites, which has inspired an often irrelevant polemic both in ancient and in modern times.

The coincidences between Seneca and St. Paul appeared so remarkable that as early as the fourth century after Christ—for it is mentioned by Jerome and Augustine—that very jejune forgery, the *Correspondence* between the Pagan and the Christian thinkers, came into circulation.[1] Actually it would be more remarkable if there

---

1. See James, *Apochryphal New Testament*, pp. 480 foll.

were no coincidences in thought and its expression between the works of two serious-minded contemporaries who belonged to the same civilised society and had passed through an intellectual training of the same general character. But the matter goes further than language and thought, for rites are but " outward and visible signs " or modes of expression, the choice of which is relatively limited. It would be strange indeed if contemporaries had not shared similar symbols for expressing similar aspirations or ideas which were in part the common property of their time.

It is, indeed, undeniably true that the form of expression affects its content. The language or rites, which men employ, cannot be wholly without influence upon their philosophical ideas. For example, I need only recall to you the chapter in Hatch's *Hibbert Lectures*,[1] in which he discusses the influence of the mystery cults upon early Christian usage, particularly in relation to the early history of the rites of Baptism and the Lord's Supper. But though, no doubt, a great deal of light remains to be thrown upon the history of the development of Christian doctrine and ritual by further research in this difficult field, the problems, which such an enquiry raises, appear to me to be questions of purely historical detail. The polemic which has centred upon the topic of " borrowings " under the impression that they affect the substantial truth of Chris-

---

1. Hatch, *The Influence of Greek Ideas and Usages upon the Christian Church*, chapter x. On this topic see also Anrich, *Mysterienwesen und Christentum*, pp. 106 foll.

tianity, seems to me largely a beating of the air. But it has not lacked unfortunate results. If the rationalist has drawn quite irrelevant conclusions from the facts, the apologist has often been tempted to deny them or to seek to explain them away. The true explanation, the obvious factor of contemporaneity, is strangely often ignored.

Again, much of early Christian literature, particularly the writings which stand as it were upon the fringe of orthodoxy, becomes intelligible only in its context in pagan literary history. Both its form and its content, its weaknesses and even some of its strength, it owes to its literary *milieu*. The character, for example, of such documents as the *Pseudo-Clementines* or the *Apocryphal Acts*, is explained by their setting as part of a contemporary literature; while Christian Gnosticism can only be understood in reference to Hellenistic mystery cults and the magical papyri.

The Christian Fathers were inevitably men of their time. Nowhere is this more clearly, if a little drearily, evident than in the barren field of polemic. Both parties are guilty of vituperation and wilful misrepresentation; the minds of both work in identical grooves. If the pagans were unfair, except in a technical sense, in branding the Christians as atheists, the Christian attack upon pagans for the unintelligent worship of stocks and stones is almost equally wide of the mark. The charge was indeed an old one, and the arguments by which it is driven home are borrowed by the Fathers from the commonplaces of the Stoic handbooks. It is a repetition of arguments which pagan thinkers had themselves brought forward in an earlier age. But that pagan idolatry was not so crude as this in the second century after Christ, a famous passage of Maximus Tyrius may remind you.[1] "God is the Father and Creator of the things that are, older than the sun, older than the heaven, master of time and eternity and of all changing Nature. To Him law cannot give a name, nor can voice describe Him, nor eye behold Him. It is because we are not able to apprehend His being that we lean upon words, and names, and animal forms, and representations of gold and ivory and silver, and plants, and rivers, and mountain tops, and groves. Craving for knowledge of Him, in our weakness we give to earthly things the name of good and beautiful from His nature. It is like the case of lovers to whose sight the representations of their beloved give most pleasure, and pleasure, too, is given by a lyre of his, a javelin, a chair, a walk and, in short, everything

---

1. Maximus Tyrius, viii, 10. Compare the noble Olympic oration of Dio Chrysostom, xii. The whole interesting question of pagan idolatry and its pagan critics is discussed in Charly Clerc, *Les théories relatives au culte des images chez les auteurs grecs du* 11me *siècle après J.-C.*, (Paris, 1915) and J. Geffcken, "Der Bilderstreit heidnischen Altertums," *Archiv für Rel. Wiss.*, xix, (1916-1919), pp. 286-316. The attack upon idolatry, which was begun by the philosophers Heraclitus and Xenophanes, was maintained by the earlier Stoicism. But after Posidonius the new defence begins to appear, which eventually takes under its wing not only the anthropomorphic gods of Greece, but even the animal gods of Egypt, which had always caused peculiar difficulty to minds rational but devout (see below p. 181). By the second century the attitude of educated pagans towards religious art had arrived very much at the position indicated by Maximus, which is, after all, not far removed from that of many Christians to-day.

which wakens the memory of the loved one."[1]

The other main line of Christian attack, logically inconsistent with the charge of blindness in bowing down to wood and stone, was the assertion that the pagan gods were devils. The first weapon was perhaps an inheritance from Judaism, for though the arguments are Stoic, the animus, which drives them home in a way which Stoicism never did, is a legacy from the Jewish hatred of idols ;[2] the second, though it draws in part upon Jewish demonological beliefs, is in the main the exploitation of an unfortunate admission by pagan philosophers. Its foundations are in a theory of demonology developed by the

---

1. For an example of this psychology in religious practice compare the chair of Demonax. Καὶ τὸν θᾶκον τὸν λίθινον, ἐφ' οὗ εἴωθει ὁπότε κάμνοι ἀναπαύεσθαι, προσεκύνουν καὶ ἐστεφάνουν εἰς τιμὴν τοῦ ἀνδρὸς, ἡγούμενοι ἱερὸν εἶναι καὶ τὸν λίθον ἐφ' οὗ ἐκαθέζετο. Lucian, Demonax, 67. It is, perhaps, interesting to find that the Moslem account of the origin of idolatry is based upon a combination of Euhemerism and this association doctrine. When Edris (Enoch) was translated, his dearest friend was inconsolable. Satan persuaded him to assuage his grief by making a statue of Enoch. In the regular contemplation of this, the friend found some comfort. He then died suddenly, and Satan persuaded his descendants that the statue of Edris was really a god which the deceased had worshipped. See Rauzat-us-safa or Garden of Purity by Mirkhond (1432-1498) trans. Rehatsek (Oriental Trans. Fund, N.S. 1891) i, pp. 74-75 where an alternative version but of the same purport is also given.

2. Two things made for the practical tolerance of Stoicism towards idolatry which it theoretically condemned, and the conformity of the older Stoics to ordinary religious practice. (1) What may be called the intellectually aristocratic temper which recognised that superstition might be useful and even necessary for the unintelligent herd (see below, p. 173). (2) The very strong conservative instinct of the ancients which again and again finds its expression in the pagan protests at the revolutionary and subversive character of Christian teaching. Maiorum . . . instituta tueri sacris caerimoniisque retinendis sapientis est (Cicero, de diu. ii, 72, 148). cf. the view of Cotta in Cicero, de nat. deor. iii, 2, 6.

new Platonism, which came to be generally accepted both by pagans and Christians alike.[1]

For the rest, the theological arguments upon both sides largely resolve themselves into a not very edifying *tu quoque*. Celsus says that Christianity is a degraded kind of Platonism, and that what is reasonable in it is filched from the Greek philosopher. The Christians retorted that pagan philosophy had borrowed or stolen its doctrines from the Scriptures. Christians again attacked the Stoics' allegorical explanation of the crudities of Greek mythology as a feeble evasion ; they themselves employed the same method in order to harmonise the Old Testament with reason and with Christian ethics or to expound the New,[2] and are in turn held up to ridicule on precisely the same grounds by Porphyry[3] and Celsus[4]. The alleged borrowing, of rites, a familiar weapon of modern rationalism, was bandied to and fro, and the Fathers explained similarities by the supposition that the Devil had inspired parodies of the sacraments.[5] This polemic does not show either Paganism or Christianity at its best, but it may perhaps serve to illustrate the truth that contemporary minds tend to work along the same lines.

A recognition of this fact may assist in clearing up a popular misconception which will later engage our attention, viz., the charge that

---

1. See below, p. 178.
2. See Hatch, *op. cit.*, pp. 126 foll., 76 foll. For examples, Tertullian, *Apol.*, 47, Clem. Alex., *Strom.*, 2, 1.
3. Eusebius, *Hist. Eccl.*, vi, 19.
4. Origen, *c. Cels.*, iv, 48-50.
5. *e.g.*, Justin, *Apol.*, i, 66. Tertullian, *de Bapt.*, 5.

Christianity stifled science and was the influence mainly responsible for that decay of the spirit of independent scientific speculation, which is characteristic of medieval as opposed to pagan learning. The implied comparison is unfairly stated. If they are set, not beside Plato and Aristotle, but beside their pagan contemporaries, the Fathers, as Mr. Bevan has rightly emphasised,[1] have nothing to fear. In intellectual vigour and independence they are here at no disadvantage, and indeed the giant stature of an Augustine or even of an Origen towers above contemporary pagan attainment. Actually the decline of rationalism had begun before the birth of Christianity, for the life of Posidonius may be said to mark the turning-point. The first great encyclopedia of medieval science, Pliny's *Natural History*, was composed at a time when the author and the social circle in which he moved, not only were untouched by Christian influence, but were in fact almost wholly ignorant of who Christians were, and what they believed.

On the other hand, but a slight acquaintance with the pagan civilisation of the Antonine age is likely to modify another popular misapprehension, viz., that Christianity was the one healthy influence in a completely evil world, and in particular that those virtues, which may be embraced under the content of the word humanity, were specifically a Christian monopoly or solely due to Christian inspiration. The facts are quite otherwise. Christianity was in a sense a

---

1. Bevan, *Hellenism and Christianity*, p. 110.

special aspect of a great moral and religious movement. The sentiment of the age was quite definitely moving in the direction of the appreciation of the fellowship of mankind, the duties of benevolence, and the dignity of work. It was Seneca the Stoic who defined slaves as " humble friends."[1]   Thus the way for the social message of Christianity was not unprepared, and many of the ethical ideas which we associate with it were already abroad.   On the other hand, it is fair to admit that Christian influence identified itself with the higher and not with the lower aspirations of the society which it penetrated, and further that it fought more effectively than any contemporary philosophy or religion for the recognition of spiritual values in a society the besetting vice of which was materialism.

The birth of Christianity and the organisation of the Roman Empire were very nearly contemporaneous.   For if the imperial idea was a legacy of Julius Caesar, its realisation was the work of Augustus, whom the victory of Actium in 31 B.C. made *de facto* master of the civilised world.   Even in a geographical sense the Roman Empire was his creation.   For the earlier possessions of Rome, like the British dominions, had been acquired, not as the result of a deliberate plan of imperial aggression, but as the accidental spoils which necessarily accrued to the victor in struggles with political rivals.   Roman territory in 31 B.C. was not continuous.   For example, although Southern Spain had long been

---

1. Seneca, *Ep.*, xlvii, 1.

Romanised, the wild mountainous districts of the peninsula were not under Roman rule, and even the immediate boundaries of Northern Italy, the Alps and Tirol, were not in Roman hands. Augustus, however, filled up the gaps, and henceforward the Roman Empire was a continuous area within definite geographical limits. These ran from the Atlantic on the West, down the Rhine and along the Danube to the Black Sea. Asia Minor was protected from Parthia by a chain of native kingdoms under Roman protection. The northern Euphrates and the desert covered Syria and Palestine, and carried the line down to Egypt which, together with the habitable fringe of Northern Africa, was bounded by the southern line of deserts. Roughly speaking, these limits defined the area of the Roman Empire; the most important subsequent additions were Britain, conquered under Claudius (43 A.D.), and Dacia by Trajan (105 A.D.)

Augustus then created an empire which was geographically a continuous unit with fixed boundaries. In spite of the constitutional fictions with which he thought it politic to veil his position, the whole area was, in fact, governed by an autocrat whose authority in the long run necessarily, if unfortunately, depended upon his sole control of the armed forces of the state. The inevitable tendency was for shams to disappear. The position of the emperor became more and more openly recognised as the autocracy which, in fact, it had always been, and the armies came gradually to learn and to abuse the sinister power which they possessed of making and unmaking emperors.

For roughly two hundred years, however, peace was established and maintained throughout this area. Augustus began, and his successors completed, a regular system of administration by which the various parts of the whole were justly and expertly governed. Although, of necessity, the conditions of recently conquered provinces in the earlier days of the empire varied from those which had long been under Roman rule, all now came under a single system. In spite of considerable minor variation, for the Romans showed a wise tolerance of local autonomy and customary law, the tendency was inevitably towards uniformity. In particular, the rude peoples of the West showed a surprising aptitude for assimilating Roman ways of life. Though it was not imposed by compulsion, their voluntary aspiration towards Romanisation was encouraged. In the tribal society of Gaul, the development of urban centres was fostered, and these in turn became Roman municipalities, though some of the modern names of French cities, e.g., Paris or Treves, still betray their origin as foci of the life of tribal communities.

With the Romanisation of the world, the extension of the Roman citizenship kept steady pace. Individual emperors, it is true, varied in their policy, but upon the whole there was a steady extension based upon the definite principle that citizen rights should be awarded in accordance with deserts as represented by the degree of Romanisation achieved. The enfranchisement of non-Italians was inaugurated by the practice of conferring the citizenship upon certain classes of individuals. Julius Caesar had granted citizenship to many tribal chieftains in Gaul, thus Romanising a tribal society from its head. The magistrates of towns, which possessed the modified citizenship known as Latin rights, were rewarded with the full citizenship for themselves and their families upon demitting office. The native who enlisted in the auxiliary troops became a citizen at his discharge. Then under the Flavians it became the practice to grant the subordinate Latin rights to whole communities, when they appeared sufficiently Romanised to have earned them, and after a further period, if the grant proved to have been justified, to complete it by bestowing the full citizenship.

That, in a compact and continuous area, governed by the authority which was centralised in an individual, upon the basis of an uniform organisation and a single system of law—an area, moreover, in which it was the ambition of the more backward communities to qualify by assimilation for the status of full membership, and in which at the same time two centuries of peace permitted and encouraged the free intercourse of commerce and constant intercommunication—there were overwhelming forces at work in the direction of homogeneity, it is hardly necessary to point out. Inevitably the various points of the Roman Empire increasingly approximated to a common type. Speaking broadly, the civilisation of this continuous geographical area became itself increasingly continuous and uniform.

A necessary corollary was the diminution in the relative importance of the Roman and even of the Italian race. With the foundation of the Empire the centre of gravity had really been shifted, and this quite rapidly became apparent. Already in the Silver Age of Latin literature the Spaniards, the two Senecas, Lucan and Martial, are as prominent as the Romans. Between Tacitus and Ammianus Marcellinus there is no Roman literary man of note. Of emperors, Vespasian is the first who was not of Roman origin, but was derived from the Italian bourgeoisie; Trajan and Hadrian were Spaniards. In the third century a medley of races is represented in the list of emperors. Thus Septimius Severus was a Punic-speaking African, Elagabalus a Syrian, Claudius Gothicus the first of the great emperors of Illyrian stock, Maximin a Thracian, Philip an Arabian, Galerius a Bulgar.

Upon the whole, as will become evident later, the centre of gravity shifted eastwards. It was the brains, financial ability and technical skill of the East which exploited the raw materials of the West. Alike in the spheres of literature and of government, the Greek tended to dispossess the Westerner. But, racially, the East never wholly conquered the West. In spite of this great levelling process, which we have indicated, and the marked tendency towards homogeneity, there remained a deep-seated line of cleavage based upon language and civilisation. In consequence, when the fabric of the Empire was subjected to external strain, it split into two parts, the Greek-speaking East based upon a civilisation older and more cultured than that of Rome, and the Latin-speaking West which had received its civilisation direct from Rome.

In the history of the Empire, the reign of Marcus Aurelius (161-180 A.D.) makes a convenient point of division. Up to this point, though it would not be true to say that Rome had had no frontier wars nor difficulties, it is roughly true that there had been no considerable nor dangerous pressure upon her frontiers. Henceforward not only was there continuous pressure from outside, but, further, that pressure was often simultaneously felt at different points. Both military and financial strain steadily increased. Armies needed to be raised and paid for. An increasing centralisation of government, while it made in some ways for efficiency, had killed local political responsibility and had thereby stifled political vitality. A deadening rigidity of organisation had sapped the resisting power of the body politic. The armies, too, as the needs of the time accentuated the importance of the military, both realised and abused their power. Troops at their caprice put forward claimants, suitable or unsuitable, for the imperial throne and refused to recognise the authority of any but the man of their choice. The inevitable result was a haphazard succession of short-lived emperors, broken by the fortunate emergence from time to time of some ruler of outstanding personal ability and character, a Septimius, an Aurelian, a Diocletian, or a Constantine.

We may notice, too, that the urgency and the scale of the ever-increasing military needs made

larger demands than a single ruler could fulfil.
Already Marcus Aurelius shared the imperial
authority with Lucius Verus, and a division of
power and responsibility became more and more
an accepted necessity, leading to the more and
more definite separation of the Empire into
Eastern and Western divisions. The emphasis of
importance was upon the East, as is shown by
Diocletian's capital at Nicomedia and, subsequently, by the founding of New Rome at
Constantinople by Constantine.

If we take, as I have suggested, the reign of
Marcus Aurelius as our dividing point, the
history of the Roman Empire up to this point
is one of concentration. Over the whole of its
area a homogeneous civilisation has been achieved.
It is very strictly administered upon uniform
principles, upon the basis of a law which runs
impartially throughout its area, by an efficient
bureaucracy under the control of an individual
who, if we may take Trajan or Hadrian as
examples, had the highest standard of his
responsibilities. After Marcus Aurelius the
tendencies are towards confusion and disintegration. A civilisation, which had been
devitalised by over-government, was subjected
in the third century to continuous external
pressure, and was exhausted by increasing financial
distress which the steady depreciation of the
currency or desperate measures like that of
Diocletian's famous edict prescribing prices,
only served to aggravate.

The machinery of government became steadily
more complicated, more expensive, and more

corrupt. The middle class was crushed out of existence. The misery of the time was increased by civil wars and anarchy due to the capricious exercise of the rude powers of brute force, which the soldiery had learned to assert. The army itself contained an increasingly large proportion of barbarian elements, which the flagging civilisation of Rome could no longer assimilate. Strong forces of disintegration had set in. In the middle of the third century the Goths were in the Ægean, the Germans had ravaged the West as far south as Tarraco in Spain, and Persian armies had entered Antioch and Cæsarea. Separatist tendencies had shown themselves in the short-lived Empire of the Gauls and in the attempted independence of Palmyra. In fact, the Empire was pulled together only by the heroic military efforts of Claudius Gothicus and Aurelian.

In the third century the Empire survived the ordeal, though with difficulty and exhaustion. In the fifth century it succumbed to similar barbarian pressure, which was not, perhaps, in itself more formidable than the invasions of the third century, but was exerted upon a body politic wearied and exhausted by the earlier struggle. But the Roman Empire, the framework of which succumbed in the fifth century, was a Christian society.

For the history of Christianity, too, the reign of Marcus Aurelius makes a convenient point of division. Of the Apostolic Age, of course, we know a good deal. We have the *Acts* and the *Epistles* to tell us how St. Paul carried the message to the Gentiles, firmly established the hold of the new religion upon the Roman Province of Asia, and made a missionary beginning in Rome itself. But of the succeeding period until the end of the second century much less is definitely known than is often supposed. The writings of Tertullian and his successors are good evidence for contemporary history, and from the end of the second century we are no longer in the dark; but the traditions of Christian history concerning events before the lifetime of the authors who have recorded them, in the opinion of some of us, have but slender evidential value.[1] There are, of course, the famous passages in Tacitus and Suetonius and the more informing correspondence of Pliny and Trajan. We have evidence of a single and local persecution by Nero at Rome, when the Christians were selected as scapegoats to appease the popular agitation aroused by the Great Fire, and there is the alleged persecution of Domitian. But, broadly speaking, before the reign of Marcus Aurelius Christianity plays no important part in the Roman world. What strikes us about Suetonius, Tacitus and Pliny is not how much, but how little they know about it. It is not, I think, until Lucian and Epictetus that you will find a classical author alluding to Galilaeans or Christians with confidence that his readers will understand without explanation what or whom he means.

---

1. I should personally agree in its general lines with the critical position taken up by Mr. Merrill in his recent *Essays on Early Christianity*.

Of course, Christianity, though unseen, was growing all the time. Asia Minor, as Pliny found, was covered with Christian organisations, and towards the close of the second century the new religion had got firm hold of the middle class even in the West, e.g., the lawyers Minucius Felix in Rome or Tertullian in Africa. " We are but of yesterday and we have filled everything, cities, islands, camps, palace, forum," boasts Tertullian (*Apol.*, 37), and roughly about the same time, if Celsus be the friend of Lucian, the new religion was thought sufficiently formidable to merit careful hostile study and the publication of a reasoned attack upon its social and philosophical position. But this growth, a *fait accompli* at the end of the second century, had taken place almost unnoticed by the Roman world as a whole. Powerful factors in its phenomenal development must have been the lively intercommunication of men, goods and ideas along the greater highways of the Empire, the increasing preponderance of the Eastern elements in Roman commerce and culture, and the social revolution of the second century. These matters we shall later discuss. The point, which I want here to emphasise, is that, thanks to this obscurity of its growth, no serious attempt was made by the State to crush it at a stage of development when such a policy might well have succeeded. The first general action, taken by the State in hostility to Christianity as such, was the decree of Septimius Severus forbidding Christians to proselytise.

The attitude of the State towards Christianity

in the early Empire,[1] if ill-defined, is perfectly intelligible. In the Greek and Italian city-states, religion had been primarily civic or communal in character ; in early Rome *ius diuinum* was an integral part of *ius ciuile*. Although the Roman state religion at an early date had admitted foreign elements, such foreign cults as were so incorporated needed to be officially adopted by the authorities and to be regulated by them. Both in Greece and Rome, however, the growth of individualism led to the propagation of cults of a different character. These were at once universal, inasmuch as they were not restricted to the members of a particular political or racial community, and individualistic, in the sense that they were concerned not with the common welfare of a politico-social group, the state or the household, but with the spiritual welfare of their individual members. Such were the Orphic brotherhoods in Greece, and somewhat similar religious fraternities were a characteristic feature of the oriental cults which, in increasing numbers, swept over the Græco-Roman world.

One oriental cult alone, that of the Great Mother of Asia Minor, was officially recognised by the Roman Republic, an action prompted by the nervous tension of the closing years of the Second Punic War. But even in this cult Roman citizens were not allowed to take an active part in the exotic and, it was felt, degrading ritual.

---

1. The best general treatment of this topic in English is still the paper of Mr. Hardy, re-published in his *Studies in Roman History* (London, 1906). For a brief statement of the nature of early Roman religion the reader may be referred to my little book in this series, *Lectures on the History of Roman Religion from Numa to Augustus*.

In actual fact, however, the private cults of foreign deities, which really did meet a spiritual need which the times acutely felt, spread rapidly in Italy in the first century before Christ, particularly among the emotional and newly emancipated women. To control and, if necessary, to suppress such private religious associations was a power which the State necessarily claimed to possess. This power indeed had been invoked in the more practicable of Plato's Utopias, and we find Ptolemy Philopator laying down regulations for the control of Dionysiac societies in Egypt, which probably formed the model for the famous legislation of the Senate against the Bacchanalian societies in Italy.[1] In theory the city-state was a religious no less than a political association for a common end. These private cults lay outside its corporate system. Further, they were secret associations and, as such, potential instruments of political conspiracy; the practices of some were more than suspected of offending public morals. They therefore needed careful watching, but, provided

---

1. Plato, *Laws*, x, 909 foll. At Athens the introduction of foreign cults without the authorisation of the Boule and the People was illegal. Compare the accusation of Phryne. ἐπέδειξα τοίνυν ὑμῖν ἀσεβῆ Φρύνην, κωμασάσαν ἀναιδῶς, καινοῦ θεοῦ εἰσηγήτριαν, θιάσους ἀνδρῶν ἐκθέσμους καὶ γυναικῶν συναγαγοῦσαν. *Frag. orat. attic.* (Müller), ii, p. 426. Upon the whole position at Athens see Foucart, *Des associations réligieuses chez les grecs*, pp. 127 foll. For the regulations of Ptolemy see Schubart, *Amtl. Berichte aus d. Kgl. Kunstsamml.*, 1916-7, pp. 189 foll., *id.*, *Einfuhrung in die Papyruskunde*, 1918, p. 352, Reitzenstein in *Archiv für Rel. Wiss.*, xix, 1918, p. 191, Cichorius, *Römische Studien*, p. 21. For the *s.c. de Bacchanalibus*, see Livy, xxxix, 8, 3 and Bruns, *Fontes Juris Romani*, 6th edition, No. 35, p. 160. For the normal Roman attitude towards private and foreign cults see Cicero, *de leg.*, ii, 8, 19 : separatim nemo habessit deos neue nouos neue aduenas, nisi publice adscitos.

that no special grounds for suspicion or scandal arose, the power of suppression, which the State never abrogated, was allowed to remain dormant.

With regard to non-citizens, the State was indifferent. It was right and proper in the general view that men should worship their own gods in their own way, provided only that this did not involve barbarities, like human sacrifice, which a civilised power could not tolerate, and that the national religion was not abused, as was Druidism, as an instrument for nationalist agitation against Roman rule.

This attitude towards alien cults in practice worked admirably. With one exception, the religions of the Mediterranean area prior to Christianity raised no political or religious questions of dispute ; they were neither nationalist in temper nor intransigently monotheistic in creed. The notable exception, Judaism, was treated with exceptional consideration ; synagogues were licensed, and special exemptions were granted to Jews. But these considerable concessions to Jewish susceptibilities in the long run failed to achieve their end. This attempt and failure to solve the Jewish question by conciliation was not without its importance for Christianity. For the policy of the State towards Christianity was complicated by the undoubted confusion between Christians and Jews, which for some time existed in the Roman mind. The view that Christians were a particular kind of Jew first gained them, in early years, something of contemptuous tolerance, and afterwards involved them in the odium which Jewish intractability had not unnaturally aroused.

The Christian communities, then, were illegal associations which had not received the sanction of the State, and, as such, were liable to suppression. Their enemies from the earliest times had charged them both with secret political aims and with gross immoralities. A further practical difficulty arose from the Christian refusal to conform to the ritual of the worship of the Emperor and Rome, with which all other peoples, except the specially exempted Jews, were perfectly willing to comply. Here was a definite test and proof of deliberate disloyalty.

Nevertheless, the State does not appear to have considered Christianity a sufficiently formidable danger to demand the consistent exercise of its undoubted powers. The general policy pursued is that explicitly laid down by Trajan. If the law is invoked, it must of course be enforced ; but there is to be no attempt to hunt Christians out.[1] This policy cannot be said to be that of deliberate persecution in the sense which applies to the conflict of Christianity and the state in the third century.

Persecutions, of course, there were in the second century, but they were due not to a deliberate policy of suppression adopted by the Roman Government, but to local popular agitation which set the law in motion. For this,

---

1. The spirit of Trajan's policy seems often to have inspired the action of individual governors. "How many rulers, men more resolute and more cruel than you are, have contrived to get quit of such cases altogether," says Tertullian, and proceeds to quote examples, *ad. Scap.*, 4.

though there can be no justification, there is, perhaps, some excuse. That " the Nihilists of the ancient world " should excite bitter hostility is hardly surprising. The disturbance of vested interests, like those of the silversmiths at Ephesus, the contempt aroused by a religion which openly appealed to the sinner, the destitute and the despised, the current belief in the incest, immoralities and infant sacrifices, which were thought to disgrace the nocturnal meetings of the sect, the uncomfortable and foolish doctrine of the proximate destruction of the world, all these no doubt played their part in exciting hatred and contempt. But the true source of animus was the way in which the new religion struck at the roots of social intercourse and menaced the time-honoured fabric of society. You have only to read Tertullian to realise the practical social difficulties which the abomination of idolatry involved. " Why, even the streets, and the market-place, and the baths, and the taverns, and our very dwelling-places, are not altogether free from idols. Satan and his angels have filled the whole world." [1]

The conscientious Christian could attend no public festival and celebrate no holiday. Hardly any trade could be found which was not in some way connected with the accursed thing. The popular view that Christians were anti-social kill-joys with a more than Jewish hatred of the human race, if mistaken, is at least intelligible. But still more deeply felt was the disturbance of

---

1. Tertullian, *de Spect.*, 8.

family life, which necessarily resulted from the conversion of one of its members. The difficulties which such scruples, as we have mentioned, would inevitably produce in the everyday life of a mixed family, are sufficiently obvious. The diversion of family property to the common fund of a communistic Christian society must often have evoked bitter feeling. But perhaps the most effective agent of exasperation was the extreme forms taken by Christian reaction against the sexual laxity of the day. Not merely did the tendency to exalt the unmarried state produce refusals on the part of converts to carry out the marriages which their families had arranged or intended, in order to lead a life of holy celibacy, but there also arose complications, of a kind which again and again recur in the stories in the *Apocryphal Acts*, where a wife after conversion refused to resume her normal relations with her pagan husband.

This brief summary may explain some of the reasons why popular animosity against the Christians became more and more inflamed. Meanwhile, the Christian community grew in numbers and became increasingly self-conscious and insistent upon its scruples. In the reign of Marcus Aurelius, the clouds were gathering, and the state was manifestly in danger. The anxious wars upon the frontier, the famine and pestilence in the land, seemed to portend celestial punishment. " The outcry is that the State is filled with Christians—that they are in the fields, in the citadels, in the islands : they make lamentation as for some calamity, that both sexes, every age and condition, even high rank, are passing over to the profession of the Christian faith." [1] The cumulative effect of popular exasperation and the reckless fury of blind panic are the explanation of the persecutions under Marcus Aurelius. Though that gentle Stoic did not effectively disapprove, they are none the less the product, not of imperial policy, but of popular feeling.

But actually at this stage the issue was being defined. Men, as Tertullian noticed, were awakening to the significance of the scale of Christianity. Further, at this crisis, as it was felt, by which the whole fabric of civilisation was threatened, Christians were conscientious objectors. The reasons why it was difficult for a good Christian to serve his emperor in the field are honourable enough, as they are set out at length by Tertullian, himself a soldier's son; but it is not hard for our generation to appreciate the effect upon the minds of pagans of this refusal in the hour of need. It is here that Celsus [2] is most compelling when he turns from intellectual criticism and pleads the urgent need of the Empire, in its danger and difficulties, for the active help of all its sons. Nor can we feel that Origen's answer that Christians, though they will not fight, are praying hard, is a completely adequate reply.

During the prosperity, then, of the Antonine period, Christianity had spread throughout the Roman Empire, and had rooted itself firmly in the

---

1. Tertullian, *Apol.*, 1.
2. Origen, *c. Cels.*, viii, 69 foll.

West as well as in the East.   It had encountered
opposition and local persecutions, but the secular
authority had not exerted the powers, which it
possessed, in a deliberate or consistent policy of
suppression.   But as Christianity increased in
numbers, the temper of the opposition to it
became more embittered.   The world, with
apprehension, was becoming alive to the scale
which the movement had achieved.   " The third
race," as it was coming to be called, appeared,
moreover, to have divergent interests from those
of the rest of society, and its members had shown
themselves prepared to refuse that obligation
which the state in time of need has a right to
expect its members willingly to fulfil.[1]   During
the third century Christianity not only increased
numerically, but in a disintegrating world it
maintained its coherence and its powers of
organisation.   It became, in fact, a highly
compact and disciplined society—a state within
the state.

Two active lines of policy were obviously open
to the political ruler.   Diocletian, who followed
the traditional policy of Rome towards associations
which might threaten the authority of the
political power, attempted, as Decius (248–251)
and Valerius (253–260) had done, to suppress it.
The attempt was a failure.   It was made too
late for prospects of success, for Christianity
was then too far developed to be crushed by
organised persecution.   Constantine adopted the
other alternative, and by making an alliance with

---

1.   τῶν θεοὺς μὴ νομιζόντων καὶ τῶν τὴν πατρίδα ἐγκαταλειπόντων καὶ
τῶν πᾶν ποιούντων, ἐπειδὰν κλείσωσι τὰς θύρας, Marcus Aurelius, iii, 16.

this powerful and highly organised institution, he enlisted the Church in the support of the State. It is probable that the fervour of personal conviction had less to do with the official recognition of Christianity than motives of political expediency, but it is not impossible that Constantine saw further than the immediate political advantages of the moment. In effect the alliance gave a sorely needed coherence and unity to a society which was in process of disintegration, and eventually in the fifth century, when the barbarians broke up the Western Empire, Christianity was in a large measure the mediator which ensured the survival of Roman tradition to form the basis of the civilisation of the nations which emerged from the ruins of the Empire.

Finally, we may notice that the transference of the political centre of gravity from Rome to Constantinople led ultimately to the very different developments of the Eastern and Western Churches. It enabled the Bishop of Rome in the West to assert and develop a position of political and religious independence of the secular power, which has been foreign to Byzantium and Russia, where so long as a national Church existed, the political sovereign remained its head.

LECTURE II

" I am by no means unaware that I might be justly accused
of ingratitude and indolence, were I to describe thus
briefly and in so cursory a manner the land which is at
once the foster child and parent of all lands ; chosen
by the providence of the Gods to render even heaven itself
more glorious, to unite the scattered empires of the
earth, to bestow a polish upon men's manners, to unite
the discordant and uncouth dialects of so many different
nations by the powerful ties of one common language,
to confer the enjoyments of discourse and of civilisation
upon mankind, to become, in short, the mother-country of
all the nations of the earth."

Pliny, *Nat. Hist.*, iii, 6, (5), 39 (trans. Bostock and Riley).

" For indeed the whole world, as though keeping high
festival, has put off the old, the beweaponed garb, and
has turned instead with complete liberty to order and to
all festivities. All other rivalries have left the cities
save one sole contention, which grips them all, to wit,
how each may present the most beautiful and most
delightful appearance. All, indeed, is full of gymnasia,
fountains, edifices, ships, workshops, schools—of certain
knowledge one can say that the sick world has been
restored anew to health."

Aelius Aristides, (Keil), xxvi, 97.

BEFORE entering upon the discussion of the
cultural aspects of the Roman Empire, it will,
perhaps, be useful to turn a rapid glance upon
its social anatomy. I propose, therefore, to

devote a lecture to the arrangements which Augustus made for the administration of the empire, the character of Roman municipalities, and the nature of the "collegia" or guilds which were so marked a feature of the social life of the early Empire. These topics can only be treated in the barest and most elementary outline;[1] even so, however, they may serve yet further to emphasise the existence of forces making for the uniformity and continuity of civilisation throughout the area which was governed by Rome.

The court poets of Augustus found a congenial and favourite theme in the text of "the world's great age begins anew," and there was more than mere adulation in their hymns. The provinces were conscious of a new and better ordering of the world, the return of an era of prosperity after dark years of misgovernment, misery and distress. This feeling finds clear, if characteristically fulsome expression in a well-known inscription of the Greek towns of Asia, establishing the birthday of Augustus as the official opening of the Asiatic year. "The birthday of most divine Cæsar we should properly regard as the beginning of all things, if we are to consider not the order of Nature, but that of utility; for nothing could have restored a fallen estate which was deeply involved in misfortune, nor have given a new aspect to the whole world, which was ready to welcome destruction, if

---

1. The best short account of Roman administration is the masterly essay by Professor Stuart Jones in *The Legacy of Rome*, pp. 91-140.

Cæsar had not been born for the common prosperity of all men."[1]

The dominions governed by the Roman Republic had been a scattered series of haphazard acquisitions, which were the result not of a deliberate policy of development, but of political accident. The method of their administration had been almost equally haphazard and arbitrary. Misgovernment of the provincials had been the rule, partly because public opinion, which regarded the provinces merely as the property of the Roman people, was completely unsound; and partly because the home authority had no effective control over the actions of a provincial governor during his term of office. The governor had been a man who had served in the home magistracies, which were unpaid but expensive to secure. He had been sent out to a province with no regular salary, but with certain allowances which could be indefinitely expanded, and with unlimited powers of despotic blackmail, at a moment when his fortune had been impoverished by the expenses of an official career. He had little interest in the work itself, which entailed exile from Rome; he had no previous experience of the conditions peculiar to the country which he was called upon to

---

1. Dittenberger, *Orientis Graeci inscriptiones selectae*, ii, No. 458. ἡ τοῦ θειοτάτου Καίσαρος γενέθλιος ἡμέρα, ἣν τῆι τῶν πάντων ἀρχῆι ἴσην δικαίως ἂν εἶναι ὑπολάβοιμεν, καὶ εἰ μὴ τῆι φύσει, τῶι γε χρησίμωι, εἴ γε οὐδὲν οὐχὶ διαπεῖπτον καὶ εἰς ἀτυχὲς μεταβεβηκὸς σχῆμα ἀνώρθωσεν, ἑτέραν τε ἔδωκεν παντὶ τῶι κόσμωι ὄψιν ἥδιστα ἂν δεξαμένωι φθοράν, εἰ μὴ τὸ κοινὸν πάντων εὐτύχημα ἐπεγγενήθη Καῖσαρ.   Beneath the flowery adulation of this decree or that of the Roman speech of Aristides, there lies a sincere appreciation of real facts, for which see Chapot, *La province romaine proconsulaire d'Asie*, pp. 18-67.

govern, and, as his tenure was normally annual, he had neither time to learn them nor an incentive to develop a long-sighted policy. Indeed, it would have been impracticable to do so, even had he possessed the necessary experience or desire, for a succession of annual changes of ruler effectively hindered continuity of policy. Further, there was no census of the resources of the province; the taxes were, in the main, inequitably assessed and collected through the wasteful, inefficient and oppressive system of tax-farmers. If a governor wished to defend his subjects from the rapacity of these middlemen, he drew upon his head the wrath of the whole capitalist body which exercised a very powerful influence at Rome.

Augustus here, as elsewhere, introduced order and system. In effect he organised two great public services, one for political and military administration, and the other for financial administration. To fill the posts in the first, he drew upon the senatorial order, i.e., the aristocracy, membership of which under the early Empire was based upon heredity tempered by imperial nomination. That is to say, while the son of a senator, provided that he possessed the necessary property qualification, was a candidate eligible for the career leading to a governorship, the emperor could in various ways secure the senatorial qualification for a suitable person. To become a governor of a large imperial province it was necessary that a man should have qualified by having held a number of posts abroad and magistracies at home in an ascending scale. He had thus been trained by a wide civil and military experience before he came to the responsibilities of his big command. He was salaried and was strictly responsible to the emperor. He held his post at the emperor's pleasure, and it became the practice both to retain good men for a considerable period, thereby supplying continuity of policy,[1] and also to appoint, as governors of a particular province, men who had already had experience of the local conditions during the earlier part of their career.

I have been speaking of imperial provinces. You will remember that Augustus had restored the Republic and had shared his power with the Senate. The emperor's share included all the frontier provinces and those with armies stationed in them. Of these, strictly speaking, he was the governor, thanks to the proconsular power which had been conferred upon him, carrying out the actual administration through his deputies (*legati*), just as Pompey, in the years immediately preceding the Civil War with Cæsar, had governed Spain by deputies while remaining himself at Rome. Hence the title of an imperial governor was *legatus Augusti pro praetore*. Under the division of power the old Romanised provinces were still under the Senate's nominal control, and were governed by proconsuls. But it will be noticed that these proconsuls were unlike their predecessors under the Republic, for they were

---

1. The policy of keeping governors for long continuous periods in command of their provinces was a prominent feature of Tiberius' policy. Maecenas is said to have advised Augustus to adopt a term of not less than three years and not more than five, in order to secure necessary continuity, while avoiding risks of rebellion.

now men who had had the training of the imperial service, and were consequently experienced administrators.

An actual example is probably the best way of explaining how the system worked, and of illustrating the points which I have tried to summarise. Agricola, the father-in-law of Tacitus, who played so distinguished a part in the history of our island, though eventually of provincial stock and probably the descendant of a Gaul who had been given the citizenship by Julius Cæsar, was himself qualified by birth for the senatorial career. His grandfather had belonged to the second social grade, the equestrian order, but his father had been promoted to the nobility. Agricola served as a military subaltern, *tribunus laticlauus*, in Britain about 60 A.D. In 64 he became *quaestor* to the governor of Asia. This was the junior magistracy, which might be held either in Rome or upon the staff of the governor of a senatorial province; its general character was that of a financial secretaryship attached to some senior magistrate; it conferred the right of sitting in the Senate. In 66 he held the now unimportant office of tribune in Rome and in 68 became *praetor*. Holding this magistracy, the tenure of which, like that of the other home magistracies, was annual, and the functions of which were judicial, qualified for the command of a legion or for a minor governorship. In 71 Agricola became commander of a legion in Britain. In 74 he was transferred to govern the small province of Aquitaine in which no troops were stationed, and remained there until

77, when he held the consulship at Rome.   He was now qualified for the higher commands and in 78 he returned to Britain as governor.   There he remained until 85, when a difference of opinion on the merits of the forward policy which he advocated, led to his honourable recall.   He was offered further employment, the governorship of Syria in 88 and the proconsulship of the senatorial province of Asia in 89, but he refused both and died in 93.

Agricola's career may serve to illustrate the peculiar merits of the system as a whole.   When he assumed the main task of his life's work, he had had practical experience of military, judicial, and financial matters;   and the province, which he was called upon to administer, was one in which he had served as a subaltern, and in which he had afterwards commanded a legion.

Under the Augustan scheme the whole financial administration of the imperial provinces was completely separated from the political and military.   For the personnel of the financial service Augustus drew upon the equestrian order, i.e., the capitalist class.   For membership, which was absolutely the gift of the emperor, a certain property qualification was demanded and, as a preliminary to employment in the financial civil service, a term of military duty.   After completing his military service the young man was eligible for the post of *procurator* or imperial agent. In the hands of these agents lay all the financial administration of the armies and the imperial provinces, and much even of that of the senatorial provinces.   The appointments were made and held at the emperor's pleasure. There was, in consequence, complete liberty to reward merit with promotion and, where desirable, to keep a good man for a prolonged period in an important post. The provincial posts naturally varied in importance ; most of them were financial. There were, however, one or two which carried with them wider powers. There existed a few districts (the Alpine districts and Judæa afford examples), which for one reason or another it was inadvisable to absorb into the neighbouring provinces, though they were too small to form provinces by themselves. Here a *procurator* was put in charge. He had, of course, no troops beyond the minimum police requirements, and he was to some extent subordinate to the governor of the neighbouring province. It seemed necessary to mention this governorship by *procurator* because of the example provided by Pontius Pilate ; but, in fact, it had always a provisional character, and when the special circumstances which had led to its adoption disappeared, the districts concerned tended to be absorbed into ordinary provinces.

The great prizes of the equestrian career were three of the four great Prefectures in Rome and the Prefecture of Egypt, a country which was governed exceptionally, not as a province, but directly on behalf of the emperor by an equestrian prefect appointed by him. Of the four Roman Prefectures the Prefect of the City, though appointed on the emperor's nomination, was a member of the senatorial order ; but the Prefect of Police and Firemen, the Prefect of the Corn Supply, and the Prefect of the Prætorian Guard,

were equestrians. The last three I have quoted
in the ascending order of their importance. As
Commander of the Household Troops, the only
military force in Italy, the Prefect of the
Prætorian Guard enjoyed a great and sinister
power under the Julio-Claudians. When the
Privy Council developed into an official body
from what had been an informal meeting of the
"friends of Cæsar," the Prætorian Prefect
became its chairman ; he also became president
of the Imperial Court of Appeal, and from the
second century onwards the office was normally
held by the leading jurist of the day. Indeed, the
Prætorian Prefect became the *alter ego* of the
emperor and, as the Empire became more autocratic, his position tended to approximate to
that of a vizier in an oriental monarchy.

It is not, perhaps, surprising to find that the
importance of the equestrian order steadily
increased.[1] This was partly due to the increasing
importance of the bureaucracy as its machinery
developed and, partly, to the increasing tendency
towards centralisation. Again, as compared with
a member of the senatorial order, the equestrian
was directly the emperor's man, and the emperor's
powers tended steadily to become more autocratic. Partly administrative convenience, and
partly deliberate policy, led to an increase in the
powers of *procuratores*. Already under Claudius

---

1. Nero is said to have thrown out unmistakable hints that he would
blot out the senatorial order from the State, and hand over the rule of the
provinces and the command of the armies to the Roman knights and his
freedmen. Suetonius, *Nero*, 37, 3. Domitian admitted equestrians to
membership of the Privy Council. Under Septimius Severus the dark
threats of Nero more or less came true.

we find them being given judicial powers. Suspicious emperors found that *procuratores* could be used as a check upon the powers of governors, and it is significant that in recorded cases of conflict between governor and *procurator*, it is the latter always who carries the day.

Under Hadrian a vast expansion of the equestrian service took place because it then took over the secretariate departments of state. Here a curious anomaly had come into existence. The small scale upon which city-state institutions had been planned, provided no official precedent for the business organisation of the Empire. In republican days when a consul took up his duties, he found no permanent office organisation to deal with official correspondence and the like; he supplied his own from his own household, which, as he was necessarily one of the wealthy upper class who alone could afford to give the unpaid service demanded by public life, he was able to do. He managed the state business with the same personnel with which he managed his private estate. The secretarial work of a large private estate was, of course, performed by trained slaves or freedmen, not by free-born Romans, who looked down upon clerical work as servile. Hence, when Augustus took over the governorship of all the frontier provinces, the secretarial work, which was connected with it, fell into the hands of the freedmen of his household. In one respect it was not unfortunate. Though sometimes corrupt and unscrupulous, the Greek freedmen were able men of business, and they, in fact, built up a highly efficient business organisation.

But it was naturally resented that the enormous powers of a secretary of state should thus be wielded by persons of servile origin, who abused their position for their own ends. In the reign of Claudius, who was under the thumb of his freedmen secretaries, the matter became a scandal. There are symptoms of a reaction under Vitellius, but it was not until the reign of Hadrian that the secretariate was definitely brought into line with the procuratorate, and the whole bureaucratic machinery was manned throughout with equestrians.[1]

This bureaucratic machinery was gradually built up, but as it became more efficient, the tendency was to tighten the control over provincial governors, and for the central authority to interfere. Thus after the revolt of Boudicca had been put down by Suetonius Paulinus, the *procurator* reported to headquarters that the governor's policy was unduly punitive, and that a milder *régime* was desirable. The result was that Nero sent a special commissioner to examine the state of affairs on the spot and to report thereon at Rome. After his report had been considered, Suetonius was recalled. This precedent was followed and developed further. Pliny is not the only example in Trajan's reign of

---

1. A more favourable view of the character of some of these freedmen ministers than that recorded by Tacitus and Juvenal, and an idea of the scale of their responsibilities will be gained from reading Statius' poems, *e.g.*, *Siluae*, iii, 3 (the father of Claudius Etruscus) and v, 1 (Abascantus). The change, however, which Hadrian effected, is not so drastic and complete as it would at first sight appear. Actually the equestrians of his time were largely of freedman and, though it is often concealed beneath Roman names, of Levantine origin. The social revolution which brought this class to the top is discussed below, pp. 119 f.

a special commissioner being dispatched by the emperor to set the affairs of a province in order, and it will be noticed as an example of the encroachment of the imperial side of government, that Bithynia, to which Pliny was sent, was a senatorial and not an imperial province.

This tendency to centralise control, as we shall presently see, had disastrous results in strangling local political life, the necessary consequence of depriving it of initiative and responsibility, and, therefore, of reality. The gradual stages of its growth it is impossible to trace in detail, for the third century after Christ is relatively one of the blank periods of history. Its perfected product is the system of Diocletian who, perhaps, more nearly resembles Sulla than any other statesman of ability, in his curiously doctrinaire belief in the efficacy of mere political machinery. Such glimpses, however, as we possess of the history of the third century, make it clear that Diocletian's arrangements were not arbitrary inventions, but the logical result of a continuous process. They systematised theory and practice, which had in the main developed under his predecessors, and the fundamental ideas of the complete separation of civil and military power and the subdivision of authority find their expression already in the speech put into the mouth of Mæcenas by Dio Cassius.[1]

But for our immediate purpose it may suffice to summarise the chief features in which the Empire at the end of the third century differed

---

1. Dio Cassius, lii, 14 foll. Upon this see Stuart Jones in *Legacy of Rome*, p. 135.

from that of the first.   The curious quadripartite division of the imperial office between two Augusti and two junior Cæsars need not detain us. Obviously it could not work in practice and, in fact, broke down at once.[1]   More significant and permanent is the altered position of the emperor, which had steadily been becoming more and more overtly autocratic.   We have moved far indeed from the cautious constitutionalism of Augustus when we enter the court of Diocletian, in which all the forms and ceremonial of Oriental despotism were deliberately adopted.

Again, for a Cicero, the state was Rome; the Mediterranean world but Rome's possessions. Even under the early Principate, Romans were the ruling race; Rome was a little more than a capital; the Italians were a privileged people.   But by the time of Diocletian, the levelling process, of which we have earlier spoken, had produced the logical result of the application of an uniform system. The concern of Diocletian is with the Empire, not with Rome; indeed, he has no prejudices in favour of the Eternal City, even as a capital. Italy, too, whose special privileges had by now disappeared, has become a province like any other.

---

1.   Diocletian wished to secure the power of the emperor beyond dispute, but it was also necessary to provide sufficient military heads for an Empire which was pressed simultaneously at more than one point.   At the same time, the experience of the third century had shown the danger of generals becoming rivals and declaring civil war in support of their claims.   Diocletian intended that, of the Augusti, one, like himself, should be master.   His idea was apparently that the normal reign would be of ten years as a Cæsar, followed by ten as an Augustus, after which his own example of abdication would be followed.   It is almost unnecessary to point out that ambition is not thus easily exorcised.

The complete autocracy of the emperor it was sought to secure by arrangements which were intended to prevent the acquisition of formidable power by any individual. The complete separation of the military and civil powers in the provinces, which had perhaps been initiated by Aurelian, was carried through. The provincial governor had now no troops at his disposal, while the provincial general was dependent upon the civil governor for his supplies. The provinces themselves were multiplied by subdivision. Whereas under Augustus there had been 29, there were now 116. Further, a new system of organised control was introduced. The new provinces were grouped in thirteen areas, called *dioceses*, which were each controlled by an officer called a *uicarius* ; the *uicarii*, in turn, were responsible to the four Prætorian Prefects at headquarters. The army, too, was reformed, and the garrison troops were supplemented by field armies, *comitatenses*, which constituted a distinct branch of the service, and the best troops in which were barbarians. Taxation was necessarily screwed up, and the *indictio*, originally an imperial decree for exceptional requisitions for an army in the field, now became a regular instrument of periodic assessment, and hence an instrument of chronology. Uniform regulations were enforced by an enlarged bureaucracy which was as corrupt as it was ubiquitous. There now came to be " more receivers than contributors." Subjects were becoming imprisoned in hereditary castes, from which there was no escape ; the serf and the municipal senator were alike savagely punished for attempted evasion of their inherited liabilities. The poor became poorer and the rich richer. The privileged classes formed a bureaucratic nobility divided into titular grades. The coinage had reached such a pitch of deterioration that taxes were exacted in kind, nor did the famous edict prescribing prices succeed in the hopeless task of defeating economic law by statute. It was indeed a sadly mistaken diagnosis which sought to cure ills, themselves largely due to over-organisation, by the prescription of yet more elaborate machinery, and the lowered vitality of the patient was ill able to stand the additional strain upon it. The expensiveness, indifference, incompetence, and almost inevitable corruption of a multiple but centralised bureaucracy, are evils which it is possible that modern society may yet learn by bitter experience. If history is any guide, the consequences, when the parasite has once developed beyond a certain size and strength, are almost inevitably fatal to its victim.

Let us now turn back from this gloomy picture to the happier days of the first two centuries! The health of any body politic eventually depends upon a satisfactory, practical compromise between the ideals of law and liberty, government and independence. The dual loyalty, upon which the prosperity of the earlier Empire was based, was, in no small measure, the result of the generous latitude which Rome had always permitted in matters of local autonomy. The general Roman principle may be said to have been not to interfere with the local customs and institutions of the peoples which she conquered, further than the

interests of Rome necessarily demanded.[1] Thus
from the first, local native law had run side by side
with Roman law in the provinces, and provincial
governors were expected, though bad governors
like Verres did not always do so, to respect its
provisions.[2] Naturally, where a conflict of laws
arose, Roman law claimed the precedence.

The degree of independent jurisdiction enjoyed
by the various urban units within the Roman
Empire varied with their status, though in this,
as in other spheres of self-government, cities
which abused their privileges might be punished.[3]
Normally, municipal magistrates were empowered
to try cases up to a degree of specified importance,
above this limit cases went to the governor's
court. Criminal cases involving a capital charge
were always reserved for Roman jurisdiction.
The Jews had no power to put Jesus to death
without the sanction of Pilate. Further, as St.
Paul reminds us, citizens arraigned upon a capital
charge had the right, under the early Empire, to
appeal to the imperial court at Rome.[4]

---

1. Characteristic is the reservation in a decree of the Delphian
Amphictyony in 130 B.C., which confirms the privileges accorded to the
Dionysiac artists of Athens. εἶναι δὲ ταῦτα τοῖς ἐν ᾽Αθήναις τεχνίταις ἐὰν
μή τι ᾽Ρωμαίοις ὑπεναντίον ἦι, Dittenberger, Sylloge, 3rd ed., 692, 60.

2. See Cicero, in Verr., iii, 6, ad. Att., vi. 1, 15, pro Balbo, 8. The matter
is discussed in L. Hahn, Rom und romanismus im griechisch-römischen Osten,
pp. 56-7.

3. See Reid, Municipalities of the Roman Empire, pp. 483 foll., where
examples will be found. We may recall the fears of the town clerk of Ephesus
in the Acts as to the consequences of a serious riot.

4. As the citizenship extended, it became impracticable to preserve the
right of appeal to Rome for all Roman citizens. In the second century it
became usual for the provincial governors to be invested with the ius gladii.
Eventually, under the later Empire, the privileged classes, honestiores, who
were also immune from the more degrading methods of torture or execution
retained a right of appeal; humiliores could be dealt with at will by the
governor. See Reid, op. cit., p. 484.

But though native laws survived and ultimately challenged the supremacy of imperial law, during the earlier centuries of the Empire convenience naturally led to the increasing dominance of imperial law, and as administration became more centralised, the adoption of uniform rules based upon precedents became universally the rule.[1] The denationalisation of Rome's native subjects was all the more effectively carried out because conformity to the Roman way was self-imposed, not forced upon them. How far denationalisation had progressed in the first century is rather strikingly illustrated by Titus' harangue to his soldiers: "My brave Romans! For it is right for me to put you in mind of what nation you are, in the beginning of my speech, that so you may not be ignorant of who you are and who they are against whom we are going to fight." This states the theme of his address which follows. Now, the enemy are the Jews, but the brave Romans, to whose nationality he appeals, were by race largely Syrians.[2]

The chief agent in thus Romanising the world was the *municipium*. Among municipalities there is some variation of detail and, in particular, there is a general distinction between the municipalities of the West, where Roman civilisation created urban life, which consequently flowed naturally into the mould

---

1. The process of building up an uniform procedure on the basis of precedents is a marked feature of Trajan's correspondence with Pliny.

2. Josephus, *de bell. Jud.*, iii, x, 2 (trans. Whiston).

prepared,[1] and those of the East, where urban life had flourished long before the Roman conquest, and where consequently there was a heritage of constitutional forms, which patriotic feeling liked to retain. But though in detail the Eastern municipalities do not follow the pattern described below so uniformly as do the Western (in the West, for instance, you will not find a town clerk, an important official in the East, like him of Ephesus who intervened to prevent a riot against St. Paul), even in the East the type is, in its general features, pretty stereotyped.

The type in general was imitated from that of the Roman colonies, which had already under the Republic proved invaluable instruments for encouraging voluntary Romanisation and, as such, had been deliberately used by Julius Cæsar both in the East and the West.[2] Already in the colony, as afterwards in the municipality, we see that eagerness to imitate Rome, even in details. Many possessed imitations of the Capitol, and in some, e.g. in Antioch in Pisidia, quarters of the town were named after divisions of Rome,

---

1. The rapidity with which the West took to Roman life is most remarkable. A curious example of the more rapid Romanisation of westerners who possessed no prior and competing civilisation is provided by the population of Emporiæ. It had long been inhabited by Greeks from Phocæa and Spaniards. After the battle of Munda, Cæsar sent Roman colonists there. " Now all the inhabitants form a single community since first the Spaniards, and eventually the Greeks too have received Roman citizenship." Livy, *xxxiv*, 9.

2. Narbo Martius specula populi Romani ac propugnaculum istis ipsis nationibus oppositum et obiectum, Cicero, *pro Fonteio* 13. For Cæsar's colonies see Hahn, *op. cit.*, pp. 59 foll., and Kornemann, *Philologus*, lx, 1901, pp. 402–426.

Vicus Tuscus, *Vicus Velabrus*, and so on.[1]   In social amusements, such as the circus, with its four factions, whose colours competed in the horse races, the municipalities throughout the empire did their best to emulate the metropolis.

The constitution of the *municipium* was everywhere timocratic in character. Men of wealth and substance alone enjoyed positions of political and social distinction. The model followed was that of Republican Rome, with its annual consuls, its powerful senate, and its popular assemblies.[2]

The normal *municipium* possessed a senate of 100 *decuriones* and three pairs of annual magistrates, *duouiri*—the chief magistrates who ranked highest in power and distinction and enjoyed powers of jurisdiction in such cases as were not important enough to go to the governor's court—two *aediles*, whose business it was to superintend the buildings, etc., and two *quaestores* to manage the municipal finance. Every five years, on the analogy of the Roman *lustrum*, the list of *decuriones* was filled up by the appointment of the senior ex-magistrates available, who were not already members. The magistrates themselves, until the second century, continued to be elected by popular vote, though popular election to the magistracies in Rome had come to an end under Tiberius.

---

1.   *Papers of the American School at Athens*, ii, Nos. 110, 115, *C.I.L. iii*, 297, 289.

2.   One of the marked differences between Western and Eastern municipalities is in the method of voting in the popular assemblies. Those in the East followed Greek precedent in voting by heads, those of the West the Roman method of voting by groups.

A number of amusing posters commending candidates for election have survived upon the walls of Pompeii, but to appreciate the real motives which swayed the voter we may perhaps listen for a moment to the small talk at Trimalchio's table: "There has been a famine for whole years now. Damn the magistrates, who play 'Scratch my back and I'll scratch yours,' in league with the bakers. I do wish we had the bucks I found here when I first came out of Asia —I remember Safinus ... He was more a mustard-pot than a man; used to scorch the ground wherever he trod. Still he was straight, you could trust him, a true friend; you would not be afraid to play *morra* with him in the dark. How he used to dress them down in the senate house ... And how kindly he returned one's greeting, calling everyone by name, quite like one of ourselves. So at that time food was dirt cheap ... Lord! things are worse every day. This town goes downhill like the calf's tail. But why do we put up with a magistrate not worth three peppercorns, who cares more about putting twopence in his purse than keeping us alive? He sits grinning at home and pockets more money a day than other people have for a fortune."

In this strain the grumbler continues further, until Echion, the old clothes dealer, breaks in: "Oh, don't be so gloomy. There's ups and there's downs as the country bumpkin said, when he lost his spotted pig. . . . (Times are not so bad.) . . . Just think, we are soon to be given a superb spectacle lasting three days. . . . And our good Titus has a big imagination and is hot-blooded:

it will be one thing or the other, something real, anyway. I know him very well, and he is all against half-measures. He will give you the finest blades, no running away, butchery done in the middle, where the whole audience can see it. And he has the wherewithal; he came into 30,000,000 when his father came to grief. . . . My nose prophesies a good meal from Mammaea, twopence each for me and mine. If he does, he will put Norbanus quite in the shade. You know he will beat him, hands down. After all, what has Norbanus ever done for us? He produced some decayed twopenny-halfpenny gladiators, who would have fallen flat if you breathed on them." [1]

Though the metropolis might make fun of the Justice Shallows of Italian provincial towns and deride their self-importance,[2] the municipal magistrate of the first two centuries enjoyed a position of local importance, power and dignity. The Roman temperament had a liking for a graded social system, and believed in the merits of doing one's duty in that state of life, to which one had been called. The *decuriones* formed a distinct local aristocracy, next to them came the *Augustales*, an order arising from the organisation of the worship of Augustus, in which the social

---

1. Petronius, *Sat.*, 44-5 (trans. Heseltine).

2. " Would you rather chose to wear the bordered robe of the man [Seianus] now being dragged along the streets, or to be a magnate at Fidenæ or Gabii adjudicating upon weights, or smashing vessels of short measure as a threadbare ædile at deserted Ulubræ ? " Juvenal, x, 99. " Nor yet one puffed up with his dignity, as a provincial ædile who deems himself somebody because he has broken up short pint measures at Arretium." Persius, i, 129.

aspirations of the rich parvenu freedmen could find an outlet. Freedmen were debarred from municipal office, but in a second generation servile origin might be forgotten, the more easily because such persons frequently took Roman names.[1] Needless to say, they acquired with ease the social prejudices of their new rank. If the *Life* is to be trusted, Juvenal was himself the son of a freedman, and though it is perhaps improbable that the inscription referring to a Juvenal as *duouir* of his native town refers to the satirist,[2] such an elevation to municipal office within a generation was by no means unusual. Below the *Augustales* came the commons. Even in the smallest matters the distinction of the social grades was observed. For instance, if largesse was distributed at a public banquet, the *decurio* got a triple share, the *Augustalis* a double, a member of the commons but a single share.

But already in the second century there are signs that people are no longer willing to come forward to take their share in political life. The Lex Malacitana[3] (82 or 83 A.D.) already recognises the necessity of providing for the

---

1. See Friedländer, *op. cit.*, i, p. 47, iv, p. 56. Professor Buckland reminds me that legally the son of a freedman, if born after his father was freed, was *ingenuus* and enjoyed the full rights of a free citizen in private law, but under the Republic and in the first century after Christ the first generation was socially regarded for practical purposes as *libertine*.

2. For Juvenal's social prejudices see below, p. 117. The facts about the inscription, which is often wrongly quoted as an indubitable reference to the satirist, are clearly stated in Ramsay's introduction to his translation of Juvenal and Persius in the *Loeb Series*.

3. Text in Bruns, *Fontes Juris Rom.*, 6th ed., No. 30, p. 147, translation Hardy, *Roman Laws and Charters*, pp. 98 foll.

possible contingency of an insufficient number
of candidates for the magistracies. Under
Antoninus Pius, Tergeste petitions for permission
to enrol new citizens to share in the burden of
office. At the end of the second century municipal magistrates ceased to be elected by the
people, because sufficient candidates would not
present themselves. A compulsory system had
to be adopted by which the local senates were
filled up from the landholders possessing the
necessary qualification, and the magistrates were
appointed from the senate. What are the
reasons for this change ?

First of all, it is essential to grasp that while
there is no period at which wealth has received
greater respect, there is also none in which so
much was expected of its possessors. Reid not
inaptly speaks of " the unwritten law that great
possessions were held on trust for public uses."[1]
By an extension of the client system, a rich man
was made patron of a municipality or a guild,
and was expected to return the honour by
munificence. If there was an element of ostentation, there can be no question of the generosity
with which the rich responded. The standard of
giving was equal to that of Liverpool's merchant
princes. The younger Pliny, for example, who
was not a portentously rich man, gave to his
native town of Como alone a library, an endowment for a school, a foundation for the nurture
of poor children, and a temple. " I do not long
for wealth," said the poet Martial, " in order to

---

1. Reid, *op. cit.*, 511.

acquire all sorts of luxurious belongings, but to make presents and to build."[1]

The municipal magistrate had to pay an honorarium, at important towns, of a considerable amount, upon taking office. But public opinion demanded a far greater expenditure. Not merely did his supporters—the people—expect to be regaled with shows and public banquets, or with free gifts of corn, but it was regarded as appropriate that he should add to the magnificence in which the municipalities rivalled each other, by the gift of some public building or aqueduct.[2] It will be readily understood that under such conditions the financial burdens of municipal office became increasingly ruinous.

The second principal cause for the decline, which we have noticed, was the decrease in the powers and responsibilities of municipal magistrates, owing to increasing interference by the central authority. This was in large measure the fault of the municipalities themselves. One has only to look at Pliny's account of the municipal finances in Bithynian towns to see that there was corruption, extravagance, and mismanagement. Nicæa had spent an enormous sum on a theatre, the foundations of which settled (x, 39). Nicomedia spent over three million sesterces on an aqueduct which was never completed, levied

---

1. Martial, ix, 22,
    Est nihil ex istis : superos ac sidera testor.
    Ergo quid ? Ut donem, Pastor, et ædificem.

2. τῶν μὲν πολιτευομένων τούτους μάλιστα ἐπαινεῖν οἵτινες ἂν πλείστας ὑμῖν τὰς εὐφροσύνας παρασκευάζωσιν, ἢ θεάματα ἀνευρίσκοντες ἢ χρήματα νέμοντες ἢ κοσμοῦντες ἐνί γέ τῳ τρόπῳ τὴν πόλιν. Aristides (Keil) xxiv, 43.

two millions for another which was abandoned, and at the end lacked a water supply (x, 37). The same town had not a single public fire-engine or bucket in the place, with the result that the greater part of it was burned down (x, 33). Under Nerva and Trajan we hear of special treasury officials being appointed to control the accounts of towns in Italy, and these officials, in the first place extraordinary, became regular institutions both in the East and in the West.

The great development in the imperial bureaucracy no doubt provided a rival and more profitable alternative to the local, municipal career. The main causes of decline, however, were the financial burdens involved in municipal office and the close supervision by the imperial bureaucracy, which ended by depriving public life in the municipality of responsibility, and, therefore, of reality. Eventually the *decurio* became merely an instrument of taxation, responsible for collecting and making up any deficiencies in the local quota. His responsibilities were riveted upon him by a compulsory heredity, and attempts to evade them were punishable by savage penalties. At the beginning of the fourth century we find that what had been the provincial aristocracy, has become not the least miserable of the hereditary castes into which society had been stereotyped.

There is another aspect of the munificence of the wealthy, which may, perhaps, merit our attention. There is to be considered not only the effect upon the givers, but the effect upon the recipients, which is hardly less important. Even under the Republic, Rome had been faced

by the problem of a large and disorderly population, a problem the acuteness of which was not
diminished by the institution of slavery, which
everywhere breeds "mean whites." In a sense, the
same political argument, which is sometimes used
to justify the unemployment dole, could be put
forward for the corn-distribution inaugurated by
Gaius Gracchus. Though his immediate object
was probably that of political bribery, there
existed a real danger of revolution, if the turbulent
and work-shy proletariate of Rome were allowed
to go hungry. Henceforward, in Rome, there
was a tacit acceptance of the quasi-socialistic
principle that it is the business of the Government to provide subsistence and of the rich to
provide amusements for poor citizens. In this,
as in other matters, the *municipia* were miniature
Romes. In the discussion on politics, which we
overheard at Trimalchio's party, the determining
factors in political candidature were the price
of food and the quality of the free amusements.
"The people that once bestowed commands,
consulships, legions, and all else, now meddles
no more, and longs eagerly for just two things
—Bread and Games." [1] "Since their needs were
largely met by others," says Professor Abbott,
"the people lost more and more the habit of
providing for themselves and the ability to do so.
When prosperity declined and the wealthy could
no more assist them, the end came." [2]

A very important social feature of the period,

---

1. Juvenal, x, 78.

2. Abbott, *The Common People of Ancient Rome*, p. 203.

which we are discussing, remains to be considered, the *collegia* or guilds.   As the *societates* or financial joint-stock companies of the Republic indicate, the Romans had always manifested a tendency towards association.   But if the *societates* were capitalist organisations, it is necessary to be careful in thinking of *collegia* of workmen as at all analogous to trades-unions.   The conditions of industry in antiquity were quite different to those of the present day.   There was neither mass production nor machinery.   " The strike is one of the rarest of phenomena in ancient society," at any rate in the sense of concerted action of wage-earners for the purpose of winning some concession from the employer.[1]   Indeed, the functions of the *collegia* were primarily social, not economic.

Nor can these associations be regarded as charitable organisations for mutual help.   The analogy of Friendly Societies or Benevolent Institutions would be hardly less misleading than that of trades unions.   The associations were formed for defined purposes, and to the expenses of carrying out these, the monies of the association

---

1.   Reid, *op. cit.*, p. 514.   The matter of strikes has recently been discussed in Buckler's paper on " Labour Disputes in the Province of Asia," *Anatolian Studies presented to Sir William Mitchell Ramsay*, pp. 27-50.   After reviewing the pertinent inscriptions in detail, his provisional conclusions are as follows. (1) strikes occurred from time to time during the period between the second and fifth centuries after Christ in the large cities of Asia Minor ;   (2) a strike of builders in the fifth century appears to be definitely a strike to secure higher wages ;   (3) to some extent strikes were controlled by working men's unions ;   (4) the authorities did not take action unless there was a breach of the peace ;   (5) if action was taken, punishment was inflicted not upon strikers as such, but upon persons charged with a breach of the peace, or with evasion of official enquiry ;   (6) if rioting occurred, the movement was suppressed and the leaders arrested.

were strictly devoted. As M. Foucart very properly emphasises with regard to Greek religious associations, the idea of the charitable relief of the indigence or hardship of the less fortunate members is quite foreign to their real character. Charitable funds of this kind were a creation of the Christian communities and, as Tertullian rightly claims, a real difference distinguishes the common funds of Christian from those of pagan societies. This practical, social aspect of the Christian doctrine of love had, indeed, no small influence in spreading the faith. Hence it is that Julian attempts to steal the weapons of the enemy, and inculcates the adoption of philanthropy upon the Christian model as an essential means towards the re-establishment of paganism.[1]

Although there existed a large number of *collegia*, the membership of which was restricted to persons locally engaged in a particular trade or profession, many had by no means this aspect of a trade guild. They included athletic clubs and social clubs, many of them, no doubt, both convivial and ephemeral, like " the Late Sleepers " and the " Late Drinkers," who have left their names upon the walls of Pompeii. Others, again, were associations united by common participation in a religious cult. In this connection we may notice an important point : the Christian com-

---

1. Foucart, *des. ass. rel.*, pp. 140 foll. Haec quasi deposita pietatis sunt nam inde non epulis nec potaculis nec ingratis uoratricis dispensatur, sed egenis alendis humandisque, Tertulliian, *Apol.* 39. ἐπειδὴ γὰρ οἶμαι συνέβη τοὺς πένητας ἀμελεῖσθαι παρορωμένους ὑπὸ τῶν ἱερέων, οἱ δυσσεβεῖς Γαλιλαῖοι κατανοήσαντες ἐπέθεντο ταύτῃ τῇ φιλανθρωπίᾳ, Julian, *Letter to a Priest*, 305c.

munities were exceptional in the closeness of their inter-relation with each other. The membership of the majority of *collegia*, even of those which were primarily religious, was purely local. The pagan exception is the guild of Dionysiac artists, whose actor members were continually on the move. This society developed a single organisation with affiliated branches throughout the Empire, its headquarters being in Rome.[1]

For obvious reasons the state had always claimed the right to suppress any private society, the activities of which conflicted with public morals, public order, or political tranquillity. In the political warfare of the last century B.C., the democrats had turned the *collegia* to use as weapons of political influence and violence. The political importance of Clodius had been similar in character to that of the Tammany boss. This had led to the wholesale suppression of the guilds. Under the early Empire, however, it became possible for an association to be registered by the state, and so to become licensed, *licitum*. As such it enjoyed an authorised legality

---

1. Reid, *op. cit.*, pp. 513 foll. For the detailed history of the guild τῶν περὶ τὸν Διόνυσον τεχνιτῶν see Poland, *Geschichte des griechischen Vereinswesens*, pp. 129-147. A further exception to the general statement is more apparent than real. The cult of Cybele was in a peculiar position, because it had been recognised as an adopted state cult under the Republic. As such, it came under the control of the Quindecimuiri. At least, in Italy and Gaul it would appear that the appointments to the priesthood in local cults of Cybele required to be approved by the Quindecimuiri. But as M. Graillot remarks, except in Rome itself this was " un simple formalité, une tradition bureaucratique." See Graillot, *op. cit.*, pp. 228-229. There is no evidence even in the cult of Cybele of any really effective centralised organisation nor anything at all comparable to the interconnection of the Christian communities.

subject to the observance of regulations, which usually restricted the number and frequency of the meetings.[1] Unlicensed associations were technically prohibited, and all through the early principate the formation of new corporations was regarded with suspicion, because of the possibility that they might be used for political purposes. Thus we find Trajan, for example, refusing to allow the formation of a guild of firemen in a Bithynian city upon these grounds (Pliny, *Ep*. x, 34). From the general interdict, however, were excluded the so-called *collegia tenuiorum*, or poor men's burial clubs. Many associations were, therefore, able to masquerade under this guise, and, further, it is clear that in practice, where the society was obviously harmless, the law was not rigidly enforced, even if no formal license had been obtained.

" Probably no age, not even our own, ever felt a greater craving for some form of social life wider than the family and narrower than the

---

1. The state control of some of the trade guilds went eventually a great deal further than this, and it was once the general view that the hereditary castes of the Theodosian code developed from the guilds of the earlier empire. It is true that by the time of the second and third centuries a number of *collegia*, mainly those the activities of which were essential to the carrying out of necessary public requirements—*e.g.*, shippers, corn-merchants, oil-merchants or bakers—received immunities from burdens of taxation or service. In return the state claimed control in essential points. The privileged member of such a guild must be a bona-fide and active member of the trade in question, he must possess the necessary implements and invest a proportion of his capital in the trade. He must further be of a certain age—*i.e.*, not too old nor too young for efficient service—and he must give a specified time to the public service. Recent research, however, has tended to show that the attractive simplicity of attributing the parentage of the castes to the guilds is not in accord with the complexity of the data so far as they are known.

State." " These colleges became homes for the homeless, a little fatherland or *patria* for those without a country." [1] Here lies the explanation and the peculiar appeal of this great movement, which affected the humblest members of society. The *collegia* were not, indeed, in the same sense as our great Friendly Societies, organisations for charity and social help ; but they satisfied the need of the humble for the pleasures of social intercourse and the dignity of self-expression. Characteristic are the burial clubs, the primary function of which was to provide members at death with a decent funeral, rescuing them from the common pit into which the bodies of the destitute were cast, and at the same time to afford the living members periodic opportunities for social reunion. At these meetings of the living the memory of the dead was kept alive, a form of vicarious immortality to which pagan sentiment attached a pathetic importance.

Along the great roads leading out of Rome, the erection of *columbaria*, which were possibly Etruscan in origin, began to be common under Augustus and Tiberius. The name, " dovecots," was derived from the rows of niches in which the urns containing the ashes of the deceased members were placed. They are the pagan counterparts to the Christian catacombs.[2] The building was

---

1. Dill, *Roman Society from Nero to Marcus Aurelius*, pp. 267, 271.

2. The latter, of course, contained burials, not urns of ashes. Both burial and cremation had been practised in Rome from very early times, but cremation had tended to become the more usual method until the Christian doctrine of the resurrection of the body ousted its practice from Europe until quite recent times.

erected under the superintendence of *curatores* appointed by the *collegium*, and paid for by a subscription of the members. It consisted normally of a subterranean building, with niches arranged in tiers for the reception of the burial urns. Some of these vaults might be of considerable size ; one has been discovered in which there are no less than nine superimposed tiers of niches. Above the vault were rooms in which the living members could meet for ceremonial and social gatherings. The system had great advantages for the poor and middle classes. The horror of the common pit, into which the bodies of paupers were cast, was intensified in a period when religious feeling was much concerned with the problems of a future life. At the same time the *columbaria* helped to solve the problems raised by the necessity of economising space and by the exorbitant costliness of ground rent, which had inevitably resulted from the concentration of population in the great cities.

The living members, however, gained from these burial clubs no less than the dead. Within the club the social distinctions of the outside world were forgotten. Distinctions there were, but they were the distinctions of seniority in the society, not those of wealth or rank outside. Slaves had an equal voice with free-born members at the meetings, and might rise to be officers of the society in due course. Thus the socially down-trodden might experience a certain social importance, and this, however lowly might be the company in which it was exercised, gratified a need of self-respect. Here was the real social merit of these institutions.

Collegia, like *municipia*, had their patrons. From the benefactions of these, the legacies of members, the entrance fees of members and office-holders, the regular subscriptions, and the fines by which the authority of the chair was supported at their meetings, the revenues of the society were derived. In the humbler burial clubs these were sometimes very small. In the *collegium* of Diana and Antinous at Lanuvium, each member paid an entrance fee of about 17s. and contributed a flagon of wine. A monthly subscription of five *asses* was demanded, and the society met once a month to collect them. In addition there were other celebrations in the course of the year—the two feast-days of Diana and Antinous and one or two meetings in commemoration of past members.

This particular club was too poor to have a *columbarium* of its own. When a member died, his legal representative was furnished with a sum for funeral expenses, provided that the dead man was not over three months in arrears with his monthly subscriptions, and that he had not committed suicide. If he died intestate, the college made arrangements for his funeral. Members were encouraged to attend funerals by a small gratuity. Special arrangements were made to provide for cases where a member died at a distance, and if the deceased member was a slave and his master refused to surrender his body, there was provision for the erection of a cenotaph over which the funeral rites were to be performed.[1]

---

1. The regulations of this college will be found in Dessau, No. 7212, or Bruns, No. 175. For further general information about *collegia* see Reid, *op. cit.*, pp. 511 foll., Dill, *op. cit.*, pp. 251-286, Abbott, *Common People of Rome*, pp., 205-234. Reference to the more specialist literature may be found under the appropriate headings in the dictionaries of Pauly-Wissowa and Daremberg et Saglio.

LECTURE III

" Cæsar seems to provide us with profound peace ; there
are no wars nor battles any more, no great bands of
robbers or pirates ; we are able to travel by land at
every season, and to sail from sunrise to sunset."
                                Epictetus, *Discourse*, iii, 13, 9.

"But he that cries up the happiness of globe-trotters who
spend the best part of their life in inns and passage
boats is like a man who thinks that the planets do better
than the fixed stars."
                                Plutarch, *de exilio*, 11, 604A.

HISTORY is not a mere logical argument nor the
presentation of a case ; it is an attempt to understand the past as lived by human beings.
Particularly when we are trying to understand
some great movement of thought, we must form,
as best we may, some imaginative picture of the
background of the material conditions under
which men lived at the time. There is, therefore,
profit as well as entertainment to be derived from
putting together some picture of the travelling
conditions of the period : for, indeed, the life
on the highways of the Empire provides an
appropriate background to the fluidity and
ferment of the intellectual life of the time.

The result of the establishment of the *pax
Romana* over the whole area governed by Rome

was the creation of a composite but single civilisation, which was in essentials the same, whether in Britain or in Borysthena. The free and constant inter-communication, the perpetual circulation throughout the veins of the great organism, was a yet more powerful agent of unification than even the increasing centralisation and uniformity of the machinery of government. Local differences of race and culture tended inevitably to be broken down. An incessant process of transplantation settled Syrians in Gaul and Gauls in Syria. It is indeed a little amusing to notice the confidence with which some anthropologists handle the racial characteristics of different parts of the Roman Empire. Actually in any place of considerable importance the population at the end of the second century must have been racially almost as mixed as that of any large American town.

That this constant intercommunication has an importance for the early history of Christianity hardly needs emphasising. It was this which enabled the new religion to spread itself almost unnoticed by the upper strata of society, first in the Eastern part of the Empire, then in Rome itself, and finally throughout the West. It was, further, the facility of communication, the constant contact of individuals from different Christian communities, the opportunity, which already St. Paul so wisely used, of issuing exhortation, advice and direction by epistolary means, which gave Christianity its corporate unity and enabled it to develop into a highly organised and disciplined state within the State.

By way of illustration we may recall the relevant passages in the *Didache*. Here regulations are laid down, first, for the itinerant missionary. " Let every Apostle who comes to you be received as the Lord, but let him not stay more than one day, or, if need be, a second as well ; but if he stay three days he is a false prophet. And when an Apostle goes forth, let him accept nothing but bread till he reaches his night's lodging ; but if he ask for money, he is a false prophet." The ordinary Christian is to be received, but again characteristic sense is shown in the care taken to avoid the exploitation of the community by frauds. " Let everyone who comes in the name of the Lord be received ; but when you have tested him you shall know him, for you shall have understanding of the right hand and of the left. If he who comes is a traveller, help him as much as you can, but he shall not remain with you more than two days, or, if need be, three. And if he wishes to settle among you and has a craft, let him work for his bread. But if he has no craft, provide for him according to your understanding, so that no man shall live among you in idleness because he is a Christian. But if he will not do so, he is making a traffic of Christ. Beware of such." " But every true prophet who wishes to settle among you is worthy of his food. Likewise a true teacher is himself worthy, like the workman of his food." Instructions follow as to the payment of such persons from first-fruits.[1]

---

1. *Didache*, xi, 3-6, xii, 1-5, xiii, 1-2.

The most usual means of communication for long distances was the sea. From the defeat of Antony and Cleopatra to the appearance of the Gothic raiders in the Ægean in the middle of the third century, the Mediterranean enjoyed one of its rare intervals of immunity from privateering and piracy. Shipwreck, of course, was still to be feared, and navigation in autumn and winter was still unsafe. Some of the smaller islands still produced wreckers and longshore pirates in a small way, and in the novel of Petronius we read of fishermen putting out to seize a disabled vessel as booty, but on finding that the survivors on board were prepared to defend their property, changing their intentions from piracy to salvage.[1] But from anything like the organised plundering of maritime commerce the seas were free. East of Suez, on the re-opened route to India, armed bowmen were a necessary addition to a ship's company to defend her against the natives of the Persian Gulf and their poisoned arrows, but within the Inland Sea merchantmen could sail care-free upon their lawful occasions. The great commercial development, which inevitably accompanied peace, had opened all the seas to enterprise. Many a merchant saw the sun sink hissing in the far Atlantic, and returned with swollen money-bags

---

1. Petronius, *Sat.*, 114. cf. Julian's reference to this longshore piracy. διαφέρουσι γὰρ οὗτοι τί, πρὸς τῶν θεῶν εἶπέ μοι, τῶν ἐπ' ἐρημίας λῃστευόντων καὶ κατειληφότων τὰς ἀκτὰς ἐπὶ τῷ λυμαίνεσθαι τοῖς καταπλέουσι ; Julian, *Or.*, vii, 210a. Upon the whole subject see Ormerod, *Piracy in the Ancient World*, in this series.

and tales of mermen and the monsters of the deep.[1]

The great centre of sea-borne traffic in Italy was Puteoli.   Here the great event was the arrival of the corn fleet from Alexandria.   Its approach was heralded by the mail boats, distinguishable by the topsails, which they alone carried in the Bay. As soon as they appeared round Capri, the whole population crowded down to the quays leaving the old philosopher, who is in no hurry to read his letters, to a welcome respite from interruption, which is warmed by the consciousness of his superiority to trivial excitements.[2] It was a number of "liberty men" from this great merchant fleet, who attended a performance of the Emperor Nero at Naples, and thus introduced him to the merits of the Alexandrian method of applauding, in which he characteristically pro-ceeded to train a body of Italian *clacqueurs*.[3]

---

1.   Veniet classis quocumque uocarit
spes lucri, nec Carpathium Gætulaque tantum
aequora transiliet, sed longe Calpe relicta
audiet Herculeo stridentem gurgite solem.
grande operae pretium est, ut tenso folle reuerti
inde domum possis tumidaque superbus aluta
Oceani monstra et iuuenes uidisse marinos.
                              Juvenal, xiv, 277.

2. Seneca, *Ep.*, lxxvii, 1-2. Philosophic calm, when the post arrives, was admired by Plutarch. " If a letter is brought to us, we must not show all that hurry and eagerness to open it which most people display, when they bite the fastenings through with their teeth, if their hands are too slow." He proceeds to narrate the politeness of Rusticus. He was listening to a lecture of Plutarch when a letter from the Emperor was brought to him. Plutarch stopped his discourse to give him an opportunity of opening it, but no, Rusticus kept it unopened until the lecture was over ! An edifying exchange of courtesies. Plutarch, *de curios.*, 522, D-E.

3. Suetonius, *Nero*, xx, 3. Puteoli was probably the home of Trimalchio, Friedländer, *Cena Trimalchionis*, p. 10. For a description of the town, see *ibid.*, pp. 73-76.

At any time if we ascended the hill by Cicero's villa and thence looked down upon the great harbour, we should see it filled with a great merchant fleet bound for all parts of the Empire. For though the plane tree and the cicadas are an obvious literary theft from Plato (*Phaedrus* 230 c and 259), the setting of the conversation between Apollonius of Tyana and the philosopher Demetrius is, in its main essentials, true to life. " You have the chance of salvation here within one step," says Demetrius. " You see all these ships ? Some of them are bound for Libya, some for Egypt, some for Phœnicia or Cyprus, some for Sardinia direct and some via Sardinia for further ports. Embark on some one of them —it is the best thing to do—and sail for any of those countries." [1] Apollonius, to whom the advice is given, had just arrived. From Smyrna he had taken ship to Corinth, where he arrived in the morning. Before nightfall he was able to get another ship bound for Sicily and Italy, and on the fifth day he had landed at Puteoli. [2] This, together with the familiar experiences of St. Paul, will give you an impression of the facility of communications by sea.

---

1. Philostratus, *Vit. Apoll.*, vii, 12, 264.

2. Philostratus, *Vit. Apoll.*, vii, 10, 260. Average times for sea journeys are not easy to establish, for our information is derived mainly from notices of record runs or from the journeys of highly placed personages who enjoyed exceptional facilities. The record voyage from Rome to Alexandria was nine days, the average summer passage probably about 18 days ; the return journey, thanks to the Etesian winds, took nearly twice as long. The record passage from Alexandria to Marseilles was 13 days, but the ordinary voyage from Alexandria to Rome must have taken from three weeks to a month. See Charlesworth, *Trade Routes and Commerce*, pp. 22, 44, 60, 86, 139, 155. Friedländer, *Life and Manners*, i, p. 285.

In fact, travel by sea was easy and was
experienced by all. Rhetorical and philosophical
common-place—though much of it, no doubt, is
of purely literary origin—is full of illustrations
drawn from the pilot, the helmsman, the shipwreck, or the big cargo vessel which responds to
so small a helm (Plutarch, *de gen. Soc*, 588 F.)
But Romans themselves were never by nature a
seafaring folk. Catullus, in his fourth poem, is
an exception; the attitude of most of his com-
patriots was that expressed by Lucretius. "How
pleasant it is to stand on shore and watch the poor
devils of sailors having a bad time." Statius
(*Siluae* iii, 2, 13 foll.) may describe a big ship
getting under way, but it is a landsman's, not a
sailor's description. Voyages are necessary as a
means of getting about, but they remain a
necessary evil. Seneca thought that a little
sailing was good for the inside (*Ep.* lxxviii, 5),
but he is hardly an enthusiastic yachtsman.
"You can persuade me into almost anything
now, for I was recently persuaded to travel
by water," is the reflection prompted by his
experience of an attempt to sail from Puteoli
to Naples, which soon ended in his forcing the
skipper to put him ashore at all costs. (*Ep.*
liii.)

From the earliest days of her political
ascendancy, Rome had inevitably been a road-
builder. As the power of the Republic had
extended in Italy, the newly-conquered territory
was secured by a net-work of military roads, with
colonies of Roman citizens (in other words
permanent hereditary garrisons) at the essential

strategic points. To all imperial powers, indeed, communications are of vital importance. Thus the Persians had, perforce, been road-builders, and railway construction has played no small part in modern imperialism. It was, there-fore, inevitable that Augustus and his successors should pay attention to so important a factor in imperial government. The great highways (*e.g.*, the *Via Egnatia*, which ran from Durazzo to Salonica, and thence, following the Royal Road which Xerxes had engineered for his invasion of Greece, to the Dardanelles and Constantinople) were maintained, and new trunk lines were constructed, notably those through the Alpine districts, which Augustus had pacified, linking Rome with the Upper Danube and the Rhine.

Thus from the golden milestone (*miliarium aureum*), which Augustus set up in the Forum at Rome, there radiated throughout the provinces a system of imperial trunk roads. Under the Republic, the *censores* had been responsible for the maintenance of the state roads in Italy, and provincial governors for those in the provinces. Now an imperial department directly under the emperor's control was created, and the *curatores uiarum* maintained the efficiency of the main lines of public communication. Apart from these imperial roads, which were maintained primarily for imperial purposes, there was a network of local municipal[1] or private roads.

---

1. For instance the question was referred to the Senate in the reign of Tiberius, whether the people of Trebia might divert a legacy which had been left them specifically for the building of a theatre, to the construction of a road. Suetonius, *Tiberius*, 31.

The state roads varied in width, but were constructed for permanence, with a solid paving upon a firmly laid foundation. They are among the most durable monuments of Roman rule, and their long, straight lines and admirable engineering will be familiar to anyone who is well acquainted with the English countryside. Distances were carefully marked with milestones, and outside a big town, as outside a Moslem city to-day, the road was flanked by tombstones with their pathetic appeals to the kindly thought of the passer-by, which have remained a convention of the literary epitaph. Here is a poet's account of the ancient navvies' task, which is taken from Statius' poem on the construction of the *Via Domitiana*.

" Here of old the traveller, moving slow in his carriage, with one wheel foundered, hung and swung in balanced torture; while the churlish soil swallowed his wheels, and in mid-land the Latins shuddered at the ills of sea-going. No swift journeying was theirs; while the suppressed ruts clogged and checked their going and the tired nags, fretting at their burden, under the high yoke crawled upon their way. But now what was a whole day's journey is become scarce an hour's travel. No barque, no straining bird of the air, will make better speed.

" The first task was to prepare the furrow, to open a track and, with deep digging, hollow out the earth; the next in other wise to refill the caverned trench, and prepare a top on which the convex surface of the road might be erected, lest the ground should sink or the spiteful earth yield an unstable bed for the deep-set blocks; then with close-knit revetments on this side and on that, and with many a brace, to gird the road. What a multitude of hands wrought together at the work! These felled the forest and stripped the hills; those made smooth the beams and the rocks with steel; these bound the stones together and wove fast the work with baked bricks and dingy pumice; others with might and main dried the thirsty pools and drained off the lesser rivulets."[1]

So much for the means of travel by land—what about its security? The band of brigands, like the by now non-existent pirates, belonged to the stock armoury of romance, and the care-free pauper who sings in the robbers' presence is a rhetorical commonplace. But allusions are too frequent to allow us to believe that the highwayman had disappeared so completely as the pirate. " A man," says Epictetus, " has heard that the road is infested by robbers; he does not dare to venture on it alone, but waits for company—a legate, or a quaestor, or a proconsul—and joining him he passes safely on the road." " Think," writes Seneca, when elaborating on the insecurity of life, " any day a robber might cut your throat."[2]

The physical characteristics of the country, in parts of the Roman Empire, made brigandage no doubt inevitable. It is still endemic in parts of

---

1. Statius, *Siluae*, iv, 3, 40 foll. (trans. Slater.)

2. Cantabit uacuus coram latrone uiator, Juvenal, x, 22. *Cf.* nudum latro transmittit; etiam in obsessa uia pauperis pax est, Seneca, *Ep.* xiv, 9; Epictetus, *Discourse*, iv, i, 91; Cogita posse et latronem et hostem admouere iugulo tuo gladium, Seneca, *Ep.*, iv, 8.

the Levant, where fugitives from justice habitually take to the hills, though Kithæron may not be permanently as dangerous as it was in Lucian's day (*Dial. Nec.* 27, 2, 438). But, although the brigand was a familiar feature of life under the Roman Empire, it may be doubted whether the roads of England in the eighteenth century were not more unsafe. The real deathblow to the profession of highway robbery has been dealt by the modern development of rapid means of communication which, in the long run, load the dice against the highwayman and make his profession an unprofitable gamble. For authority is now enabled to get almost immediate news of the commission of crime, and thus at once to close or watch the robber's avenues of escape.

In detail, what general organisation existed under the Roman Empire for the policing of the roads is a matter of some obscurity. In brigand infested areas like Palestine, upon frontier routes like the passes of the Caucasus, or upon threatened but important stretches of road like that to Myos Hormos, the port for the Far Eastern trade, the imperial government stationed military posts.[1] " Military stations," declares Tertullian, " are distributed through all the provinces for tracking robbers. Against traitors and public foes, every man is a soldier ; search is made even for their confederates and accessories." [2] We hear of a *praefectus arcendis latronibus* at municipal centres, and normally in settled areas

---

1. See Charlesworth, *Trade Routes*, pp. xvi, 22, 40 foll.
2. Tertullian, *Apol.*, 2.

it would seem probable that the duties of maintaining security fell upon the local authorities.

It is, at any rate, certain that an enormous
amount of traffic passed continuously to and fro
along the Roman highways. This was not the
least of the benefits conferred by a strong central
government. In the troubled century, which
preceded the accession of Augustus—a century of
civil wars and proscriptions—Italy had been
filled with broken men, runaway slaves and the
outlawed victims of injustice. It had then been
not uncommon for travellers to be kidnapped
upon the highways, and to be sold as slaves to
work in the plantation gangs of large estates.
This state of things Augustus stamped out, and
persons, like Ballista, who pleasantly combined
the trades of schoolmaster and footpad, were
forced to give up their nefarious double life.[1]
The only considerable brigand in Italy during the
first two centuries of our era is the admirable
rogue, Felix Bulla. He is an instructive exception,
for his career is, in fact, a sign of the times—a
symptom of the beginning of the period of
disintegration at the close of the second century.

Septimius Severus, by disbanding the Prætorian
Guard, had deprived the high-spirited youth of

---

1. Suetonius, *Augustus*, 32. His work in Italy was completed by Tiberius,
Suetonius, *Tiberius*, 37. Juvenal complains that the stamping out of highway
robbery in Italy has brought all the footpads and assassins to Rome.

> Interdum et ferro subitus grassator agit rem ;
> armato quotiens tutae custode tenentur
> et Pomptina palus et Gallinaria pinus,
> sic inde huc omnes tamquam ad uiuaria currunt, iii, 305.

Ballista was the theme of what was said to be Vergil's earliest attempt at verse.

> Monte sub hoc lapidum tegitur Ballista sepultus ;
> nocte die tutum carpe, uiator, iter, [Suetonius], *Life of Vergil*, 17.

Italy of a safe outlet for their martial energies. From this material Bulla created a band of six hundred men which, for two years, defied the utmost efforts of the authorities. He worked the road between Brindisi and Rome, and his agents in the capital and in the port kept him well informed of arrivals and intended departures. He was clearly a man of great personality and daring, and a born leader of men. His hold upon his band was strengthened by the numerous feats of which he was the hero. For instance, when an officer was sent to catch him, Bulla presented himself in disguise and offered to act as guide to the unfortunate representative of the law, and so personally led him into his own clutches. Upon another occasion two of his men had been captured and sentenced to be thrown to the beasts. Bulla, impersonating a high official, presented himself at the prison in which they were awaiting execution and persuaded the warders of the authenticity of alleged official instructions to hand them over to him. A woman's jealousy eventually led to his capture. Unrepentant to the last, when asked by the great jurist Papinian from the bench, " Why did you become a robber ? " he retorted, " Why are you a prefect ? " He was, of course, condemned and thrown to the beasts ; his band, which had been held together by their leader's personality, at once collapsed.[1]

Occasionally, no doubt, if alienated by some act of violence, the local population of the

---

1. *Dio Cassius*, lxxvi, 10.

countryside, like the villagers in Apuleius, would attack the brigands, and, taking the law into their own hands, would inflict summary punishment, hurling them over some precipice, or cutting their throats, and leaving them to lie unburied. If they fell into the hands of justice, like the English highwaymen, the robbers received no mercy. They were often crucified and left to rot by the roadside, as a warning to others and a testimony to the vigilance of the authorities; and Galen mentions the somewhat gruesome opportunities for anatomical observation which were provided by their exposed remains. Sometimes they were condemned to fight under the most barbarous conditions. Seneca, in a passage of considerable ethical interest, expresses his condemnation of this form of brutalising cruelty. "You may retort. 'But he was a highway robber; he killed a man!' 'And what of it? Granted that, as a murderer, he deserved this punishment, what crime have you committed, poor fellow, that you should deserve to sit and see this show?'"[1]

The practical reason which lay behind the creation and maintenance of a highly developed system of imperial roads was the necessity of securing rapid and frequent communications between the central authority and the provinces. Indeed, the exchange of despatches inevitably

---

1. Apuleius, *Met*, vii, 13; Petronius, *Sat.*, 111; Galen, *de anat. adm.*, iii, 79, 145 in *Medicorum Graec. Op.*, ed. Kühn, vol. ii, p. 385; Seneca, *Ep.*, vii, 5. cf. Tertullian, *Apol.*, 9. "It is the blood of a beast-fighter, you say. Is it less, because of that, the blood of a man? Or is it viler blood because it is from the veins of a wicked man? At any rate it is shed in murder." cf. homo sacra res homini iam per lusum et iocum occiditur, Seneca, *Ep.* xcv, 33.

increased in number and frequency as the hold of the central office became firmer, and it became customary to refer even matters of detail to headquarters for the Emperor's decision. Hence it is not surprising to find a regular system of post-houses in use. For this the model lay ready to hand in the East, where the successors of Alexander had extended and improved the postal system of the Persian Empire, which Herodotus describes (v, 52).

At intervals of twenty-five Roman miles, rest-houses (*mansiones*) were erected and, in some provinces at least, *prætoria* or *palatia* were attached to them, in which officials travelling upon business could be housed. At lesser intervals were *mutationes*, where the imperial couriers could change horses. The earlier practice seems to have been for the couriers to hand on despatches in relays, but although this had the advantage of rapidity, the more secure, if slightly slower, method of sending a single responsible messenger right through, came to be preferred. This postal service was official and was limited to official use. Permission to travel by the imperial post might be given as a favour, and in a case of urgency, for instance to Pliny's wife (*Ep.* x, 120, 121) ; but, no doubt necessarily, such privileges were more and more sparingly conferred upon private persons. Of private companies for providing posting facilities for ordinary travellers there is some evidence in Italy, where associations of *iumentarii* and *cisarii* (horse and carriage jobbers) are recorded in inscriptions.

The inns and accommodation for travellers do not appear to have been very inviting or excellent. Of course, our evidence on the subject is not conclusive. To grumble at the fleas and bugs in the inns or at the extortions of innkeepers is one of the stock topics of the hardships of travel. For the former complaint, which is attested by the Elder Pliny,[1] I cannot resist quoting by way of illustration the delightfully comic miracle of St. John in the *Apocryphal Acts*. St. John and his disciples came to a deserted inn and made themselves at home for the night. The bed proved to be infested with bugs, whom St. John thereupon addressed : " I say unto you, O bugs, behave yourselves, one and all, and leave your abode for the night and remain quiet in the one place, and keep your distance from the servants of God." On the next morning, when the disciples opened the door, " we saw at the door of the house which we had taken, a great number of bugs standing." St. John then " sat up on the bed and looked at them, and said, ' Since ye have well behaved yourselves in hearkening to my rebuke, come into your place.' And when he had said this, and risen from the bed, the bugs running from the door hasted to the bed and climbed up by the legs thereof and disappeared into the joints." [2]

For the second complaint I would quote a philosopher's illustration. " How glad we are at

---

1. Pliny, *Nat. Hist.*, ix, 47 (71), 154.   Adeo nihil non gignitur in mari ut cauponarum etiam aestiua animalia pernici molesta saltu aut quae capillus maxime celat exsistant.

2. *Acts of John*, 60 foll., James, *Apocryphal New Testament*, p. 242.

the sight of shelter in a desert, a roof in a storm, a bath or a fire in the cold—and how dear they cost in inns." [1]

In the big towns there were, of course, taverns and low pot-houses, some of which were little better than gambling dens or brothels. The public-houses in which Lateranus hobnobbed with ostlers (Juv., viii, 156), and, perhaps, even the old taverns of Claudius' youth, the disappearance of which he publicly lamented (Suetonius, *Claudius*, 40), were probably pretty disreputable places. But in large urban centres there was at least a choice. As an example of foolish weakness Plutarch gives the incapacity to resist the persistence of the hotel tout, " lodging in a paltry inn when better accommodation is to be had, to oblige the landlord who has cringed to us " (Plutarch, *de vit. pud.*, 8, 532 B). Certainly, at the big centres of exchange, like Aquileia, and at such places as Canopus, the Egyptian pleasure resort, or Berenice, the port for the Eastern trade, as Strabo expressly tells us,[2] there were admirable hostelries. Among the amenities of the springs of the Clitumnus, which the younger Pliny recommends (*Ep.* viii, 8, 6), were the municipally owned baths and hotels.

Inns, like those of our coaching forbears, had signs and often animal names. Thus at Pompeii was found a notice of a restaurant to let called *The Elephant*, which its owner, Sittius, had recently " done up." Its sign was the painting

---

1. Seneca, *de Ben.*, vi, 15.
2. Strabo, xvii, 17, 801, 45, 815.

of an elephant encircled by a snake and attended by a pygmy. In one of the many curious dreams recorded by Artemidorus, a man dreamed that he interrupted a game of draughts between Charon and a man. Charon, infuriated, pursued him ; he fled into an inn called *The Camel* and just slammed the door in time to shut his pursuer out, but grass then began to grow upon one of his thighs. The dream came true, though the explanation is, perhaps, a little far-fetched. It signified an escape with a minor injury to the leg from the accidental collapse of part of the dreamer's house.[1]

Naturally enough, the inn figures largely in the picaresque novels of adventure of Petronius and Apuleius, just as it does in those of Fielding and Smollet. A modern, though more estimable parallel to Meroe was of some service to the Allied cause in the Levant during the war, though the lady, of whom I am thinking, did not reinforce the elderly charms, which she was far from depreciating, by the practice of witchcraft.[2]

As in Greece to-day, the traveller could not be sure of finding a hostelry and must sometimes seek quarters in a private house. One of the best and most realistic passages in Heliodorus (v, 18) is the description of Calasiris' interview of cross

---

1. Hospitium hic locatur, triclinium cum tribus lectis Sittius restituit Elepantu. See Mau, *Pompeii*, p. 393. Artemidorus, *Oneirocrit.*, I, 4, 12. There is a good deal of random information in Firebaugh, *The Inns of Greece and Rome* (Chicago, 1923), but the work is untidy, undocumented and unpleasantly journalistic.

2. For the stock story of the murder in the inn, which originates with Chrysippus, see Cicero, *de diu.*, i, 27, 57. For further references see the notes in the elaborate edition by Professor A. S. Pease. cf. the story in Cicero, *de inu.*, 2, 14, 15. For Meroe see Apuleius, *Met.*, i, 7.

questions and crooked answers, with the deaf old
fisherman at Zacynthus, who at length under-
stands what he wants, and, as no local inn exists,
agrees to take them in, provided that they don't
want much accommodation or service, into the
cottage which he and his two sons inhabit. But
even in the country delightful inns must have
existed, if we may trust Epictetus' illustration of
the man who is so attracted by the pleasantness
of a good inn, in a beautiful country, that he
stays on and on and forgets the goal of his
journey (*Disc.*, ii, 23, 36).

No doubt, however, in the main the country
inns were simple and primitive. In part this was
due to the institution of slavery. The rich man
travelled with a luxurious retinue of slaves, and
his extensive cortège was self-sufficing. The
average man in antiquity, as in the Near East
to-day, aimed little higher than the *khan*, a
place, that is to say, where the traveller can
obtain lodging for the night for himself and
his beasts. To-day in Greece, outside the
Europeanised hotels of Athens, the functions of
inn and restaurant are distinct. In the inn the
traveller hires a bed—not even a room unless
he pays for all the beds in it. His food he either
brings with him or must procure outside in a
café or restaurant—in a *popina* in fact.[1] It was

---

1. Polybius notes " the exception, which proves the rule," in the Po
valley. It is a remarkable sign of the richness of the country and the cheap-
ness of food that " travellers in this country who put up in inns, do not bargain
for each separate article they require, but ask what is the charge per day
for one person. The innkeepers, as a rule, agree to receive guests, providing
them with enough of all they require for half an *as* per day, *i.e.*, the fourth
part of an obol, the charge being very seldom higher." Polybius, ii, 15, 5.

no doubt in such *khans* along the road from the Rhine to Rome that Vitellius curried favour by his affability to the travellers and mule-drivers.[1]

The doubtfulness of accommodation and the difficulties of synchronising arrival with that of the baggage increased the accidental discomforts of the traveller, as they still do in the Levant to-day. The god sent one of his usual peremptory messages to Aristides, that martyr to vanity, superstition and hypochondria, to leave Smyrna forthwith. It was summer, and very hot, so the baggage was sent on ahead, while Aristides waited in a suburb for the cool of the day. At sunset he came to the khan (καταγωγίον) on the Hermus, but he did not like the looks of the building, and his baggage was still ahead, so he pushed on. In late evening he got to Larissa, but the khan was no better, and still they had not caught up their gear. At midnight they got to Kyme and found everything locked up, and so on to Myrina which they reached at cock-crow. Here they found their baggage and the carters in the street in front of one of the inns. The place had been locked up before they had arrived, they said. There was a truckle-bed in the porch of the inn, and they spent a while carrying it round; but wherever they put it, it was equally miserable. They knocked at doors, but could make no one hear. At long last they got admission to the house of a connection of one of the men. Here the doorkeeper had put out the light, and there was no fire, big or small, in

---

1. Suetonius, *Vitellius*, vii, 3.

the house, and they had to grope their way in blindly in the dark. By the time they got settled in, the day dawned.[1]

The rich, as I have said, travelled luxuriously with a large retinue, and the envious complaints of their poorer brethren are among the commonplaces of Silver Age literature. Runners preceded them and their cortège carried the necessities and even the luxuries of life with them. Nero "never made a journey with less than one thousand carriages, his mules shod with silver and their drivers clad in wool of Canusium, attended by a train of Moorish horsemen and couriers with bracelets and trappings" (Suetonius, *Nero*, 30, 3). This is an extreme of extravagance, but to balance it here is the nearest ancient analogy to our walking tour. Seneca expatiates upon the delights and merits of the simple life. He has just spent two days on tour with his friend Maximus in a country cart, attended by *no more slaves than would go into a single conveyance !* He tells us that it was great fun and, upon philosophical grounds, wholly admirable, but he could not help feeling a little self-conscious and shy about meeting anyone on the road (Seneca, *Ep.*, lxxxvii).

The well-to-do man seldom walked ; physical exercises (Seneca, *Ep.*, xv, 4) might satisfy the requirements of a literary man's body. If he went into town he went in his litter. The

---

1. Aristides (Keil), li, 2-7. For the discomforts of a person, suffering amongst many other maladies, from earache and toothache, when making a winter journey from the Hellespont along the *Via Egnatia* to Rome, see Aristides (Keil), xlviii, 60 foll.

motion was good for the liver, and study or, if the windows were shut, sleep were not interfered with.[1]

For travelling, a litter[2] or a carriage, two-wheeled or four-wheeled, was used. The vehicles were fitted up with means for relieving the tedium of travel. Reading, writing and dictation could be carried on undisturbed. In the coldest weather the indefatigable Elder Pliny ceaselessly dictated his notes, and his nephew mentions a characteristic piece of thoughtfulness, the long sleeves which he invented to keep the fingers of his amanuensis from getting cold (Pliny, *Ep.*, iii, 5).

Writing, at any rate of not too exacting a character, could be conducted in a two-wheeled carriage.[3] Claudius, who was so notoriously devoted to dice that the satirist, anticipating the Mikado's maxim, condemned him in hell to rattle dice eternally in a box without a bottom,[4] had a dice-board fitted up in his travelling

---

1. " Riding in a litter shakes up the body (cf. *Ep.*, lv, where Seneca takes· litter exercise) and does not interfere with study : one may read, dictate, converse or listen to another." Seneca, *Ep.*, xv, 6.

  si uocat officium, turba cedente uehetur
  diues et ingenti curret super ora Liburna.
  atque obiter leget aut scribet uel dormiet intus ;
  namque facit somnum clausa lectica fenestra.

Juvenal, *Sat.*, iii, 239. Of Aristo the philosopher, who was never seen to walk but was always carried about in his litter, a wag said, " Anyway, he is not a Peripatetic." Seneca, *Ep.*, xxix, 6.

2. Non turba seruorum lecticam tuam per itinera urbana ac peregrina portantium. Seneca, *Ep.*, xxxi, 10.

3. quaedam enim sunt quae possis et in cisio scribere, Seneca, *Ep.*, lxxii, 2.

4. Seneca, *Apocolocyntosis*, 14-15.

carriage.[1]   The studious Julian carried a library
with him, even on his campaigns.[2]

The Roman Empire of the first two centuries
was a travelled society like our own.   In the
upper classes it would be the exception to find
an Aelian who had never been abroad.[3]   Official
duty scattered the upper class over the Empire.
"A senator," says Epictetus, "must spend most of
his time abroad, in command or under command,
or as a subordinate to some office, or as a soldier
or judge." [4]   In Statius' reflections on the after
career of pupils at the school, which his father
kept, those of us who have been members of
any of the larger public schools will detect a
familiar note.   "Now of that company one,
perchance, is governor of Eastern nations, and
one controls the races of the Ebro; one from
Zeugma beats back Achaemenid Persian; those
bridle the wealthy peoples of Asia, these the
Pontic lands; these by peaceful authority purify
our courts; those in royal leaguer guard their
camp" (i.e., are in the Guards).[5]   But travel
for pleasure was also common, as is shown by
the frequency of the allusions in Seneca's *Letters*.
His favourite topic that travel is no cure for
discontent (*e.g.*, *Ep.* xxviii) is, of course, a hoary
commonplace, our old friend *coelum non animum*

---

1.   Suetonius, *Claudius*, 33.

2.   Julian, *Or.* iii, 124-125.

3.   It was a source of pride to Aelian that he had never been outside
Italy and had never set foot on a ship, Philostratus, *Vit. Soph.*, ii, 31, 625.

4.   Epictetus, *Disc.*, iii, 24, 36.   For instance, Bolanus had served in
Armenia and in Britain, and had been proconsul in Asia, Statius, *Siluae*,
v, 2, 29 foll.

5.   Statius, *Siluae*, v, 3, 185.

mutant qui trans mare currunt. " If you really want to enjoy travel, make healthy the companion whom you must take with you (si uis peregrinationes habere iucundas, tuum comitem sana," *Ep.* civ, 20), gives it a new turn. " Those who spend their life in travel have many acquaintances, but few friends" (*Ep.* ii, 2), may well be the result of direct observation.

Like modern urban dwellers, the ancient enjoyed a change of air. In the summer particularly, everyone, who could afford it, left the unhealthy metropolis for the sea-side. The rich, like Cicero, had always had their several villas or country houses in Italy,[1] many of them at Baiae. Here on the Bay of Naples was the great pleasure city of the rich and the middle class, and it was a favourite resort of Nero. With its demi-mondaines, its coloured boats, its roses, its serenaders, and its sailing parties, it must in many ways have resembled Monte Carlo in the season. A nearer sea-side resort, the Southport as it were of Rome, was Ostia. Thus a typical *controuersia*, or set subject in the rhetorical schools, began " some young men from the city went to Ostia in the summer season, and arriving at the shore found some fishermen

---

1. For Cicero's villas see Warde Fowler, *Social Life at Rome in the Age of Cicero*. The Laurentine and Tusculan villas of Pliny the Younger (*Ep.* ii, 17 and v. 6) have lately been discussed in an excellent and well-illustrated monograph by Miss Tanzer, *The Villas of Pliny the Younger* (Columbia University Press, 1924). Further villas of Pliny (huius in litore plures uillae meae, sed duae ut maxime delectant ita exercent; the rival charms of watching fishermen or being able to fish yourself from your bedroom window) *Ep.* ix, 7.

drawing in their nets." But you will, no doubt, have visited it with Minucius Felix and his friends, and will remember how they escaped from the city on a summer's evening and walked along the shore, while they watched the boys playing " ducks and drakes " and discussed the rival merits of paganism and the new religion.[1]

The well-to-do travelled widely farther afield and, like their modern successors, from various motives. Some because travel was the right thing to do, some because of a real curiosity and a genuine desire to acquire knowledge, some in search of health and some for distraction from care. It was as much the fashion for the educated upper class to visit Greece or Egypt as it is for Americans to visit Europe. Like modern tourists, they scratched their names upon the monuments of antiquity, and, like Mr. Pontifex senior, they were liable to lapse into poetry. From an Egyptian pyramid come the following pathetic verses, with a terrible false quantity in the last line :

" I have seen the pyramids without you, my dearest brother, and here, it was all I could, I poured sad tears for you and grave this plaint in memory of our grief. The lofty pyramid knows the name of Decimus Gentianus to be that of a pontifex

---

1. For Baiae see Seneca *Ep.* li, Suetonius *Nero*, 27. For an interesting account of the journey from Baiae to Naples by the short-cut through the Naples tunnel see Seneca, *Ep.* lvii. For Ostia, Suetonius, *de rhet.*, i; Minucius Felix, *Octauius*. It is amusing to find parallels to the mementoes, which cram the shop window in Douglas or Blackpool, in the glassware from Baiae with pictures of the lighthouse, Nero's pond, the oyster pond, the park, etc. See Friedländer, *op. cit.*, i, p. 337.

and companion, Trajan, of thy triumphs, and within thirty years a censor and a consul." [1]

It was evidently one of Plutarch's greatest pleasures to act as cicerone to distinguished visitors at Delphi, and for what better informed or more delightful guide could any traveller wish ? Thus the treatise on the decay of oracles arises out of the conversation of two such visitors—Demetrius the grammarian, who was on his way back from England, where he had lived, to Tarsus, where he had been born ; and Cleombrotus the Spartan, who knew Egypt like a book, and from scientific curiosity had travelled both in Africa and in the East.[2] A good example this of the extent and motives of travel and the consequently high degree of intercommunication of ideas and knowledge.

One of the main motives of travel was sight-seeing. "The first thing a man does in a strange city is to ask the citizens ' what are the sights ? ' " (Epictetus, *Disc.* iii, 7, 1), like Lucius at Hypata. "As soon as the sun, new-risen, had banished night and restored day, I woke from slumber and at once left my bed, for I was most anxious to make myself acquainted with the rarities and

---

1. The dead brother was Terentius Gentianus, whose memorial has been found at Sarmizigetusa, *C.I.L.*, iii, 1463. Terentio Gentiano trib. militum quaestori trib. pl. pr. leg. Aug. consuli pontif. cens. provinc. Maced. colonia Ulpia Traian. Aug. Dac. Sarmizegetusa patroni. The lines "suitable to the day and scene" which Mr. Pontifex wrote in the visitor's book at Montanvert (Butler, *Way of All Flesh*, cap. iv) are quite characteristic of the latest, early Victorian, stages of the Grand Tour. A youthful diary of my grandfather abounds in exercises in verse of a similar technical and sentimental merit.

2. Plutarch, *de def. orac.*, i. It is interesting that two bronze tablets found at York may be dedications of this Demetrius, see Dessau, "Ein freund Plutarchs in England," *Hermes*, lxiv, (1911), pp. 156 foll.

wonders of the place" (Apuleius, *Met.* ii, 1).
" You travel to Olympia," says Epictetus,
" that you may see the works of Pheidias, and
each of you thinks it a misfortune to die
without visiting these sights, and will you
have no desire to behold and to comprehend
those things for which there is no need of
travel ? " [1]

An opportunity of inspecting a celebrity or a
famous work of art, which the chances of travel
might afford, was eagerly seized ; but too often,
mainly, with the motive of being able to say that
the traveller had "done" them.   " 'I met
Epictetus. It was like meeting a statue.' 'Yes,
for you just saw me, and no more.' 'We are
passing through Nicopolis ; while we wait to
charter our ship, we can see Epictetus ; let us
see what he is saying !' Then when you leave
you say, ' Epictetus was nothing ; he talks bad
Greek, outlandish stuff.' " " How few," says
Tacitus, " when they visit the capital from Spain
or Asia, to say nothing of our Gallic neighbours,
ask after Saleius Bassus ! And indeed if anyone
does ask after him, having once seen him, he passes

---

1. Epictetus, *Disc.* i, 6, 23. An excellent description of doing the
sights at Delphi, the garrulous professional guides, etc., in Plutarch's treatise
upon *Why the Pythia no longer gives oracles in verse.* How admirable is the
accomplished and travelled young connoisseur of art ! " The guides were
going through their lectures as prepared, showing no regard for our entreaties
that they would cut short their periods and skip most of the inscriptions.
The stranger was but moderately interested in the form and workmanship
of the different statues ; it appears that he has seen many beautiful objects
of art. What he did admire was the lustre on the bronze, unlike rust or
deposit, but rather resembling a coat of deep shining blue." Plutarch
op. cit., 2, 395a (Prickard, p. 83),

on and is satisfied as if he had seen a picture or a statue." [1]

Places of historical interest, famous temples, which were also, in fact, museums of art, and natural curiosities attracted the educated sight-seer. It was indeed the spirit of the Grand Tour. Greece, for obvious reasons, had a special attraction, and the detailed catalogue of Pausanias, the forerunner of Herr Baedeker, shows the interest which society in the second century took in Hellenic monuments.

For romantic scenery, which indeed is a very modern taste, the Romans cared little. The Alps, for instance, they regarded not with enthusiasm but with aversion, and the prayer of the mediæval traveller, Adam of Usk[2] (1377–1421), at the summit of the Great St. Bernard, " Lord, restore me to my brethren, that I may tell them, that they come not to this place of torment," would not have struck them as inappropriate. The scenery, which they preferred, was that of the sea-shore or of some well-wooded and well-watered valley. Of water—to look at—they were particularly fond. But wildness did not appeal to them, and adventure beyond the limits of civilisation had no attraction for them. There were not many Roman explorers. I can think only of the Roman knight, who may well have been

---

1. Epictetus, *Disc.*, iii, 9, 12 foll., Tacitus, *Dialogus*, 10. Compare the story of the man from Gades who came to see Livy. Numquamne legisti Gaditanum quemdam Titi Liui nomine gloriaque commotum ad uisendum eum ab ultimo terrarum orbe uenisse, statimque ut uiderat abesse. Pliny, *Ep.* ii, 3, 8.

2. Miss Skeel, " Some Mediæval Travellers to Rome," *Proc. Class. Ass.*, xxi, p. 35. The scenery did not alleviate Seneca's exile. For him the beautiful island is *Corsica terribilis*, *Anth. Lat.*, 236, 237.

of non-Italian origin, who was sent by Julianus, the manager of the gladiatorial exhibitions under Nero, to explore the route of the Baltic amber trade.[1]

The kind of travelling, which we have so far been discussing, helped, it is true, in the circulation of ideas, but hardly at all in the mixing of nationalities, and, but to a limited extent, in the fusing of national modes of thought and living into a single cosmopolitan blend. More important here than the luxury travel of the rich was the professional travelling of the middle and lower classes and, what I may call, the vocational transplantation of peoples by commerce, slavery, and military service. It should be remembered in this connection that there was no bar to racial intermixture like the colour prejudice, of which antiquity seems to have been unconscious. An English family may be settled for generations in India, its members may belong to a distinguishable Anglo-Indian type, but they do not cease to be even pugnaciously English. But in the Roman Empire the general process was one of denationalisation, and with the possible exception of the Jews, extraneous racial elements in any given area tended, like the white peoples in America, to become absorbed into the population.

Perhaps between luxury travel and commercial travel comes educational travel. At many places, notably at Rome, Athens, and Rhodes were famous universities, to which students

---

1. Pliny, *Nat. Hist.*, xxxvii, 3, 11, 45.

flocked from all over the Roman Empire. Indeed
it was alleged that the purity of the Attic dialect
was destroyed, and that the local spoken variety
became the worst, instead of the best, kind of
Greek owing to the numbers of foreign students.
The fame of Epictetus drew students, even from
remote provinces, to Nicopolis. Of the typical
young hopeful " the people at home say ' he
will come back knowing everything.' I did
indeed wish to return one day, if I could, having
learnt everything," Epictetus represents him as
grumbling; "but it needs hard work, and no one
sends me anything, and the baths are shockingly
bad in Nicopolis, and I am badly off in my
lodgings and in the lecture room " (*Disc.* ii,
21, 13–14). And then, as now, when the
graduate at last returned, his friends at home
sometimes complained that he had learned little
but self-assertiveness and how to set everybody
right about everything.[1]

The traveller, again, like the Balliol man of
the story, was likely to find college friends in
most out of the way places. Thus in Thessalian
Hypata the ædile in charge of the market turns
out to be an old class-mate of the African
Lucius and welcomes him warmly with recollec-
tions of the lectures of Clytius, which they
had attended together at Athens University
(Apuleius, *Met.* i, 24). Again, just as the Scots,
to Dr. Johnson's indignation, discovered London,
so ambitious Gauls and Spaniards invaded Rome.
Some of them, like Martial, eventually retired

---

1. For instance, Plutarch's young fellow-townsman, Niger, *Quaest.
Symp.*, vi, 7, 1, 693b.

to their native land ; others, like the Senecas, did not.[1]

The professions, as opposed to the crafts, were, upon the whole, migratory. The travelling teacher had always been a part of the Greek tradition, whose wise men—Solon, Pythagoras, Democritus—or the professional sophists of the fifth century, had travelled the world to learn and to disseminate their learning. Both motives were operative under the Empire. Galen travelled widely to get first-hand experience and the knowledge of medical remedies at their source ; for to get his drugs pure and genuine was no easy matter for the ancient doctor. Indeed Galen's practice is itself illuminating testimony to the efficiency and facility of communications. In Rome the great specialist was consulted and gave advice by correspondence to patients in remote provinces. For example, he was consulted for cases of ophthalmia from Asia, Gaul, Spain and Thrace ; and he procured medicines direct from Syria, Palestine, Egypt, Cappadocia, Pontus, Macedonia, Spain and Mauretania.[2]

The pseudo-scientist, too, was often an industrious researcher. Artemidorus, the author

---

1. Ex municipiis et coloniis suis, ex toto denique orbe terrarum influxerunt. alios adducit ambitio, alios necessitas officii publici, alios imposita legatio, alios luxuria, opulentum et opportunum uitiis locum quaerens, alios liberalium studiorum cupiditas, alios spectacula. Seneca, *Cons. ad Helu.*, 6, 3.   For the cosmopolitan crowd in Rome, where all sorts of strange Eastern costumes were to be seen, see *Dio Chrys.*, lxxii, 3-4 (von Arnim, ii, p. 185).   For the view that this speech was made in Rome after Dio's exile see von Arnim, *Leben und Werke des Dio*, p. 276.

2. Friedländer, i, p. 303.

of the dream-book which has dominated subsequent European superstitious treatises on this subject, travelled indefatigably all over the Empire to collect his material. Aristides, the rhetorician, travelled widely as a distinguished peripatetic master of oratory and then, for twelve years, from cure to cure in search of a remedy for his disease, an Odyssey of nervous hypochondria which is chronicled in his *Sacred Orations*. The chairs at the universities, again, were filled with international, not with local talent. For instance, Philostratus, the author of the *Life of Apollonius*, who had been the chief star in the *salon* of Julia Domna at Rome, eventually held chairs first at Athens and afterwards at Rome. Lucian the Syrian practised rhetoric in Gaul, and at the end of his life held a post in Egypt.

Besides the great men there was naturally a host of lesser fry—educationists, doctors, quacks, prophets, and actors—continually upon the move. The companies of actors, who journeyed all over the empire to the great festivals and to provincial fairs, had even, as we have seen, a single organisation with its headquarters in Rome. In this in some degree the profession resembled Christianity, whose arrangements for co-operation and for the mutual help of travelling members we have already seen to be laid down in the *Didache*.

Perhaps it is in the company of the hero of Apuleius' novel that we get the best idea of the busy life on the roads of the Empire. We meet with him the Greek travelling vendor of cheeses with his pack (i, 5), Diophanes, the fraudulent Chaldaean seer (ii, 12 foll.), Zatchlas, the Egyptian miracle worker (ii, 28), the rascally band of priests of the Syrian Goddess preying upon the piety and the superstition of the simple country folk (viii, 24 foll.), or the swaggering legionary who robs and metes out soldier's justice to the poor old gardener.[1]

Since Rome first rose to greatness she had been a commercial power. If the economic life of Greek civilisation in its great days had ultimately been based upon the carrying trade, that of Rome was based upon finance. The successful wars of the second century B.C. concentrated the capital of the world in Roman hands, and the natural resources of the provinces were exploited by Roman financiers. Already in the time of Cicero the Roman banker was ubiquitous, and not a transaction took place in Southern Gaul except through his books. The number of Italian merchants, who were massacred by Mithradates in the province of Asia, was certainly large, the minimum estimate was 80,000, the maximum 150,000. The enterprise of the Roman banker had indeed been a very effective, indirect influence in Romanising the world.

The activity of commercial life under the Empire naturally increased with the establishment of the Roman peace. It still took Italians far afield. Thus, for instance, the father of Vespasian was born at Reate in Italy, farmed the import

---

1. Apuleius, *Met.*, ix, 39 foll. cf. Petronius, *Sat.*, 82. For soldier's justice see Juvenal, *Sat.*, xvi. For the young intellectuals' dislike of the "stupid soldier," see Persius, *Sat.*, iii, 77, viii, 189.

tax in Asia, and subsequently carried on a banking business in Switzerland, where he died. (Suetonius, *Vespasian*, 1, 2–3). But under the Empire the current was rather the other way; the control of commerce came mainly into the hands of the Eastern provincials. The cosmopolitan character of early imperial Rome is too well known to need emphasis or elaboration. "The Orontes," in Juvenal's words, "had long been pouring into the Tiber." But it is not always remembered that as commerce developed under the peaceful conditions ensured in a large area controlled by a single political authority, all the big centres of exchange—the knots as it were in the net of the road system, like Aquileia, or the ports like Puteoli—became big cosmopolitan cities with a similarly variegated population. Merchant cities kept factories in such places. "Berytus, Damascus, and other Phœnician and Syrian cities had factories at Puteoli. Tyre, in the fourth century still the greatest commercial city in the East, had one as Puteoli and one at Rome." In particular the national genius of the Syrians for commercial enterprise found ample scope under the Empire, They spread everywhere and "wandered," in the words of St. Jerome, "throughout the world," until in Gaul in the fifth century "Syrians," like "Lombards" in the Middle Ages, had come to mean "bankers." [1]

---

1. See Friedländer, *op. cit.*, p. 313. For Roman traders in Petra, Cimmerian Bosphorus and with Maroboduus in Bohemia, see Charlesworth, *op. cit.*, p. 11. On the other hand, for Bithynians at Moguntiacum and Burdigala, a Lydian in Switzerland, Cappadocians, Carians and Asiatic Greeks at Lindum in Britain (" It was the turn of the tide "), *ibid.*, p. 96.

The goods of all the world were to be bought in Rome. The trade with the Far East had been reopened during the governorship of Egypt by the ill-starred Gallus, envoys from India visited Augustus, and an embassy from Ceylon came to Rome in the lifetime of the Elder Pliny. There was indirect trade with China through the intermediation of the Hellenised Bactrian kingdom, though it was not until towards the end of the second century that a Roman embassy (probably some merchant adventurers who gave themselves out to be an official body) penetrated to the court of China itself. This Far Eastern trade, however, was economically a source of weakness rather than of strength. Like the ostentatious building of the municipalities it represented an economic drain, a capital expenditure on luxury.[1] Baltic amber, which was also the product of indirect trade, was so plentiful in Italy that, as Pliny notes (*N.H.*, xxxvii, 3, 11, 44), it was used for amulets by the peasant women of the Po valley. But for our purposes more important was the internal circulation of goods which was both rapid and continuous. For example, the Younger Pliny (*Ep.* ix, 11) learns to his pleased surprise that his books are on sale in Lyons. Most of the better pottery, found upon Roman sites in Britain, was made in the kilns of Southern

---

1. Promiscas uiris et feminis uestes atque illa feminarum propria, quis lapidum causa pecuniæ nostrae ad externas aut hostiles gente transferuntur ? Tacitus, *Annals*, iii, 53. Cf. Pliny, *N.H.*, xii, 18, 41, 89.

Gaul.[1] This circulation of goods is, for our topic, particularly significant because, under ancient conditions of commerce at any rate the smaller merchants travelled with their wares. This indeed is still largely the practice in the Levant to-day, as I have good reason to know from my experience as a Naval Examination Officer.

In fact, one should realise that there was an incessant circulation of individuals, goods and ideas, along the veins of imperial commerce. Let me take a Christian example of the resulting cosmopolitan influences. These are the teachers to whom Clement of Alexandria acknowledges his indebtedness. In Greece he sat at the feet of an Ionian; in Magna Græcia one of his teachers had been a native of Cœle Syria and another an Egyptian ; in the East he had learned from an Assyrian and a Hebrew ; and, finally, in Egypt from " the true Sicilian bee," by whom he probably means Pantaenus.[2]

That the institution of slavery had an enormous effect upon the racial population of the Empire is obvious. It transported large numbers of aliens in a constant stream to countries other than those in which they had been born. " We have in our households nations with different customs to

---

1. On the whole topic as regards Britain see Haverfield, *Romanisation of Roman Britain*. Signed vases of Syrian Greeks have been found at Rome and in Africa, Gaul, and Germany, Charlesworth, *op. cit.*, p. 52 ; lamps from the factory of Sempronius, in Mauretania, turn up in Baetica and Sardinia, *ibid.*, p. 141 ; granite from Syene has been used in Belgian villas, *ibid.*, p. 24.

2. Clement Alex., *Strom.*, i, 1.

our own, with a foreign worship or with none at all," says a speaker in Tacitus.[1]

The influence of Christian slaves in spreading the gospel message is notorious. Further, as we shall see, the ex-slave often became a man of commercial, and even of political and social importance, and it was no uncommon thing for his son or grandson to become a senator. Here, too, we may remark that the balance of influence is from the East to the West. For the higher-grade slaves, who became ready candidates for manumission, were mainly orientals.

A word, too, must be said about the army. That it was an important factor in the blending of races is obvious. There were Gauls and Germans in the bodyguard of Herod the Great, and already at the battle of Philippi there had been Gauls, Lusitanians and Spaniards serving with the armies of the East under Brutus and Cassius. It is not true, as an American anthropologist mistakenly supposes, that foreign legionaries profoundly affected the racial population of Italy ; for the legions were never stationed in Italy itself. Mainly, the population affected was that of the frontier provinces.

Augustus' system had been to concentrate field armies at strategic points along his frontiers. Each striking force consisted roughly of an equal number of legionaries and auxiliary troops brigaded together. The former, the heavy-armed infantry, were recruited solely from Roman citizens. In the first instance this implied for

1. Nationes in familiis habemus, quibus diuersi ritus, externa sacra aut nulla sunt, Tacitus, *Annals*, xiv, 44.

practical purposes Italians; but as the area covered by the franchise extended, the provincial element inevitably increased. Actually Italians ceased to serve as legionaries after Vespasian, though they continued to enlist in the Prætorian Guard until this *corps d'élite* was disbanded by Septimius Severus. In two ways the legions promoted the process of assimilation. During foreign service they were susceptible to foreign influences.[1] The critical moment of the second battle of Betriacum in 69 A.D. provides a dramatic illustration. The German armies in support of Vitellius hurled themselves upon the hated armies of the Danube, and all night long there raged a soldiers' battle of almost unexampled ferocity. At dawn, the soldiers of the Third Legion turned, as they had learned to do during their stay in Syria, to salute the rising sun. The false rumour immediately spread among their opponents that Mucianus and the main armies of the East had come up. Consequently they broke, and the day was lost.

Of the second way in which the army aided the

---

1. Although upon the whole the armies of the Eastern and Western halves of the Empire were normally kept in the East or West as the case might be, there was a good deal of shifting about of legions on service. Thus, Legio iii Gallica was stationed in Mœsia under Augustus; under Claudius in Germany, in 59, under Nero, it went to Syria for the Parthian War; in (?) 68 it was transferrred to Mœsia. After the battle of Betriacum it wintered in Capua and then went back to Syria. Other legions which took part in Nero's Parthian War were Legio xv Apollinaris from Pannonia, Legio iv Scythica from Mœsia and Legio v Macedonica from Mœsia. These remained in the East until the fall of Jerusalem. Then Legio xv was transferred to Pannonia, and after Trajan is found stationed in Cappadocia; Legio iv remained in Syria; Legio v was transferred to Mœsia; subsequently under Trajan it fought in Dacia, Parthia and Palestine. Besides the shifting of regiments there must also be taken into account the cumulative effect of the frequent shifting of individuals, particularly of centurions,

process of assimilation, Mithraism may provide an example. The extension of the franchise opened the door of enlistment to provincials. It can hardly be doubted that the importance of Anatolia as a recruiting-ground for the legions was mainly responsible for the phenomenally rapid propagation of Mithraism throughout the Roman army during the latter half of the second century.

The auxiliaries were a native militia, which replaced the mercenary troops or subject levies from which the later Roman Republic had drawn its cavalry and light-armed troops. Here, as elsewhere, Augustus standardised an existing system. Under the early emperors these native troops served in their own country, often under their own Romanised chiefs as officers. The danger of this system was terribly brought home by the great rebellion on the Rhine in 69–70, the Indian mutiny of the Roman Empire. This led to the adoption of a new policy, viz., that of shifting the auxiliary troops to alien provinces, and of never employing native regiments in their own district. Immediately this must have involved a considerable shifting of racial factors, but there were strong influences at work for localisation, and we must not exaggerate its importance. The researches of Cheesman[1] have shown that, no doubt because of the trouble and expense of maintaining a supply of drafts from their original home, the tendency was to keep up the strength by recruits from the locality in

1.   Cheesman, *The Auxilia of the Roman Army*.

which they were stationed. A Gaulish regiment in Mœsia, let us say, would be fed by local enlistment rather than by drafts from Gaul. The exceptions were the oriental auxilia, which seem regularly to have received drafts from their native province.

But even allowing for this, the presence under one command in Dacia, in 110 A.D., of regiments from Palestine, Spain, Thrace, Gaul, Rhaetia and Britain is not without significance. " In the military cemeteries the most diverse nations lie together ; inscriptions of officers and men in Mainz show them to have come from the Rhine, Holland, Brabant, Hungary, Carinthia, Styria, the Tyrol, Dalmatia, Rumelia, Syria, Spain, France, and Italy, North and South." [1]

Now upon discharge the member of an auxiliary regiment received the citizenship for himself and his children. As is well known, he most usually did not return to his native land, but settled down near his old regiment, and his son probably enlisted as a citizen in one of the legions with which it had been brigaded. In this way towns grew up round the military stations, a large element of the population of which was of military origin and ultimately of the most mixed racial descent.

In the second century, Hadrian and his successors introduced a system of frontier fortifications, the army was immobilised and became a garrison force until the necessities of the third century brought about the changes which

---

1. Friedländer, *op. cit.*, i, p. 302.

culminated in Diocletian's reforms. These, in fact, created a new field army to supplement the garrison troops, and incidentally they involved the barbarisation of the Roman army, which fatally depended more and more upon the blackmail system of employing earlier barbarians to keep out the later. The maximum influence of the army in effecting racial interchange was before the reign of Hadrian. In the propagation of some cults, notably of Mithraism, it played an important part. Directly it had little to do with Christianity, for there were special reasons of conscience which made it difficult for a Christian of the second century to become a soldier.

LECTURE IV

SOCIETY AND SOCIAL ETHICS.

" So let the tribunes await their turn ; let money carry
the day ; let the sacred office give way to one who came
but yesterday with whitened feet into our city. For
no deity is held in such reverence amongst us as Wealth ;
though as yet, O baneful money, thou hast no temple
of thine own."

Juvenal, Sat., i, 109.

" Nay, rather let us offer to the gods what the blear-eyed
progeny of the great Messala cannot give out of his
lordly salver :— a heart rightly attuned towards God
and man ; a mind pure in its inner depths, and a soul
steeped in nobleness and honour."

Persius, ii, 71.

To analyse the character of a highly civilised
society is obviously no easy task. Sharp moral
contrasts there are almost bound to be, and where
huge fortunes are in the hands of individuals,
there are likely to be outstanding examples of
folly and vice. Of these, Tacitus and Juvenal
have made full use. Both, in their different ways,

are masterly artists, and it is not surprising that the picture, which they have painted, has impressed itself upon the imagination of posterity and has dominated tradition. But this picture is of one small section only of a large community, nor is either artist guiltless of deliberately deepening his colours in order to obtain his effect. It would, indeed, be as reasonable to brand our own times on the evidence of the sensational Press, the divorce reports or the freak dinners of American millionaires, as to accept the estimate of the satirist or of the master of pathological psychology as a true and final verdict upon theirs.

We may, perhaps, begin by noticing certain characteristics ingrained in the Roman temperament, which stamped themselves with Roman institutions and Roman municipal life upon the Empire as a whole. Worst, perhaps, is a certain hardness and indifference to cruelty, a vice which was fostered by the growth of large slave households and the demoralising effect of the possession of arbitrary power to treat human beings as chattels. Here, Romans contrast with Greeks. It is easy to be over-sentimental about the ancient Greek, but the difference seems to me this, that while the Greek was not too scrupulous where an object was to be gained by cruelty, purposeless cruelty was abhorrent to him. Gladiatorial shows never became popular in Greece itself, except at cosmopolitan Corinth, and when it was proposed to set up an amphitheatre at Athens, the sarcasm of Demonax, who bade his fellow-citizens first remove the altar of Pity, sufficed to put an end to the project.[1]

Again the Roman temperament, perhaps like that of the English, was a little unimaginative. The Roman had other qualities, but hardly the artistic, and his guide to social conduct was rather convention than native taste. It is a result that his vices do not " lose half their evil by losing all their grossness," and they are in consequence the more repellent. Gluttony is the characteristic Roman vice.

From the earliest times, respect for convention had been a dominant note in the Roman character. That, too, we find running through

---

1. The general insensitiveness of the Roman world to the intrinsic barbarity of the gladiatorial shows and to their demoralising effect upon the spectators is indisputable, see Friedländer *op. cit.*, ii, pp. 76 foll. The sensational excitement which they aroused is described by Tertullian *de Spectaculis*, 16, and the fascination which they exercised is vividly pictured in the account of Alypius' experience, Augustine, *Confessions*, vi, 8. Though introduced into the Greek East, they never became comparably popular with a race of softer and more humane fibre. Occasionally, in the West, feeling might be outraged, as in the case of Nero's grandfather who gave " a gladiatorial show, but with such inhuman cruelty that Augustus, after his private warning was disregarded, was forced to restrain him by an edict," Suetonius, *Nero*, 4. The action of Trebonius Rufus, a *duumuir* who abolished the games at Vienne, was brought before the Privy Council, where Junius Mauricus supported his action and added, " I wish the games could be abolished at Rome as well." The Council decided that the contest should be abolished " because it corrupted the morals of Vienne, just as our contests have corrupted the world." Pliny, *Ep.*, iv, 22. Cicero, *Tusc.*, ii, 17, 41, indicates a not very effective disquietude in some minds : crudele gladiatorum spectaculum et inhumanum non nullis uideri solet, et haud scio an ita sit, ut nunc fit ; compare his distaste for the beast fights which inaugurated Pompey's theatre, *ad Fam.*, vii, 1, 2–3. But the only voice consistently raised in protest against the inhumanity and degrading character of these exhibitions was that of Seneca (See above p. 77 and *Ep.*, vii, 2-7, xc, 45, xcv, 33, *de tranq. an.*, 2, 12).

society under the Empire. There is throughout an exacting social code with strictly marked grades of social dignity and reciprocal social duties, which were enforced by public opinion in their relation to each other. Something of this we have already seen in discussing the municipalities and the *collegia*. Very characteristic is the relation of client and patron, with its mutual obligations of homage and attendance on the one hand, and of protection and generosity upon the other.

Another very characteristic Roman trait is a love of pageantry that inspired the processional ceremonial which, throughout its history, has been characteristic of Roman religious ritual.[1] The call of this passion for gratification had led, even under the Republic, to a great development and multiplication of spectacular shows. In the somewhat ostentatious and materialistic age which we are considering, the cry of the populace throughout the great cities of the Empire was for " Bread and Games." The passion for racing more than equalled the zeal of our democracy for professional football. The rivalry of the four factions, distinguished by their racing colours, was everywhere acute and upon

---

1. " The stately processions remained, and could be watched with pride by the patriotic Roman all through the period of the Empire, until the Roman Church adapted them to its own ritual and gave them, as we was, a new meaning. As the cloud-shadows still move slowly over the hollows of the Apennines, so does the procession of the patron saint pass still through the streets of many an Italian city." Warde Fowler, *Religious Experience of the Roman People*, p. 218.

more than one occasion gave rise to serious rioting.[1]

Both Juvenal and Tacitus have depicted with a masterly literary skill and with the passionate emotion inspired by the memory of the silent shame of their experience under the tyranny of Domitian,[2] the vices of the imperial court. We get from them the impression of a society which is irredeemably rotten, and move in a circle which has exhausted the ingenuities of vice and even the crude blackguardism of the pot-house and the stews in the vain effort to stir palates which have been jaded with satiety. It is true that from the latter years of the soured and almost insane Tiberius to the accession of Vespasian, the vices of the court circle can neither be denied nor palliated. In the Julio-Claudian

---

1. For the scene at the Megalensian Games see Juvenal, xi, 193. "Meanwhile the solemn Idæan rite of the Megalensian napkin is being held; there sits the prætor in his triumphal state, the prey of horse flesh; and (if I may say so without offence to the vast unnumbered mob) all Rome to-day is in the Circus. A roar strikes upon my ear which tells me that the Green has won; for had it lost, Rome would be as sad and dismayed as when the consuls were vanquished in the dust of Cannæ." cf. *Sat.*, x, 36. For the scholar's isolation broken only by the distant shouts during the games, see Seneca, *Ep.*, lxxxiii, 7. Though Pliny (*Ep.*, ix, 6) is as lukewarm as was Gibbon in his appreciation of race meetings (*Memoirs of My Life* (*London*, 1814) p. 118), for the average man the greatest hardship in leaving Rome was missing the games, Juv., xi, 52, iii, 223. This Nero would never do (Suet., *Nero*, 22, 1). Caligula, himself an unscrupulous partisan of the Green Faction (Suet., *Cal.*, 55), had his rest disturbed by people taking their seats in the Circus the night before (*ibid.*, 26). Epictetus quotes in illustration the man who was so nervous that when the horse, which he had backed, was running, he covered his eyes, and when it unexpectedly won, fainted and needed first aid to bring him round, *Disc.*, i, 11, 27. For the racehorse see Juvenal, viii, 56. Further matter will be found in a popular article upon "Horse-racing and Magic under the Roman Empire," in *Discovery*, iii, April, 1922, pp. 99-102, and a store of information and references in Friedländer, *op. cit.*, ii, pp. 1-130.

2. Tacitus, *Agricola*, preface.

family there was undoubtedly a strain of madness, and the fashionable world was led and terrorised in turn by the monster Caligula, the grotesque and animal Claudius, and the vicious *poseur* Nero. The latter's short-lived successors—the incompetent Galba, the spendthrift Otho, a surviving boon-companion of the notorious *noctes Neronis*, and the gluttonous Vitellius—were little better. With the homely, bourgeois Vespasian came a change to frugal decency; but his sons, the facile and showy spendthrift Titus,[1] and the sinister and cruel Domitian, brought back the bad old days.

But let us remember that the picture is of the court circle only,[2] and the court, after all, did not comprise the whole of society. That it affected for evil the general moral tone is, of course, undeniable; but we must not forget the existence of men like Agricola or Verginius Rufus, upright, clean-living members of the aristocracy. English society was not destitute of honourable men and pure women when the First Gentleman in Europe so lamentably led the fashionable world.

Under Trajan and his successors a different tone was set. The change is comparable to that from the Regency to Victorian society, which in other respects than those of morals

---

1. Amor ac deliciae generis humani, Suetonius, *Titus*, i.

2. To give the devil his due, whatever the shortcomings of their private lives, the provinces did not suffer. The reign of Claudius, at home a dreary catalogue of palace intrigues and crimes, marked a definite epoch of development in imperial administration, and even Otho seems to have done well as a provincial governor. Prouinciam administrauit quaestorius per decem annos moderatione atque abstinentia singulari, Suet., *Otho*, 3, 2.

presents a parallel to the social revolution which was taking place. Fortunately, in the correspondence of the Younger Pliny we possess a record of the new aristocracy. It presents indeed a striking contrast to the picture drawn by his friend and contemporary, Tacitus, and we find ourselves moving, as we read the letters, in a society humane and civilised, among gentle-men distinguished, not merely by generosity, but inspired by genuine kindness and a real delicacy of feeling in their relations with their friends and dependents.[1]

It is, perhaps, Pliny's failing, as he says of himself, to think well of his friends; he has even a word of regret for the old scoundrel Marcus Regulus (vi, 2) and if, with Modestus, he admits him to have been the most detestable of bipeds (1, 5), he admires ungrudgingly his professional industry and skill as a pleader. But Regulus is almost the only bad man to be met with in Pliny's circle, and we should agree, on the whole, that his friends deserved his appreciation.

The Younger Pliny's was no idle life.[2] He takes seriously both his work at the bar and also his literary studies (vii, 9); if he is fastidious himself in his amusements, he has a pleasant

---

1. *E.g.* The delicacy with which the present of a dowry is made to Quintilian's daughter (vi, 32) or his correspondence with Corellia, when the generous deceit is discovered by which he had allowed her to profit by 200,000 sesterces at his expense (vii, 14).

2. The amazing industry of these people must strike anyone familiar with the writings of the period. cf. Seneca, *Ep.*, viii, 1. Nullus mihi per otium dies exit. Partem noctium studiis uindico. Non uaco somno sed succumbo, et oculos uigilia fatigatos cadentesque in opere detineo.

tolerance for others' tastes [1] ; he is punctilious in the performance of his social duties (i, 13). Few of his contemporaries will have equalled the prodigious industry of Pliny's uncle, the Elder Pliny, who would begin his literary work at midnight, visit the emperor Vespasian, himself a night-worker, before dawn, and then spend a long day in administrative work (iii, 5), but even the nephew takes note-books with him, when he goes boar-hunting (i, 6). In business affairs, we find this lawyer strictly honourable, preferring equity to his legal rights.[2] Towards dependents and friends he is uniformly affectionate and thoughtful. Thus having given a small property to his old nurse, he asks a friend to look into the business side of it for her (vi, 3). A consumptive freedman is sent to Egypt for a cure, and when his malady recurs, the country air and fresh milk of a friend's farm are solicited on his behalf (v, 19). In helping his friends, Pliny is tireless, whether it be by the exercise of his political influence (*e.g.*, ii, 9) or in such matters as the selection of a husband (i, 14), or a tutor (ii, 18 ; iii, 3) for their children. An especially pleasant trait is his eagerness to help and encourage younger men in his own profession (vi, 11 ; vi, 23).

Very characteristic of the difference between the two pictures presented by Pliny and the

---

1. Demus igitur alienis oblectationibus ueniam, ut nostris impetremus ix, 17. cf. viii, 22.

2. *E.g.* The modification of his contract with the wine dealers whom the accidents of the crop would otherwise have involved in serious loss (viii, 2) or his honouring of codicils in a friend's will though they were not legally valid (iv, 10).

satirists is the strongly contrasted impression of
the Roman lady. The pages of Tacitus are
dominated by the Messalinas, Agrippinas or
Poppæas ; in the main such examples of female
virtue as he allows us, are drawn, like the freed-
woman Epicharis, faithful on the rack, from a
lower class, and serve to throw up by contrast
the selfish and cowardly vices of the aristocracy.
But in Pliny's own letters to his wife (*e.g.*, iv, 19 ;
vii, 5), and in his references to his friends, like
Macrinus and his wife (viii, 5) who had lived
together thirty-nine years without a quarrel,
we find, what is noticeably absent from the
pages of Juvenal and Tacitus, a simple and very
genuine domestic happiness, which, in Pliny's
case, was marred only by the disappointment of
the mutual longing of Calpurnia and himself
to have a child. Statius' poem to his wife and
his references to his married friends or Plutarch's
consolation to his Timoxena show that the
inscriptions, which are usually less delicately
articulate because more conventional in form,
tell no lying tale. In fact, in all grades of society
married happiness and the virtues upon which
it is based, were no more uncommon than with
us.[1]

In matters of sexual purity, no doubt the age

---

1. Statius, *Siluae*, iii, 5. Statius' friends, *Siluae*, ii, 2, 143 foll., v, 1.
Perhaps the most pathetically sincere of the inscriptions is Dessau, No. 8190.
dis manibus Meuiae Sophes C. Maeuius Cimber coniugi sanctissimae et
conseruatrici, desiderio spiritus mei, quae uixit mecum an. xiix menses iii
dies xiii, quod uixi cum ea sine querella, nam nunc queror aput manes eius
et flagito Ditem, aut et me reddite coniugi meae, quae mecum uixit tan con-
corde ad fatalem diem. Maeuia Sophe, impetra, si quae sunt Manes, ne
tam scelestum discidium experiscor diutius.

was lax, though it may be doubted whether the practice of virtue in this respect has ever been extended beyond a lamentably small section of society. For precept, if the vicious ladies of Juvenal were claiming sexual equality to sin, Musonius the Stoic was preaching a single standard of chastity for men as well as women.[1] Dio Chrysostom in no measured terms condemns the indignity and disgracefulness of venal and promiscuous vice.[2] But here it must be admitted that the crusade of Christianity on behalf of sexual purity was in opposition to a lower contemporary standard, a fact which at once explains and excuses the exaggerated form which it sometimes took. The exhortation of Epictetus is to " avoid impurity to the utmost of your power before marriage, and if you indulge your passion, let it be done lawfully. But do not be offensive and censorious to those who indulge it, and do not be always bringing up your own chastity."[3]

---

1. Men are just as bad as women : respice primum/ et scrutare uiros ; faciunt nam plura, sed illos/ defendit numerus uinctaque umbone phalanges, Juvenal, ii, 44. For the teaching of Musonius see the quotation from his περὶ ἀφροδισίων in Stobaeus, *Flor.* vi, 61, and Zeller, *Die Philosophie der Griechen*, 3rd edition, iii, 1, p. 737.

2. Dio Chrysostom, vii, 133-152 (von Arnim, vol. i, pp. 214-219). Pudicitia utraque, et illa, cui alieni corporis abstinentia est, et hac, cui sui cura, Seneca, *Ep.*, xlix, 12.

3. Epictetus *Manual*, 33, 8. It is fair to remember, however, that the last sentence is not inspired by any wish to condone vice, but by Epictetus' characteristic hatred of humbug and self-righteousness. His teaching upon the importance of moral purity is unequivocal, and impurity of intention or the lust of the eye are as explicitly branded as they are by Jesus, see *Di course* ii, 18, 15. Smutty talk should be avoided. If no occasion offers to rebuke the offender, you should make it plain that you don't like it, *Manual*, 33. For avoiding conversation about gladiators and horses, etc., and still more ill-natured gossip about men, " who touches pitch will be defiled," see *Discourse*, iii, 16.

But if this is a practical rather than an ideal standard, it is nevertheless certain that the sixth satire of Pliny's contemporary, Juvenal, is over-drawn. It was not true of Roman ladies as a class that they habitually indulged guilty passions with slaves and gladiators, or without exception practised poisoning and abortion.[4] But, further, it is a most noticeable feature of Juvenal's diatribes, and not least of this satire, that offences against convention and moral delinquency arouse in equal measure his savage indignation. To him the blue-stocking is no less detestable than the adulteress. The vicious debauchee, unworthy scion of some great Roman *gens*, is the object of not more scathing contempt than the successful artisan or man of business. He hates Crispinus for his crimes, but he hates him not less because he had once hawked fish on the quays of Alexandria.[5]

By the time of the accession of Trajan the old aristocracy of the Republic had died out or had

---

Epictetus' personal view of women was low, and he does not seem to have shared the enthusiasms of the day for sex equality. "The battle is an unequal one when it is between a pretty maid and a young man beginning philosophy. 'Pot and stone,' as the saying is, 'do not agree,'" *Discourse* iii, 12, 12, cf. *Manual*, 40; *Frag.*, 15, women only read Plato's *Republic* to get a justification of free love from it.

Upon marriage he held the usual Stoic principle of doing one's duty by society (*Discourse*, iii, 7, 19), but he regarded the celibacy of the Cynic teacher as justified by the freedom, which it conferred, from ties which are necessarily a distraction from his high vocation, *Discourse* iii, 22, 67 foll. He himself was unmarried, and the retort of Demonax will be remembered. Epictetus advised him to marry and do his duty by society. "Willingly," replied Demonax, "if you will give me one of your daughters." Lucian, *Dem.*, 55.

4. Of course, Juvenal is not tilting at windmills. Libido atque luxuria coercente nullo inualuerat, (Vespasianus) auctor senatui fuit decernendi, ut quae se alieno seruo iunxisset, ancilla haberetur, Suet., *Vesp.*, 11. But Juvenal exaggerates the degree and extent of the evil.

5. Juvenal, i, 26, iv, 1-33.

become submerged.   Even in the fourth century there were a few survivors in the circle of Symmachus and Macrobius who could trace their descent to one of the old families, but these are individual exceptions.   The process of extinction had begun before the Empire, and Augustus had found it politic to finance more than one impoverished, noble house in order to enable it to keep its social footing.   The reckless extravagance of the Julio-Claudian courts had ruined many, not only of the older noble families, but also of those, who, like the Vitellii, had come to the front during the civil wars.   Calculated childlessness helped to bring great lines to a close, and of self-indulgent vice it is literally, as well as allegorically, true that the wages of sin is death.   It was the aristocracy, too, which had excited alike the avarice and the fears of the worst emperors, and the senatorial class had been decimated by persecution in the reigns of terror of Nero and Domitian.   For those who had gambled away or dissipated their means of subsistence, there was no opportunity for recovery.   As a class they became submerged.   The conventional ban upon commercial callings, which was aggravated by the existence of slavery and the consequent contempt for menial occupations, erected a barrier against their making good by adopting some lucrative trade.   They and the middle-class Roman, whose point of view Juvenal very much represents, were too proud to work, sank consequently into obscurity and swelled with their descendants the idle mob of the big cities. Umbricius shakes from his feet the dust of Rome, where men of alien birth achieve wealth and position, and thrust aside the less supple and less industrious native, and goes to find a refuge in the rustic obscurity of some small Italian village. Were he to turn to and become, say, an auctioneer and so redeem his fortunes, he would be no hero for Juvenal.[1]

Juvenal, in fact, represents the old-fashioned social sentiment fighting helplessly against the inevitable results of an inexorable economic process. It should not be difficult for us to appreciate the position. It was but recently strange with us for a gentleman to "go into trade," and how long ago is it since the occupations of the upper social class were limited to learning, religion, diplomacy, politics, and one branch of the law ? Even the standing of the professions is relatively recent, and I can remember a very old relative of my own expressing her horror at the strange and desperate action of "a gentleman" who had become a dentist.[2]

In part the increased scale of society under the Empire, as with us in the nineteenth century, helped to accelerate the process. The new aristocracy was in the main Italian or even provincial, for Claudius, it will be remembered, in spite of the opposition of prejudice, had enrolled Gauls in the senate. The younger Pliny, who was a member of a family which had

---

1. Umbricius laments that there is no reward in Rome for his *labores*, but it does not appear that he means by these more than the performance of a client's duties to his patron.

2. The underpaid professions with which Juvenal has sympathy as being the employments of a gentleman, are poetry, history, law and higher education, see *Sat.*, vii.

long held a leading position in Como, is a very
fair example of the provincial land-owning class
which now assumed the lead. But this was but a
transition stage ; the processes, which we are
about to discuss, changed the Roman senate into
an imperial senate, and every Chiote, Galatian
and Bithynian was ambitious to become a senator
and to hold the higher magistracies.[1]

We may, perhaps, note in passing, though we
have not time to discuss it in detail, that the
emergence of a new aristocracy drawn from a
wider class brought with it a tendency to break
with other social conventions. The lack of
dignity of the modern young Roman, his
indecorous appearance as a gentleman driver at a
race meeting or his performance upon the music-
hall stage supply a constant spur to Juvenal's
indignation. Even Pliny thinks that the younger
generation show too little respect for their
elders' guidance, and are become a law to themselves, *ipsi sibi exempla sunt.*[2] Feminine emanci-

---

1. " Der Senat verwandete sich im Laufe der Kaiserzeit, in dem Senat
des Reiches," Mommsen, *Staatsrecht*, iii, 2, 876. Plutarch, *de tranq. an*,
10, 570c. ἄλλος δέ τις Χῖος, ἄλλος δὲ Γαλάτης, ἢ Βιθυνὸς οὐκ ἀγαπῶν,
εἰ . . . δόξαν καὶ δύναμιν ἐν τοῖς ἑαυτοῦ πολίταις εἴληχεν ἀλλὰ
κλαίων ὅτι μὴ φορεῖ πατρικίους καλτίους · ἐὰν δὲ καὶ φορῇ, ὅτι μηδέπω
στρατηγεῖ Ῥωμαίων, ἐὰν δὲ μὴ στρατηγῇ ὅτι μὴ ὑπατεύει. As early as the
reign of Nero, we find allusion to the ennoblement of freedmen's sons.
" For a long time he would not admit the sons of freedmen to the
Senate, and he refused office to those who had been admitted by his
predecessors," Suet., *Nero*, 15, 2.

2. Pliny, *Ep.*, viii, 23, 3. An interesting, though hardly typical example
of the relationship between the old generation and the new is provided by
the anxiety of the eccentric old lady Ummidia Quadratilla not to shock
her exemplary grandson by her own somewhat lurid tastes (Pliny, vii, 24).
By a happy accident the name of one of her freedman actors is recorded upon
an inscription at Puteoli (*C.I.L.* x, 1946=Dessau, 5183). Of the temple
and amphitheatre which this remarkable lady presented to Casinum (*C.I.L.* x,
5183=Dessau, 5628), the ruins of the latter are still extant.

pation again, though the history of the movement
goes back beyond the Empire, finds reasoned
support among thoughtful people.   Thus Seneca
and Plutarch, almost in modern tones, deny the
alleged inferiority of the sex, and affirm its
equal intellectual and moral capacity and its
consequent right to equal opportunity.[1]

For our purpose more important than the
change in the aristocracy, is the revolution which
was taking place in the middle class.   This it is
which rouses Juvenal's most indignant wrath.   He
might, perhaps, in a Roman have recognised the
patent of nobility conferred by sheer merit and
have agreed with Tiberius' *mot* " it seems to me
that Curtius Rufus is his own ancestor "[2]   Such
he would have regarded as worthy a place, though
perhaps a second place, with a scion of one of
the old families who had not betrayed his lineage.
What rouses his fury is the rise of the quick-
witted Greeks and pliable Orientals who from
humble, not seldom from servile beginnings,
build up a fortune, elbow out and ultimately
patronise the true-born son of Rome.

" The Orontes had long been flowing into the
Tiber," and the shrewd Levantine, who did not
share the prejudices of the Roman nor feel his
distaste for mean but lucrative occupations, took
full advantage of the great commercial opportunities of the time.   Industry and a low standard

---

1.   Seneca, *ad Marc.*, 16.   Plutarch, *Conj. Praec.*, 48, 145c. Plutarch
wrote a treatise on the theme, *quod mulieres etiam erudiendae sint*, of which
only inconsiderable fragments survive.

2.   Tacitus, *Annals*, xi, 21.   Is Statius on Rutilius Gallicus (genus ipse
suis permissaque retro nobilitas, *Siluae*, i, iv 68) another reminiscence of
this anecdote ?

of living enabled him to put money by, and with a little capital in hand the racial genius of Syrian and Greek for financial operations, in which in all ages they have shown a combination of courage in speculation and sagacity in skilful investment, enabled them to build up large fortunes. Juvenal would add, and no doubt there is some truth in his complaint, that they will sacrifice any personal dignity to gain their end. They will fawn on the great and make themselves unscrupulously useful to men of influence. The whole of their great abilities are concentrated upon self-advancement and money-making, nor will any scruple deter them from taking advantage of any means, however base, ignoble, or even criminal, in order to achieve their end.

But the animus is that of the stupider ruling race which finds itself outwitted and outstripped by peoples whom it has conquered and despises; it is the feeling of the Turk for the Armenian. The Roman despised the Levantine as a creature of inferior clay, and the free citizen looked down upon the slave. The new rich were mainly both Levantines and of servile origin. It is, therefore, hardly surprising that their prosperity provoked not merely envy but a rancorous hatred and disgust.

When speaking of the reversals of fortune and the position to which some ex-slaves attained, Seneca mentions Callistus, who became a powerful freedman of Caligula. " I have seen," he tells us, " standing in the line before the door of Callistus the former master of Callistus. I have seen the master himself shut out, while others were welcomed—the master, who once fastened the ' For Sale ' ticket on Callistus, and put him in the market along with the good-for-nothing slaves. . . . The master sold Callistus, but how much has Callistus made his master pay for ! " [1] Such incidents inevitably evoked bitter feeling.

We have already noticed how the accident that secretarial work was normally regarded as a servile occupation, had provided the freedmen of Cæsar with the opportunity to exercise their talents of business organisation upon an imperial scale. As a result, in the reign of Claudius, the Empire was virtually governed by the great freedmen secretaries of state. A process of the same kind was going on in the middle class. The great commercial development and· activity of the early empire gave the Levantines their opportunity ; many of them built up huge private fortunes, and a large part of the commerce of the world was in their control. This silent revolution must have played a more important part than is sometimes realised in the conversion of the middle class to Christianity. Prosenes, the freedman of Marcus Aurelius, who rose to be chamberlain under Commodus, was almost certainly a Christian, and his case, one would imagine, was not an isolated one.[2]

Of the successful ex-slave and plutocrat we possess in Trimalchio a character study of con-

---

1. Seneca, *Ep.*, xlvii, 9.
2. For the career of Prosenes, see Friedländer, *op. cit.*, iv, p. 53.

vincing and cynical realism.[1] It did not the
more endear them to Juvenal and his like, that
these displayed to the full the tasteless follies of
the parvenu. Like the new rich in all ages they
endeavoured to cover their social unease by an
exaggerated imitation of a culture which they
imperfectly understood, and aped the least
admirable features of the social class to which
they now aspired, while retaining much of the
grossness of their humble origin. Trimalchio's
banquet is a tasteless attempt to outdo the
extravagance of a Neronian feast, the freak
dinner of a millionaire. The host is by way of
being a well-read man. He keeps a Greek and
Latin library and knows all about Homer,
though he thinks that Iphigenia was the wife of
Achilles and that Helen was the mother of
Diomede and Ganymede ! He is fond of telling
his guests how much he and his belongings
are worth, and scales are sent for to prove the
weight and value of his wife's rings. She,
poor lady, soon gets sadly maudlin and
reminiscent. The conversation of the guests is
admirably done to the life with its *banale*
chatter liberally besprinkled with copy-book
platitude.

Yet with it all, we feel that the grotesque
Trimalchio is not such a bad old fellow at heart.
He has the obvious defects of the self-made man,
whose capacities have been exercised exclusively

---

1. Compare the historical Caluisius Sabinus, who "et patrimonium
habebat libertini et ingenium." He, too, had grotesque aspirations to be
thought a Homeric scholar, Seneca, *Ep*. xxvii, 5. Freedmen's ostentation
was proverbial. 'Et adhuc plebeias fistulas loquor : quid cum ad balnea
libertinorum peruenero," Seneca, *Ep*., lxxxvi, 7.

in money-making. He is, however, a kindly, generous creature and possesses a quite genuine bonhomie. No doubt, not all the members of his class became millionaires upon this scale, nor developed the same means or taste for vulgar ostentation; but without becoming millionaires, the barber, the auctioneer and the leather-seller became men of considerable wealth. Their sons became members of the equestrian order and it was not at all unusual for the grandson of a slave to attain senatorial rank.[1]

Some of the lesser but prosperous fellows of Trimalchio we meet at his table. They are the products of an era of peace and material development. Again we might cite the analogy of the nineteenth century. Business is their real interest; their heart is with their money bags.[2] That is perhaps the true vice of the age, as indeed it may be thought to be of our own. We notice a practical materialism and, in spite of a great deal of humanitarian sentiment, a real insensitiveness to other than cash values. It is by this standard that men are measured at Trimalchio's table. "Don't make the mistake of looking down upon his freedman friends" the guest is warned, "they are very warm men"; a man's value, declares another speaker,

---

1. Juvenal, 1, 24, x, 225, xiv, 203; Martial iii, 16, iii, 59. The sons of panders, auctioneers, gladiators and trainers in the equestrian seats at the theatre, Juvenal, iii, 154.

2. Lucri bonus est odor ex re qualibet (cf. Vespasian's *mot* that money does not stink, Suetonius, *Vesp.* 23). Unde habeas quaerit nemo sed opportet habere. Juvenal, xiv, 203 foll. Mane piger stertis "surge," inquit Auaritia, "heia! surge." negas. instat; "surge," inquit, "non queo." "Surge," Persius, v. 132.

is what he is worth.   *Assem habes, assem ualeas.*[1]

We may note, further, a sadly familiar attitude towards education.   " I have a young scholar ripening for your trade," says the old rag-dealer to the Greek Agamemnon.   " He has good wits and never raises his head from his task.   He paints with a will. . . . He has begun Greek and has a real taste for Latin. . . . I have bought the boy some red-letter volumes that he may get a tincture of law for domestic purposes.   That is what gives bread and butter.   He has now had enough of literature.   If he gives it up, I think I shall teach him a trade—a barber's or auctioneer's or pleader's—something that only death can take from him.   Every day I din into his ears: Primigenius, my boy, what you learn you learn for profit.   Look at the lawyer Philero.   If he had not learned his business, he could not keep the wolf from the door.   Why, only a little ago, he was a hawker with a bundle on his back, and now he can hold his own with Norbanus. Learning is a treasure, and a trade that can never be lost." [2]

---

1. Petronius, 38, 77, cf. 43, ab asse creuit et paratus fuit quadrantem de stercore mordicus tollere. itaque creuit, quicquid creuit, tanquam fauus. Protinus ad censum de moribus ultima fiet quaestio, Juvenal, iii, 140. I have myself heard, and am not likely to forget, two wealthy manufacturers loudly express in a public place that an individual of their acquaintance, whose decoration with the Victoria Cross was announced in that day's newspaper, was a man " not worth more than thirty bob a week." Utrum illum pecunia impurum effecit an ipse pecuniam inspurcavit ?   Quae sic in quosdam homines quomodo denarius in cloacam cadit. Seneca, *Ep.*, lxxxvii, 16.

2. Petronius, 46.   dicant sine his in foro multi et adquirant, dum sit locupletior aliquis sordidae mercis negotiator et plus uoci suae debeat praeco. Quintilian, *Inst. Or*, I, xii, 17.   For the converse extreme view cf. de liberalibus studiis quid sentiam, scire desideas : nullum suspicio, nullum in bonis numero, quod ad aes exit.   Meritoria artificia sunt, hactenus utilia, si praeparent ingenium, non detinent.   Seneca, *Ep.*, lxxxviii, 1.

All through the temper of society of the time runs this materialism, and in the middle class it is money which makes the man. The whole structure of local society emphasised, as we have seen, the social deference paid to wealth. In return the great generosity expected of, and displayed by, the wealthy class pauperised the lower orders and encouraged a decay of initiative and effort. The failure of intellectual and creative power in literature, which is lamented by Pliny and Statius, is no doubt in part a concomitant.

We may, however, notice two less gloomy aspects of this social movement. Firstly, it helped throughout the Empire to assist in breaking down the humble citizen's contempt for labour. Free labour was on the increase and was more conscious of its own worth. In part this may have been due to the decrease of slave competition, which adversely affects free labour not merely by economic rivalry, but also by branding certain types of employment as unworthy of a freeman. Manumission was increasingly practised,[1] and there was no longer, as under the Republic, the constant influx of the slave captives of war. I am also inclined to think that the prejudices of a Juvenal were more pronounced in Rome than in what had been subject countries. St. Paul was

---

1. For the numbers of freedmen in Rome in 56 A.D., see the speech in the Senate, Tacitus, *Annals*, xiii, 27. Persius satirises manumission, v, 75 foll. "O soul barren of truth, you who think that one twirl of a thumb can make a Roman citizen! Look at Dama here; an understrapper not worth three groats; blear eyed from drink; a man who would tell a lie about a half-feed of corn. His master gives him one spin, when lo and behold! in the twisting of a top, he comes forth as Marcus Dama." Everyone trusts citizen Marcus Dama. Haec mera libertas, haec nobis pillea donant!

evidently not ashamed of being a tentmaker. Something again may be attributed to the influence of the Cynics, who preached the essential merit of work; of this doctrine Dio Chrysostom, partly, no doubt, as the fruit of the personal experiences of his exile, is also an adherent.[1] In any case, whatever the reason, the inscriptions show us, as Dill has rightly emphasised, that a new consciousness of the dignity of labour was emerging. The apple seller, the cooper, or the blacksmith display upon their monuments the implements of their trade: "This pride in honest industry is a new and healthy sign."[2]

Secondly, materialism provokes its own reaction, and there developed a widespread and almost pathetic longing for a gospel of spiritual values. This longing, though naturally more articulate in the upper strata of society, was not confined to them.[3] For the ubiquity of the Cynic is the measure of the popular opportunity, of which Christianity made full use.

From the freedmen we may pass naturally to the class from which they rose—the slaves—and the fact of their emergence to social importance

---

1. For Cynic attitude to work as possessing value in itself see von Arnim, *Leben und Werke des Dion*, p. 497, for Dio's sentiments, see *Or.* vii, Euboicus, especially sections 109-113. For Dio's life as an exile see von Arnim, *op. cit.*, pp. 246 foll. Philostratus, *Vit. Soph.* i, 7, 488, tells us that "he planted and dug, drew water for baths and gardens, and performed many such menial tasks for a living." No doubt it was this experience which gave him his marked sympathy for the "underdog" in the social system (see von Arnim, *op. cit.* pp. 491 foll.).

2. Dill, *op. cit.*, p. 253.

3. Compare the scathing attacks upon the rich which run throughout Lucian's writings. The same moral as that conveyed by his pictures of the judgment of the rich in the next world, is expressed by the tombstone: "Bene fac, hoc tecum feres."

is in itself evidence that the lot of the slaves was not so hopeless as is often supposed. Not that the evils of slavery are to be condoned. As everywhere it had worked havoc with the ruling race. On the one hand, the vast slave households of the very rich had bred the minor vice of absurd dependence upon servants. "A Roman noble," said the moralist, "needed to be assured by a slave that he was really seated before he felt comfortable in his chair."[1] But far worse was the effect upon character, and the results of the brutalising influence of irresponsible power over human beings. Juvenal has drawn an unforgettable picture of the great lady's capricious cruelty to her servants. "You complain," says Seneca, "of the loss of liberty, when every great household is a tyranny in miniature." "As many enemies as there are slaves, says the proverb. But it is we that have made them so."[2] Further, the idle and turbulent urban rabble, which already in Gracchan days it had become advisable to feed and to amuse, was directly a social product of the institution of slavery.

But when we turn to the second century, we find ample evidence of a new and humane attitude, and the status of the slave was definitely improving. Indeed, the nature of the services of the domestic slaves have always, in households of moderate size, tended to give them the position

---

1. Seneca, *de brev. vit.*, 12, 6.

2. Juvenal, vi, 219, vi, 475 ; deinde idem de republica libertatem sublatam quaeris quam domi sustulisti, Seneca, *de ira*, iii, 35. What a contrast to the early Romans qui " domum pusillam rempublicam esse iudicauerunt ! " Seneca, *Ep.* xlvii, 14, cf. Pliny, *Ep.* viii, 16 seruis respublica quaedam et quasi civitas domus est ; Seneca, *Ep.*, xlvii, 5.

of family retainers.   Think, for example, of the
nurses in Greek tragedy.   Only in the very
large establishments of the rich, where personal
relations might be lost, was this not the rule.
It may also be remembered that at Rome the
slave was often better educated than his master.

Even the best hated of emperors inspired loyal
affection in a slave.   It was his nurse, Phyllis,
who cared for the corpse of Domitian, and his
nurses Egloge and Alexandria with his freed-
woman mistress Acte, who placed the ashes of
Nero in the family tomb of the Domitii.[1]

There were still cruel masters in Pliny's day,
and we read some ugly stories of men being
murdered by their slaves or freedmen, or of a
master who set out on a journey with a large
slave retinue and completely disappeared.[2]   But
Pliny himself is uniformly kind to his slaves ;
he is solicitous for their health and deeply distressed by their illness or death.[3]   The spirit of
the forty-seventh Letter of Seneca, indeed, not
infrequently found expression in the practice of
his contemporaries.   The love of Martial for the
little Erotion is famous[4] ; less familiar, perhaps,
though equally tender, are the consolations
addressed by Statius to his friend upon the loss
of Glaucias, a slave child whom Melior had

---

1. Suetonius, *Domitian*, 17, *Nero*, 50.

2. Pliny, *Ep.* iii, 14, viii, 14.   Cf. intelleges non pauciores seruorum
ira cecidisse quam regum, Seneca, *Ep.* iv, 8.   Primum detraxit illis metum
et indicauit tunc familiam adire, cum incertum esset, an mors domini uolun-
taria fuisset, Seneca, *Ep.* lxxvii, 7, cf. the debate in Tacitus, *Annals*, xiv,
42 foll.

3. Pliny, *Ep.* viii, 1, viii, 16, v, 19.

4. Martial, v, 34, v, 37, x, 61.

adopted as his own, or to Flavius Ursus upon the death of a favourite slave.[1] Countless inscriptions also bear testimony to the mutual affection of slaves for their masters and mistresses, and of these for their " humble friends."

Manumission in this period became increasingly common and the slave whose savings (*peculium*), though technically held only as a grace from his master, were actually though not legally his property, could purchase his freedom. Skilled labour has always enjoyed consideration. Ultimately, for any except the roughest and least skilled work, the good-will and interest of the worker are essential to success. In the skilled trades many masters found it profitable, as well as equitable, to give the slave a pecuniary interest in the profits of his labours. In fact, given the necessary proficiency and thrift, a skilled slave could in a relatively short space of time put by enough to purchase his freedom, if he so desired.

The general tone of the age is, indeed, inspired by the Stoic ideal of the brotherhood of man. The slave and the emperor are alike members of the universe and alike partake of the Divine Principle. *Unus omnium parens mundus est.* It is typical of the Stoicism of the second century that its two great figures are Epictetus the slave and Marcus Aurelius the Emperor, and it is even characteristic that the works of the former, which were never written for publication, have

---

1. Glaucias in Statius, *Siluae*, ii, 1. " Bitter it is to sigh for a sister or to weep a brother lost. Yet men of other blood than ours steal into our hearts, so that a lighter wound touches us more nearly than a greater grief. 'Tis for a slave, Ursus, that you mourn, a slave—since thus with blind hands Fortune confounds the name and discerns not the heart." *Siluae*, ii, 5.

survived in the notes taken of his lectures by one who became an imperial official of high rank.

Humanitarian sentiment and the obligation to social service runs throughout the higher thought of the day. For a summary of pagan ethics in this period I may refer you to Dill's sympathetic study of Seneca, the philosophical director, or to Hatch's not less excellent account of the teaching of that yet greater man, Epictetus.

The practical standard of conduct, which is preached by the moralists of the time, is one with which Christian ethics will find much in common. It is true enough that preaching or rebuke imply the existence of the evils which evoke them. On the other hand, it would be difficult to maintain that similar exhortations, which are voiced to-day, have become superfluous. That they were uttered, if it admits the existence of certain evils, no less affirms the existence of ideals which recognised them as such. The Stoic teachers inculcated the practice of the social duties of forbearance, loyalty and humanity towards one's fellow-men. This duty towards others rests fundamentally upon two cardinal principles of Stoic doctrine, (1) the essential unity of the universe, of which all men are parts; (2) the demands of self-respect. God also, in the Stoic view, is immanent both in the universe and in man and, at least in the new Stoicism, the performance of social duty is sanctioned by an appeal to religious emotion as much as to logic.

Man is a member of the great commonwealth

of the universe, the great city state.[1] His relationship to his parents or his children, to his city or to
the Empire, impose upon him duties (*Disc.* ii, 10).
The same is true of the wider fellowship of the
universe. He must here exercise his natural
faculty of trust, his natural gift of affection, of
beneficence, of mutual toleration.[2]

If we are not doing good to others, we are
doing harm. The nature of man and the
constitution of the universe make it a positive
obligation to seek the welfare of our fellows.
" You must live for others if you wish to live
for yourself."[3]

All men are members of the universe, whether
bond or free ; all are of flesh and blood ; to the
philosopher, distinctions which are based upon
the accident of circumstance, have no reality.[4]
" When the slave does not come at once with
warm water, is it not pleasing to the gods that
you should not be angry or break into a passion ?
Men must bear with one another as children of
one father." " Man, if you must needs harbour
unnatural feelings at the misfortune of another,

---

1. ἡ μεγάλη πόλις, Epictetus, Disc. iii, 22, 4. πολίτην ὄντα πόλεως
τῆς ἀνωτάτης ἧς αἱ λοιπαὶ πόλεις ὥσπερ οἰκίαι εἰσίν, Marcus Aurelius,
iii, 11, cf. *ibid.* iv. 4, Cicero, *de nat deor.*, ii, 62, 154.

2. Seneca, *Ep.* lxxxviii, 30, xc, 3, *de ben.* iii, 28, Cf. Epictetus, *Disc*, i, 9,
ii, 10. hoc primum philosophia promittit, sensum communem, humanitatem,
et congregationem, Seneca, *Ep.* v, 4. Cf. the attack of Epictetus upon
Epicureanism for its selfish isolation of the individual and its denial of his
responsibilities to his fellows, *Disc.* iii, 7.

3. Seneca, *de otio*, xxx, 5 ; *id.*, *Ep.*, xlviii, 2. Cf. Deus est mortali iuuare
mortalem et haec ad aeternam gloriam uia, Pliny, *N.H.* ii, 7, 5, 18.

4. Mitem animum et mores modicis erroribus aequos/ praecipit atque
animas seruorum et corpora nostra/ materia constare putat paribusque
elementis, Juvenal, xiv, 15. Si quid est aliud in philosophia boni, hoc est,
quod stemmata non inspicit, Seneca, *Ep.* xliv, 1.

pity him rather than hate him : give up this spirit of offence and hatred." Revenge is wrong and unworthy of your true self : you should be gentle to those who revile you.[1]

Humane behaviour towards others is an obligation consequent upon our common fellowship in the universe, and it is also an obligation to ourselves. " If, instead of man, a gentle, sociable creature, you have become a dangerous, aggressive, and biting brute, have you lost nothing ? Do you think you must lose cash in order to suffer damage ? " " The very act of imprisoning his slave is his penalty, and this you will admit yourself, if you will hold fast to the principle that man is not a brute, but a civilised creature." Pity, says Juvenal, and the gift of tears, are the greatest boon which nature has bestowed upon man. The gratification of revenge is a womanish vice, which gives pleasure only to a petty mind. To return evil for evil is only harm to ourselves.[2]

In the later Stoicism the appeal to obligation is sanctioned by religious emotion, for while in strict Stoical theory the Divine Principle immanent in the universe is an all-pervasive, rational, and material essence, and therefore, in logic, an impersonal force, the language of Seneca and Epictetus is again and again appropriate only to a personal Deity. God is within

---

1. Epictetus, *Disc.* i, 13, 2, i, 18, 9, iv, 5 ; *Manual*, 42.   Compare Marcus Aurelius, ii, 13, iii, 11, vi, 6, vii, 26, x, 30, xi, 9.

2. Epictetus, *Disc.* ii, 10, 14 ; *ibid.* iv, 1, 120 ; mollissima corda/ humano generi dare se natura fatetur/ quae lacrimas dedit ; haec nostri pars optima sensus, Juvenal, xv, 131 ; Juvenal, xiii, 190 ; Epictetus, *Disc.* ii, 10.

us. Prayer is communion with Him. "We do
not need to uplift our hands towards heaven or
to beg the keeper of a temple to let us approach
his idol's ear, as if in this way our prayers were
more likely to be heard. God is near you, He
is with you, He is within you."[1] The voice of
conscience, upon the authority of which the
moralists of the period repeatedly insist,[2] is
His voice. "What avails it that something is
hidden from man ? Nothing is shut off from the
sight of God. He is witness of our souls." " If
your deeds are honourable, let everybody know
them ; if base, what matters it that no one knows
them, as long as you know them yourself ? O
wretched man, if you despise this witness."[3]

God is the great example. It is upon His
nature that the ideals of conduct are based, and
this nature is described in terms, not of cold
abstract excellencies, but of warm benevolence
and loving-kindness. "The next thing is to
learn the true nature of the gods. For whatever
their nature is discovered to be, he that is to
please and obey them must try, so far as he can,
to make himself like them. If God is faithful,
he must be faithful, too ; if free, he must be free,
too ; if beneficent, he, too, must be beneficent ;
if high-minded he must, in fact, as one who
makes God his ideal, follow this out in every act
and word." As God is long-suffering, so should

---

1. Seneca, *Ep.* xli, 1.

2. To the terrors of a guilty conscience, Juvenal devotes his XVIth Satire.
Compare Plutarch, *de ser. num. vind.* 9, 554.

3. Seneca, *Ep.* lxxxiii, 1, Cf. *Ep.* xli, 1 ; *ibid.*, xliii, 5. God sees all
things, Epictetus, *Disc.* i, 14, 12.

we be merciful and generous.   " The gods are
not disdainful nor envious ; they open the door
to you ; they lend a hand as you climb upwards."
Worship is love, and love of God casteth out
fear. Hoc qui dixerit, obliuiscetur id dominis
parum non esse quod deo sat est.   Qui colitur
et amatur ; non potest amor cum timore misceri.[1]

Such passages could easily be multiplied, and
indeed to the topic of this personal Deism of the
later Stoicism we shall have to return in another
context, but sufficient evidence has been cited
to show that Tertullian's verdict of *anima
naturaliter Christiana* was not, what indeed we
should hardly expect from him, a charitable
exaggeration of the facts.   Nevertheless, in spite
of obvious similarities, and in spite of the fact
that the successful practice of the precepts of
Stoicism and Christianity as regards our duty
towards our fellowmen would result in identical
actions, there is a very real and fundamental
difference in their respective motives and in
their way of looking at the relation of men to
each other.   Between the two points of view I
am not called upon to judge nor to express any
opinion, either as to which is the higher ethical
ideal or as to which is the more nearly practicable.
I am concerned solely to record a difference, which
I feel to be radical.[2] Apart from its intrinsic

---

1. Epictetus, *Disc.* ii, 14, cf. Seneca, *Ep.* xcv, 50, uis deos propitiare ?
bonus esto. Satis illos coluit, quisquis imitatus est ; Seneca, *de ben.* iv,
4, 5, iv, 28, *de ira*, iii, 26, Marcus Aurelius, ix, 11 ; Seneca, *Ep.* lxxiii, 15 ;
Seneca, *Ep.* xlvii, 18.

2. Here I agree entirely with Mr. Bevan, *Stoics and Sceptics*, pp. 66 foll.
' I think it is important to realise that mankind has two different ideals
before it ; and I do not see how the ideal of Detachment is compatible with
the ideal of Love," *ibid.*, p. 69.

importance, it perhaps reveals the roots of some of the antagonism between the higher pagan and Christian thought.

The teaching of Christianity, as I understand it, is based upon the positive motive force of a love which is prepared to proceed to the extreme limit of self-sacrifice. Here the Christian Saviour, who redeemed man by self-sacrifice—an idea which in essence was repugnant to many pagan philosophers' view of the Divine nature—was completely unlike the saviour gods of the mystery religions. To this we must later direct our attention ; here we are concerned with the motives of social duty. In this, too, the ideal motive force is positive love for others and sacrifice of self. The sinner and the outcast, the intellectually as well as the morally feeble, have all souls of equal value in the sight of God. The ideal Christian will act benevolently and humanely towards his fellows, not merely in fulfilment of the obligation of a common kinship in the Universe or even in God, not from enlightened self-interest, nor solely out of self-respect, but because he actively loves them. That the ideal is consistently, or perhaps even frequently, realised in practice, I am not suggesting, but that surely is the ' idea,' in the Platonic sense, at the embodiment of which the perfect Christian life would aim.

Now in spite of their recognition of the common fellowship of all men in God and of the love of God to man, of this Christian attitude I do not think that Seneca and Epictetus would have had understanding. Stoicism was essentially self-centred. Its appeal is not to complete self-sacrifice, though it may indeed demand material, or even physical sacrifice, in the interests of the higher spiritual self. Self-respect is its driving force rather than love.

Again, though Stoicism denies the reality of the world's distinctions of rank, wealth, freedom and slavery, the Stoic view of mankind was yet essentially aristocratic. If material distinctions were unmeaning, it did not thereby deny the reality of other distinctions. Indeed, this was inevitable, for the basis of all philosophical ethics was intellectual. Hence Origen is perfectly justified in bringing the charge of, what may be called, "spiritual aristocracy" against the higher pagan thought. "See, then, if Plato and the wise men among the Greeks, in the beautiful things they say, are not like those physicians who confine their attention to what are called the better classes of society and despise the multitude."[1] Here he is reacting to the pagan view of Christianity. "Let no one come to us who has been instructed or who is wise or prudent (for such qualifications are deemed evil by us); but if there be any ignorant or unintelligent or uninstructed or foolish persons, let them come with confidence. . . . They manifestly show that they desire, and are able to gain over, only the silly and the mean and the stupid, with women and children."[2] It is not only social prejudice nor even a resentment at the methods

---

1. Origen, *c. Cels.*, vii, 60.
2. *ibid.*, iii, 44.

of Christian propaganda,[1] though these may
account for some bitterness, that prompt Celsus'
attack. It is rather that Christianity, as judged
by the pagan standards, seemed to ignore moral
values in its direct appeal to sinners and criminals,[2]
and its basic doctrine of spiritual democracy
appeared to run counter, as indeed it did, to that
intellectual conception of virtue which is cardinal
to pagan ethics.

For though the Stoic believed that the Divine
spark was immanent in all men, in some it flickered
but feebly. His view of mankind as a whole was
pessimistic ; from past history he drew no hopes
for the future, and he cherished no illusions as
to the moral progress of the ages. True that
moral values do not correspond with material
or social distinctions, but they have, nevertheless,
their own different gradation. The ruck of
men are incapable of rising far above the brute.
Ages have differed, not in viciousness so much
as in the forms which vice has assumed. The
simple age of primitive man was less wicked, for
the possibilities of wickedness have developed
with the increasing luxury and complexity of
civilisation. It is hardly to be called more
virtuous, for virtue depends upon moral choice
and cannot be predicated of ignorance or of
lack of opportunity. There is, therefore,
individual moral progress ; but general standards
have not altered for the better, nay rather, in

---

1. Origen, *c. Cels.*, iii, 55.
2. Origen, *c. Cels.*, iii, 59.

practice, with the growing complexity of civilisation, they have degenerated.[1]

The Wise Man, in his relations with the common herd, will obey the dictates of the kindly self-interested virtue which is proper to him, and will render their due to fellow members of the universe. His actions will not be unworthy of himself, but he will not feel called upon to love them nor to suppose that they are in any real sense his spiritual equals.[2]

But it is, perhaps, time to leave the philosophic basis of the social ethics of Stoicism and return to the world of practical life. Here we have still to enquire what effect, if any, had this preaching upon the ordinary standards of conduct. Do we find evidence of a more humane temper, and a new ideal of social service, actually expressing itself in practice ? The question has, in part, been previously answered. The remarkable generosity of the wealthy to their poorer fellow-

---

1. See Seneca, *Ep.* lxxiv. Of primitive man he says "non erant illi sapientes uiri, etiam si faciebant facienda sapientibus " ; similarly of animals " sine nequitia, sine fraudibus degunt." Ignorance is not virtue. Ignorantia rerum innocentes erant. Multum enim interest utrum peccare aliquis nolet an nesciat, *Ep.* xc.

2. σοφὸς μὲν γὰρ ἢ εἷς ἢ καὶ δύο κατ' αὐτοὺς γεγόνασιν, ἐν οἷς μόνοις ὁ λόγος κατώρθωται, οἱ δὲ ἄλλοι φαῦλοι πάντες. κἂν οἱ μὲν ὦσι προσκόπτοντες, οἱ δὲ χύσιν τῆς φαυλότητος ἔχοντες, εἰ καὶ πάντες ὁμοίως λογικοί, Porphyry, *de abst.*, iii, 2. Hence the attitude that the ritual and mythology of popular polytheism are allegorical expressions of truths which the vulgar are incapable of understanding, see my *Lectures on the History of Roman Religion*, pp. 130–159. The general position is well expressed in Strabo i, 2, 8-9, 19-20. " For the mob of women and of all the uneducated masses cannot be brought to reverence, piety and faith by the reasoning or exhortation of the philosopher. There is therefore a need for the instrument of superstition and this cannot be aroused without myths and marvels. . . . Philosophy, however, is for the few, but poetry, particularly Homer's, has a greater popular influence and can get its message across (θέατρα πληροῦν δυναμένη)."

citizens and to the public amenities of their native towns, cannot merely be dismissed as a necessary response to the demands of public opinion or to the vanity of ostentation. It is undoubtedly inspired by a real sense of obligation. Characteristic of the time are the foundations for the maintenance of the aged poor or for the upbringing of poor children (*alimenta*), which were endowed by private benefactors, like Pliny, or, under Trajan and the Antonines, by the State. Bequests to cheapen the necessaries of life or to provide free baths for the poor are common. A spice dealer left a sum of money to provide free medicine for the poor of his native home.[1]

In other and less material ways the growing humanity of the age displays itself. We may notice, for instance, the preoccupation of the time with the problems of education, or the emphasis which again and again is laid upon the paramount necessity of good example and the importance of early influences upon character in its formative stage. Pliny's rebuke to the man whom he caught thrashing his son, or Quintilian's quite admirable exposure of the defects of the use of corporal punishment in the classroom, may again remind us of the humane

---

1. Pliny's foundation, *Ep.* vii, 18. For *alimenta* and benefactions see Dill, *op. cit.*, pp. 195, 227, Reid, *op cit.*, p. 462. The earliest private foundation dates from the reign of Augustus ; State endowment was inaugurated by Nerva. An ingenious double purpose was secured by a system by which the State lent capital to landowners at low interest, thereby providing a needed stimulus to agricultural prosperity : the interest on the money was earmarked to form the annual endowment of *alimenta*.

For further examples of donations and bequests for charitable purposes, see Friedländer, *Cena Trimalchionis*, pp. 52 foll.

tendencies of the time.[1]   Again, a good deal about
ordinary standards of human conduct is implied
in Plutarch's attack upon superstition as essentially
an insult to God.   " I, for my own part, had
much rather people should say of me that there
never is nor ever was such a man as Plutarch,
than that they should say, Plutarch is an unsteady,
fickle, froward, vindictive and touchy fellow :
if you invite others to sup with you and chance
to leave Plutarch out, or if some business falls out
that you cannot wait at his door with the morning
salute, or if when you meet with him you don't
speak to him, he'll fasten upon you somewhere
with his teeth and bite the part through, or catch
one of your children and cane him, or turn his
beast into your corn and spoil your crop."   If
this is negative testimony, let me conclude with
some sentences from the passage in his life of
the elder Cato, in which the ruthless treatment of
slaves as living tools, which was recommended
by that hard business man, moves the gentler
Plutarch to righteous anger.   " But we may
extend our goodness and charity even to irrational
creatures :   and such acts flow from a gentle
nature as water from an abundant spring.   It is
doubtless the part of a kind-natured man to
keep even worn-out horses and dogs . . . not to
use living creatures like old shoes or dishes, and
throw them away when they are worn out or

---

1.   Pliny, *Ep*. iii. 3, Juvenal, xiv ; Pliny, *Ep*. ix, 12 ; Quintilian, *Inst.
Or*. i, 1, 3, 13. [Plutarch], *de lib. educ.*, though a poor work from a literary
point of view, illustrates the prevalence of excellent educational sentiments.
Defects of corporal punishment, 8F, use of example, particularly in the
mastery of anger, 10B, advice to fathers to temper severity with kindness and
discretion, 13D foll.

broken with service. . . . As to myself, I would
not so much as sell my draught ox on account of
his age, much less for a small piece of money sell
a poor old man and so chase him, as it were,
from his own country, by turning him not only
out of the place where he has lived a long while,
but also out of the manner of living to which he
has been accustomed." [1]

---

1. Plutarch, *de superstit.* 10; for Plutarch's contrast between superstition,
a thing of gloom, and religion, a source of radiant joy, see *non poss. suav.,
uiu. sec. Ep.* 21, 1101c; Plutarch, *Cato Major,* 5.

LECTURE V

EASTERN AND WESTERN ELEMENTS IN GRÆCO-ROMAN CIVILISATION.

Διὰ γὰρ τὸ θαυμάζειν οἱ ἄνθρωποι καὶ νῦν καὶ τὸ πρῶτον ἤρξαντο φιλοσοφεῖν·

" The sense of wonder is and was the stimulus which made men begin to be philosophers."

Aristotle, *Met.* i, 11, 8.

Ἀρχὴ φιλοσοφίας, παρά γε τοῖς ὡς δεῖ καὶ κατὰ θύραν ἁπτομένοις αὐτῆς, συναίσθησις τῆς αὑτοῦ ἀσθενείας καὶ ἀδυναμίας περὶ τὰ ἀναγκαῖα.

" The beginning of philosophy with those who approach it in the right way and by the door, is a consciousness of one's own weakness and want of power in regard to necessary things."

Epictetus, *Disc.*, ii, 11,

" ' And the soul, the soul itself,' I went on, ' has it not been imprisoned in the body contrary to nature, a swift, and, as you hold, a fiery soul in a slow cold body, the invisible within the sensible ? Are we therefore to say that soul in body is nothing, and not rather that, Reason, that divine thing, has been made subject to weight and density, that one which ranges all heaven and earth and sea in a moment's flight, has passed into flesh and sinews, marrow and humours, wherein is the origin of countless passions ? Your Lord Zeus, is he not, so long as he preserves his own nature, one great continuous fire ? ' "
Plutarch, *de fac. in orb. lun.*, 12,926c, (Prickard, p. 271).

It will hardly be disputed that Christianity is one of the forces in which Eastern and Western

forms of thought are blended. The Apostle of
the Gentiles belonged to a different social status
from the peasant disciples, who listened in person
to the teaching of Jesus. If the mystical
experience of his conversion had given him a
simplicity of conviction and purpose no less
determined than that of the fishermen of Galilee,
he was, unlike them, equipped for his task of
interpretation by a mastery of both Greek and
Hebrew learning. The mission, which he felt
to be imposed upon him, indeed aroused misgiving
and prejudice among some of the older disciples,
but it was carried out with conspicuous success,
and Christianity, in consequence, became more
than the peculiar doctrine of a Jewish sect.

It is true that St. Paul in the face of a Greek
audience mistrusted his mastery of the rhetorical
tricks of the schools, and wisely decided to
rely upon the eloquence of simple conviction
(1 *Corinthians*, ii, 1). In fact, in a purely literary
sense, he created a new style, truer and more
genuinely eloquent than that of contemporary
artifice, because it was fired by burning faith
and a more direct contact with passionately
realised truth. He is a far more individual
author, in proportion as he is a far greater
religious genius, than the Christian philosophers of
a later generation, who despoiled pagan learning
in the service of apologetic. But, nevertheless,
he is essentially one of the ' not many wise
after the flesh,' (1 *Cor.* i, 26) and was profoundly
versed in Hellenistic culture.

It was that which made him an almost perfect
instrument for his mission, for he could employ a

language and an imagery which his Greek-speaking hearers understood. If the Founder of Christianity was born in Bethlehem of Judæa, His message in order to reach the larger world was necessarily dressed in Hellenistic garb. The form in which Christian metaphysic and theology are expressed, consequently has its roots in Greek philosophy and literature. On the institutional side, on the other hand, Christianity perhaps owes most to the West. For it assimilated the practical political capacity of the ruling race, and from Rome it derived its instinct for corporate discipline and solidarity.

I spoke of St. Paul as being versed in " Hellenistic " culture, avoiding the word " Greek " of deliberate intent, for there is a distinction which is important. It is important, even in detail. For example, when St. Paul uses the analogy of a mystery, he is not, as commentators seem often to suppose, thinking in terms of the Eleusinian Mysteries of Periclean Athens, but of the mystery religions of his own day, whose vocabulary indeed he frequently borrows for his own purposes.[1] But the thought and language of the religion and philosophy of

---

1. Upon St. Paul's use of the vocabulary of mystery religions, see Reitzenstein, *Die hellenistische Mysterienreligionen.* Farnell (*Cults of Greek States*, iii) is inclined to maintain that the Eleusinian mysteries remained to the end unaffected by syncretism, one of the few points upon which he would agree with Foucart. In spite of this authority the view of Anrich, *op. cit.*, p. 40, and Otto Jahn, *Hermes*, iii, 1869, p. 327, is more probable. Upon general grounds it is unlikely that Eleusis would remain unaffected by the other mystery cults in an age of religious syncretism, and, though for obvious reasons our information is not as explicit as could be wished, that Eleusinian doctrine was actually so influenced in imperial times, is surely implied by such passages as Plutarch, *Quaest. conviv.* iv, 6, 1, 671, C-D.

his Greek-speaking contemporaries were themselves products of a fusion of Oriental with
Greek ideas.

Civilisation develops—I will beg no questions
by the use of the word progresses—by alternate
processes of individualisation and assimilation.
An analogy may perhaps be found in the psychological experience of our own mental development.
A part of our gains is the product of what our
individual and peculiar mind has worked out for
itself in relative independence ; a part, hardly less
in importance and greater in amount, is the
product of assimilation from persons and ideas,
with which we have been brought into contact,
and from whom we have borrowed. Inevitably
the two processes are always continuously at
work, but I am not at all sure that if we look
back upon our lives that we should not find
that there were periods rather markedly distinguished by the predominance of one or other
characteristic. Indeed it is one of the difficulties
which beset all educational tests, that the fruits
of the periods of assimilation are difficult to
evaluate while the process is going on, and shallow
precocity may often outstrip the delayed but
eventually riper products of a wider and deeper
mental experience.

At any rate an appearance of this kind is
presented by the history of the civilisation of the
ancient Mediterranean world. Of course, peoples,
like our individual, have never evolved a civilisation quite independent of contacts, borrowing,
or external stimulus, but at the same time there
is a marked contrast between periods, on the one

hand, of relative political or cultural isolation, during which individual peoples work out independently, with a success proportionate to their native genius, their own peculiar civilisation; and periods, on the other hand, in which a variety of cultures which have been created along independent lines, are brought by political or other circumstances[1] into close interrelation. There results what is called a period of syncretism. The contributions of the various individual civilisations are adjusted and harmonised, as well as may be, with one another. Some immediate intellectual confusion is inevitable; there is a loss of definite precision. Such periods are assimilative rather than creative; they tend to be characterised by scientific industry and learned erudition rather than by imperishable monuments of artistic or literary genius. But their importance is often unduly neglected. They are the great formative epochs, and it is their humbler but invaluable task to provide the broader basis of a wider experience for those periods of creation, which are as rare in the history of the race as in the experience of the individual.

When civilisations are thus thrown into a single cauldron, the result of the process of fusion is inevitably different from all or any of the constituent elements, though it is probable that one, in virtue of its special circumstance or

---

1. Thus it is the development of printing and of facility of communication rather than political unity, which has made the civilisation of to-day in a real sense international.

quality, will predominate in the composite product. A process of the kind which I have indicated, must have taken place in the Middle East when, in the middle of the sixth century B.C., the Persian Empire formed a political unit, the fringes of which touched Hellenism on the west and India upon the east. In this Empire, united culturally by the use of a single official language, Aramaic (just as later Hellenistic civilisation was united by the use of a standardised Greek, the *Koine*), the civilisations of Egypt, Chaldæa, and Iran were brought together, that of Mesopotamian Babylon on the whole predominating. But this fusion of the old Oriental cultures, though we shall notice evidence of its influence upon the history of Mithraism, I have neither the time nor indeed the knowledge to investigate, although I fancy that a deeper analysis of the Oriental elements of Hellenistic thought than we can undertake, would reveal a perhaps unsuspected degree of its importance.

We have already noticed that the Roman Empire united in a single political whole the countries of the Mediterranean sea-board. These fall, roughly, into two distinct groups, the West which derived its civilisation from Rome, and the East which in a large measure had given its civilisation to Rome. For Roman culture had been itself derivative ; captive Greece had conquered her conqueror. Greek models had inspired Roman literature, and, long before Augustus, the Roman of education regarded Greek language and letters, no less than Latin,

lis indispensable heritage.[1] In the Eastern
 of the Empire Greek, not Latin, remained the
current speech. Her law, her institutions, her
genius for order and political government, Rome
imposed upon the East, together with less
admirable products of the Roman temperament,
the crude and cruel taste for gladiatorial shows,
the convention of rigid social grades and the
institution of clientship. Thus the ruling race,
it is true, imposed an ordered organisation and
something of a Roman stamp. But the vital
forces of culture were, and remained, Græco-
Oriental.

In fact, as the Empire proceeded, the dominance
of the eastern half became more and more
pronounced. Superficially, it is true, the earlier
Principate is marked by apparent actions and
reactions. In a sense Augustus himself had
conquered Antony as the representative of the
West against the minion of an Oriental queen,
whose ambitions were plainly to found an Eastern
Empire upon the eastern model. It is significant
that Augustus, who as *triumuir* founded a temple
of Isis, as emperor inculcated contempt for all
forms of Eastern religion and attempted to revive
the forms of the national worship of Græco-
Roman Italy.[2] Indeed, his policy throughout is

---

1. The bilingual culture of Rome in imperial times is illustrated by a
story of Claudius. " Cuidam barbaro Græce ac Latine disserenti, ' cum
utroque,' inquit, ' sermone nostro sis paratus,' " Suetonius, *Claudius* 42.
The lampoons, in which popular feeling against Nero found expression, were
scribbled upon the walls of Rome indifferently in Latin or Greek, Suetonius,
Nero, 39, 2. Non possum ferre, Quirites, Graecam urbem, Juvenal, iii, 60.

2. For a short account of the religious policy of Augustus, see my *Lectures
on the History of Roman Religion*. The defeat of the eastern gods at Actium
has inspired a famous passage in Vergil, *Aeneid*, viii, 675 foll.

inspired by a deliberate appeal to national
sentiment. But Eastern culture was too strong
for the Western reaction to be permanent.
Already Nero, the devotee of a somewhat decadent
Hellenism, despises other cults, except that of the
Syrian goddess, and has dreams of sitting at
Jerusalem upon the throne of an oriental despot.[1]
In the struggle for mastery between the legions
of the West and of the East, which followed
Nero's downfall, the legions of the East were
victorious. Their nominee, however, was of
Italian bourgeois stock, and their victory resulted
in some measure in a temporary western reaction.
But these political fluctuations are but surface
ripples. The force of ideas was irresistible.
From the reigns of Trajan and Hadrian, Spaniards
though they may be by race, Hellenism flows in
a steady and increasing tide. The centre of
gravity of Mediterranean civilisation more and
more openly shifted to the East.

The process was inevitable. The derivative
character of his own literature and art was
confessed by the Roman, and Greek influences
had all the prestige of a language and literature,
which formed the basis of polite education and
provided the acknowledged masterpieces of
thought and expression. The ancient civilisations
yet further east impressed the Roman, as they had
done the Greek before him, with awe for their
immense antiquity. To intellectual reverence
may be added economic and social causes.
Industry, technical skill, artistic productivity,

---

1. Suetonius, *Nero*, 56 and 40.

intelligence, science—all these, as Cumont has said, passed by peaceful penetration from East to West.[1] We have already noticed how their business aptitude distributed the Greeks and Syrians throughout the Empire along the great commercial ways. Skilled clerks from the Levant filled the offices of the imperial bureaucracy, and we have remarked how in the social and economic revolution of the second century, the Greek or Syrian business man exploited his social opportunities, until Roman society itself ceased largely to consist of Romans by blood.

Politically, too, the influence of the East inevitably increased.   Where else was to be found the precedents for monarchy upon a large scale ? It was, for instance, in Egypt of the Ptolemies that Rome found the model for an organised system of taxation.   As the importance of Rome and Italy declined in relation to the provinces, as the control of the central authority was tightened, as the position of the emperor became more and more openly autocratic, the Eastern analogy became more and more compelling. The overt oriental despotism of Diocletian's court is the logical result of an inevitable bias.

Again, the religious movements which seriously affected the life of society are without exception of Eastern origin or influenced by Eastern thought.   The rude cults of Gaul and the West had no contribution to make.   Druidism, as an

---

1. Cumont, *Les Réligions Orientales dans le Paganisme Romaine*, p. 4. The economic exploitation of the raw material of the West by the technical skill and commercial ability to the East is well brought out in Charlesworth, *Commerce and Trade Routes of the Roman Empire*.

agent of political nationalism, was ruthlessly suppressed. To Celtic deities, no doubt, the legionary paid local worship and identified them as forms of gods which he knew, but no great religious movement came from the West.[1]

Now the Greek influences, with which Rome had been brought into direct contact by the conquest of the East, were not those of the independent Greek city-states. Characteristic of these small and intensely independent communities had been their social attitude towards life. The individual was primarily a member of a small political community, a part of a living organism, in the life of which he shared. Man, said Aristotle, is a political creature (πολιτικὸν ζῷον),[2] that is to say, he could not be considered, nor did he consider himself, out of relation to the small society of which he was an essential member. He did not feel himself to be isolated, a single individual face to face with an enormous world. Even his religion was essentially corporate, and its higher functionaries were civic officials, not professional priests. His religion, again, laid emphasis not upon faith, but upon works, in the sense of the proper

---

1. When they did spread, the western cults tended to remain national. Thus the cult of Epona, the ostler's goddess, by whom the horsey Lateranus swears (Juvenal, viii, 156) and whose picture hangs in Thessalian stables (Apuleius, *Met.*, iii, 27), has no importance for the civilisation of the Empire as a whole. And though it achieved a wide distribution, thanks in the first place to Gallic soldiers, on ne voit pas qu'elle ait obtenu les hommages de nombreux étrangers. Cumont, *Les Rel. Or.*, p. 38.

2. That is to say a member of a *polis* or city state. With this contrast the Stoic definition, coined perhaps by Chrysippus, that man is a κοινωνικὸν ζῷον, *i.e.* a member of the universe, Epictetus, *Disc.*, ii, 10, 4. Compare the Latin equivalent sociale animal et in commune genitus, Seneca, *de ben.*, vii, 1, 8.

performance of prescribed ritual duty, and it had relatively very little interest, certainly no vested interest, in theology or scientific speculation.   The Greek, in consequence, attacked the problems of the universe fearlessly and from a detached objective standpoint.   For him man was the gauge of all things ; in the face of nature he was curious but unafraid.   It is quite true that even in the fifth century we can trace a growing influence of oriental contacts upon Greek religious belief, and in the steadily increasing vogue of Orphism, which was not primarily of oriental origin, the growth of ideas of universalism and individualism in religion, the development of a sense of sin, and the tendency to shift religious interest from this world, with which the city-state worship was primarily concerned, to another in which individual deserts would receive reward or punishment.

To trace the gradual development of these ideas in the Greek world before Alexander would be an interesting, but for us too long and difficult a task.   It is convenient to take the exploits of Alexander as marking a decisive change. Inevitably they altered the whole horizon.   For the city-state was substituted the idea of a world empire, and though it is true that none of the Successors succeeded in holding more than a share of Alexander's conquests, all regarded themselves as legitimate heirs to the whole. Not only the particularism of the city-state, but even the wider boundaries which separated Hellene and Barbarian had been broken down.

The individual was no longer an important unit
in a small, free community, but politically felt
himself to be a powerless entity in a vast monarchy,
and physically a microscopic atom in an immense
universe. Individualism is a necessary corollary
of universalism. Man's attitude to the universe
was no longer detached, confident, or unemo-
tional. Philosophy was now called upon to
undertake a new task, to justify the ways of God
to man. Certain tendencies towards emotionalism, individualism, and other-worldliness there
already were at work. These were now reinforced
by closer contact with the old civilisations of the
East. Here for centuries the individual had been
the slave of an arbitrary monarchy,[1] and science
had been the monopoly of a priestly caste.
Eastern conceptions of the universe were consequently influenced by the analogies of human
autocracy, the helplessness and dependence of
the individual subject, and a theological and
emotional, rather than a secular and detached,
attitude towards the problems of science.

The centre of Hellenistic culture was at
Alexandria in Egypt, the greatest of Alexander's
foundations. Here East and West met and
blended. Their mutual influence upon each
other was inevitable, and it was also deliberately
fostered. A mutual assimilation, it would seem,

---

1. "But among barbarians no distinction is made between women
and slaves, because there is no natural ruler among them : they are a community of slaves, male and female." Aristotle, *Politics*, i, 2, 4, 1252b.
The facts were openly recognised in conventional speech. The King of
Kings officially addressed his subject as "slave." E.g. the letter of Darius
to the satrap of Western Asia Minor begins "The King of Kings, Darius,
the son of Hystaspes to his slave Gadates saith as follows." Hicks and
Hill, *Greek Historical Inscriptions*, No. 20.

had been one of Alexander's hopes. In such a cult as that of Serapis, which was an artificial creation of Greek and Egyptian elements by the first Ptolemy, may be seen a good illustration of the forces at work under his successors.[1]

This hybrid god was a Saviour, and salvation is henceforward the characteristic promise of the cults of the eastern Levant. The political circumstances of the eastern Mediterranean after the death of Alexander were unhappy. The confused rivalry of great powers, constant warfare, social and economic upheavals combined to render the individual a helpless victim of circumstances which he could neither control nor foresee. "Much more keenly in evil days do men turn their minds to religion,"[2] and the peculiar miseries of the chances and changes of their mortal life added special force to men's hopes of a just redistribution of happiness in a world to come.

In this world, indeed, the lot of the individual

---

1. The policy of fusion by the identification of Greek with Oriental gods was actively pursued by the Successors, and we may notice, corresponding to the monotheistic tendency of contemporary philosophy, a tendency towards monotheism or at least henotheism in cult. There are comfortable affinities between autocracy on earth and autocracy as represented by solar henotheism in heaven. Thus, under the Seleucids the cult of Zeus Olympios was established at Antioch by identification with Baal, that of Dionysos in Cappadocia. Ptolemy even attempted to identify Dionysos Sabazios with Sabaoth. But the national spirit of the Jews proved too intractable for syncretism to conquer. See Pedrizet, *Rev. des Ét. Anc.*, xii, 1910, pp. 226-247. The development of the philosophical and theological moral of the analogies between the universe and the world state ($\dot{\eta}$ $\mu\epsilon\gamma\dot{\alpha}\lambda\eta$ $\pi\dot{\alpha}\lambda\iota s$)=the Roman Empire, and between the supreme god in the universe, the sun, and the Roman emperor, furnishes a common topic in the second century after Christ, e.g., Dio, xxxvi, 22 foll., $\pi\epsilon\rho\dot{\iota}$ $\beta\alpha\sigma\iota\lambda\epsilon\dot{\iota}\alpha s$ ii, 42, iii, 50, Plutarch, *ad princip. inerudit*, 3.

2. Lucretius, iii, 53.

appeared to bear no intelligible relation to his skill, forethought, or deserts. Characteristic of the time is the worship of Tyche, the Blind Chance by whose caprice events seemed to be directed. But on a different plane to the ordinary individual were the powerful kings. At their pleasure wars were declared or peace restored, and the unrecking whim of these remote great ones spelt catastrophe or security for helpless individual lives. Their power was more than mortal in as much as they were powerful to save. Hence arose the cult of the deified living monarchs, the Saviours (Σωτῆρες), as they were called. No doubt in part this doctrine of the divinity of kings is based upon the survival in the oriental monarchies of the idea, which is widely spread among mankind at a certain stage of culture, that the ruler is a temporary personification of the national god. Pharaoh had thus been identified with Ra[1] and the king of Babylon with Marduk. On the Hellenic side the way had been prepared for the acceptance of the doctrine by the practice of hero-worship. Hero-cult, which had in the first place consisted mainly of the worship of the great men of legend, had been extended to the founders of colonies, and already in the Fifth Century it had been awarded to distinguished persons, like the Spartan general Brasidas, immediately after their death.

When a political power, which showed itself mightier than any of the oriental monarchs, began to play an active part in the East, it was

---

1. E.g. upon monuments of Rameses iii, "thou art Re . . . when thou risest, the people live." See *Cambridge Ancient History*, ii, p. 341.

natural that honours no less than those awarded
to them should be paid to her.   In 166 B.C.
a king of Bithynia addressed the Roman senate
as " saviour gods " ($\theta\epsilon o\grave{\iota}$ $\sigma\omega\tau\hat{\eta}\rho\epsilon\varsigma$), and Flamininus,
the Roman liberator of Greece, received divine
honours in his lifetime at Chalcis.   To the
goddess Roma and the Fortune of Rome were
erected temples throughout the Greek East.[1]

In consequence, Augustus had forced upon
him, rather than himself forced upon the world,
the worship of Augustus and Roma.[2]   In his
eastern provinces it was a native plant of well-
established growth, and thence it spread all over
the Empire.   In Italy, it is true, Augustus
deprecated direct worship of himself, and even
the practice of the deification of the dead emperor,
for which he provided the model by his apotheosis
of the divine Julius, upon occasion aroused
mockery in Rome.[3]   But in a modified form the

---

1. Prusias II of Bithynia, Polybius, xxx, 16. Cult of Flamininus at
Chalcis, Plutarch, *Vit. Flam.*, 16. The titles of Roman emperors in the
Greek East carry on the Hellenistic tradition, e.g. Tiberius $\kappa o\iota v\grave{o}s$ $\tau\hat{\eta}s$
$o\grave{\iota}\kappa o\nu\mu\acute{\epsilon}v\eta s$ $\epsilon\grave{\nu}\epsilon\rho\gamma\acute{\epsilon}\tau\eta s$, *I.G.*, xii, 2, No. 206; Claudius $\sigma\omega\tau\grave{\eta}\rho$ $\tau\hat{\eta}s$ $o\grave{\iota}\kappa o\nu\mu\acute{\epsilon}v\eta s$,
I.G., xii, 2, No. 541, or $\theta\epsilon\grave{o}s$ $\grave{\epsilon}\pi\iota\phi\alpha v\acute{\eta}s$, *I.G. ad r. R. pert.*, iii, No. 328. Nero
$\grave{o}$ $\grave{\alpha}\gamma\alpha\theta\grave{o}s$ $\delta\alpha\acute{\iota}\mu\omega v$ $\tau\hat{\eta}s$ $o\grave{\iota}\kappa o\nu\mu\acute{\epsilon}v\eta s$, *C.I.G.*, iii, No. 4699; Trajan $\theta\epsilon\grave{o}s$ $\theta\epsilon o\hat{v}$
$\nu\acute{\iota}os$ $\grave{\alpha}v\epsilon\acute{\iota}\kappa\eta\tau os$, *C.I.A.*, iii, No. 462. See further Wissowa *Religion und
Kultus der Römer*, p. 283, Hahn, *Rom und Romanismus*, p. 30. Cult of Dea
Roma in Smyrna (195 B.C.), Tacitus, *Annals*, iv, 56; at Alabanda in Caria
170 B.C.), Livy, xliii, 6. In general, see Wissowa, *op. cit.*, pp. 281, foll.

2. For the pressure put upon the emperors by their Eastern subjects
in this matter, and the reluctance of the more sensible of the earlier rulers
to allow extravagant extensions of the worship of the living emperor, see the
very important *Letter of Claudius to the Alexandrians* in Bell, *Jews and
Christians in Egypt* (London, 1924), pp. 1-37. "I deprecate, however, the
appointment of a high-priest to me and the erection of temples, for I do not
wish to be offensive to my contemporaries, I hold that sacred fanes and the
like have by all ages been attributed only to the gods as peculiar honours."

3. For example there is Vespasian's jest "ut puto deus fio " (Suetonius,
Vesp.. 23) or Seneca's satire on the pumpkinification (Apocolyntosis) of
Claudius.

cult of the living emperor took root even in Italy, where Augustus encouraged the worship not of himself but of his *genius*, a distinction with but little difference for the uneducated masses. Not all his successors were so modest. I am not thinking of the claims of the insane Caligula, but of the gradual assimilation of the emperor to a divine monarch of the oriental type. From the end of the second century onwards *inuictus* and *aeternus*, epithets properly belonging to solar henotheism, became conventional titles attached to the imperial office and implicitly identified its holder with the eternal and unconquered Sun.

Politically the worship of Augustus and Roma, the worship, that is to say, of the great distant emperor and the mighty power of Rome, formed a valuable prop to imperial monarchy and a sentimental link which bound the distant provinces to the crown. The formal fulfilment of its prescribed acts of worship upon official occasions offended no consciences but those of Christians, for Christianity was unique in being exclusive. Hence emperor worship provided a test of loyalty by which Christians alone necessarily failed, and refusal to comply with its formal requirements inevitably brought them to the hostile notice of the secular power.

That the widened horizon of intellectual and emotional sympathy which, after Alexander, embraced not merely fellow citizens in a small community but the human race, and the secular political and social difficulties of the time, necessarily affected the whole trend of philosophy, we have already suggested. Thought was no longer inspired by detached and disinterested curiosity. Philosophy now constructed systems, and its function was less to discover an abstract truth than to formulate a way of life, while giving a rational and coherent explanation of the universe of which its view was fundamentally pessimistic.

Of the two great schools of thought which were most profoundly to influence the Roman mind, Epicureanism was upon the whole sceptical. This system adopted the atomic theory of Democritus and consequently offered a mechanical explanation of the universe. The attitude of the school towards Heaven may be said to be agnostic. If gods exist, and the evidence of dreams suggests that they do, they are nevertheless transcendent, and as such are too remote from humanity to exhibit interest in mundane affairs. It is, indeed, a necessary condition of their perfect beatitude in completely realised freedom from disturbance (ἀταραξία), that they should be completely aloof.

Now the human need to which philosophy and religion are called upon to respond in this period, is the need for comfort or reassurance in a world of miserable circumstance. Religion in the main offered the consolation of the prospect of a posthumous readjustment in accordance with deserts. Philosophy followed the Greek tradition of attacking, instead of evading, the problem of this life. It had become, as we have seen, essentially applied philosophy, and its problem is to discover a way of life by which its admittedly evil circumstances can be ignored or be made unreal. How is happiness to be attained?

The answer of Epicurus was that happiness consists in a freedom from disturbance (*ataraxia*), which may be attained by the exercise of a wise and enlightened self-interest. His doctrine is a form of quietism. Obviously happiness of this kind is not to be obtained by self-indulgent Hedonism and the mere gratification of the senses, but rather by the suppression of needs, appetites and desires.

Some followers of Epicurus, notably Lucretius, attacked the illusory hopes and fears with which in their view religion has unnecessarily tortured mankind, and the rewards and punishments of a future life had no meaning for those who believed that at death the individual was dissolved into the atoms of which he was composed. Epicureanism, unlike Stoicism, could not make terms with the human craving for hopes of immortality; its tendency in religious matters was sceptical, and in the second century after Christ we find Epicureans and Christians bracketed together in the popular mind as the two main types of atheist.[1]

More important in the extent and depth of its influence on Græco-Roman civilisation was Stoicism. The founder of the school which met in the Painted Porch in Athens, was Zeno, a Semite from Kition in Cyprus, and of the greatest

---

1. " If there be any atheist or Christian or Epicurean here spying upon our rites, let him depart in haste; and let all such as have faith in the God be initiated and all blessing attend them ! " He led the litany with, " Christians, avaunt ! " and the crowd responded, " Epicureans, avaunt ! " Lucian, *Alexander*, 38.

of his successors a large proportion were of
Eastern birth—Chrysippus of Tarsus, Diogenes of
Babylon, Posidonius of Apamea, Antipater of
Tyre.

Stoicism was based upon a cosmological theory
and a geo-centric system of physics ; to its
support more than to any other single cause was
due the long reign of astrology.   It found in the
contemplation of the universe, which was regarded
as finite, irrefutable evidence of a controlling
power or Reason.   The regular revolution of the
stars was evidence of an inexorable and eternal
system.   Destiny or Providence ($\epsilon i\mu\alpha\rho\mu\acute{\epsilon}\nu\eta$, $\pi\rho\acute{o}\nu o\iota\alpha$)
controls the inevitable progression of the universe
through cycles of eternity, each cycle being an
exact replica of its predecessors.

The argument from design, which this ordered
universe presents, established the existence of
God.   The Divine was, therefore, envisaged as
directing Reason.   Clearly this Divine Reason,
however multiple its manifestations, must be
itself one.   The famous Stoic hymn, from which
St. Paul quoted at Athens, gives eloquent expression to the essential monotheism of the Stoic
creed, its doctrine of resignation to the will of
Providence, and its belief that the soul is part of
God in us.   " As certain even of your own poets
have said, ' For we are also his offspring.' "
(*Acts*, xvii, 28.)

For the Stoics regarded God, not as transcendent, but as immanent in the universe.   The
soul is, as it were, a fragment of the Divine,
obscured and hampered by its bodily encum-
brance and its attendant irrational desires,

pains, and pleasures. Man is a microcosm of the universe.[1] It is this indeed which saves Stoicism from the indifferent passivity of a mechanical fatalism, for though the individual cannot alter his predestined circumstances he can, thanks to the divine spark within him, rise superior to them. This divine element, immanent in man and the universe, was not immaterial, but was conceived as an extremely subtle and tenuous fiery substance.

The ideal at which Stoicism aimed, was that of the Wise Man, who so orders his life as to be in harmony with the universe and to become indifferent to the accident of circumstance. Monism met the difficulty of the problem of Evil by a defiant denial of its reality. Apparent evil is not really evil when seen in relation to the great whole,[2] and it is the instrument, as the

---

1. The universe was regarded as ζῷον λογικὸν καὶ ἔμψυχον, see von Arnim, *Stoicorum Veterum Fragmenta*, ii, pp. 191 foll. Man is a microcosm; quid mirum noscere mundum/ si possunt homines, quibus est et mundus in ipsis,/ exemplumque dei quisque est in imagine parua? Manilius, iv, 885-7. This doctrine of the microcosm and macrocosm, which became one of the general intellectual presuppositions of Graeco-Roman civilisation, naturally ent itself to mystical developments in theosophy and magic. There is thought to be an analogy between parts of the universe or God and parts of the human body. Thus the stars are analogous to the eyes, the sun to the heart, the earth and sea to the stomach and bladder, Plutarch, *de fac. in orbe lun.* 15, 928B (Prickard, p. 275), cf. Macrobius, *Sat.*, i, 20, 16-18. But if the sun and moon are the eyes of God (Plutarch, *de Is. et Os.*, 52, 372 B), and man is a microcosm, there will be a mystical affinity between them and his corresponding organs, which are also, therefore, organs of God. Thus a text in a Leyden papyrus quoted by Reitzenstein, *Poimandres*, pp. 15-16, runs, οὗ ὁ ἥλιος καὶ <ἡ> σελήνη ὀφθαλμοί εἰσιν ἀκάματοι, λάμποντες ἐν ταῖς κόραις τῶν ἀνθρώπων. ᾦ οὐρανὸς κεφαλή, αἰθὴρ δὲ σῶμα, γῆ δὲ πόδες, τὸ δὲ περὶ σὲ ὕδωρ ὁ ὠκεανός. "Da der Mensch der κόσμος in kleinen ist, leuchten die Augen des Hermes auch in ihm."

2. See, for example, Marcus Aurelius, v, 8, vi, 44. Referring to his lameness, Epictetus exclaims, " Slave, do you mean to arraign the universe for one wretched leg ? Will you not make a gift of it to the sum of things ? . . . Do you not know what a little part you are, compared with the universe ? " Epictetus, *Disc.*, i, 12.

stimulus to moral struggle, by which "God's athletes," as Epictetus calls mankind, attain to good.[1] Stoicism, therefore, did not need the sanction of posthumous reward or punishment as a basis for conduct, but maintained the truth of the paradox that virtue is its own reward and that the good man is happy on the rack.

The Stoic attitude towards survival after death was never strictly defined. The system, it is true, maintained that the soul, though material, was divine, and was liberated after death to be united with the divine fiery essence, of which it was a spark. Clearly, such a doctrine by itself does not fulfil the desire for personal survival, but many Stoics never went beyond this impersonal indestructibility of reason. Thus Panætius, Epictetus and Marcus Aurelius, for example, may all be called sceptics as regards personal immortality. On the other hand, longing has often greater force than logic. Many Stoics were distinctly more hopeful, and an assimilation of the religious ideas attaching to Babylonian cosmology enabled Stoicism to develop a theory of astral immortality which harmonised with its general account of the universe.

Some of the reasons why Stoicism attained its dominant position in the thought of the Empire will be obvious. It provided a complete and intelligible account of the universe, adequate to satisfy minds which were neither preoccupied with nor peculiarly endowed for subtle metaphysical

---

1. " God's athletes," Epictetus, *Disc.*, iv, 4, 32. " What do you think would have become of Heracles, if there had not been a lion?" etc. Epictetus, *Disc.*, 1, 6.

speculation.[1] The virtues of conduct which it
particularly inculcated, were eminently those
which appealed to the sympathy and admiration
of the Roman's inherited tradition. But, above
all, its elasticity and adaptability enabled it to
reconcile existing religious practice with its
tenets and to absorb into itself alien philosophical
theories.

The main instrument of reconciliation was
allegory. The gods of Greek mythology were
regarded as picturesque descriptions of the
operations or manifestations of the immanent
god in special elements or spheres of activity.
The stories about them were explained away as
allegorical representations of the operation of
the forces of Nature. The theory of the existence in man of a divine element of reason
permitted of the justification of the worship of
the living emperor, and the doctrine of astral
immortality sanctioned the apotheosis of his
predecessors. The emphasis laid upon the
unalterable progression of the universe supplied a
rational line of defence for the belief in astrology
and divination.

In the process of absorbing the tenets of other
systems of thought, Stoicism was itself modified.
It became more emotional if less logical. A
compressed summary, such as I have given, of
the main features of its system may give an
exaggerated impression of its aridity, while it
also may unduly conceal the degree of transformation which Stoicism underwent in the

---

1. This virtue its critic Cotta allows it. etiam si minus uera, tamen apta
inter se et cohaerentia, Cicero, *de nat. deor.*, iii, 1, 4.

course of its development. Actually the
emotional and religious note becomes increasingly
prominent in the later Stoicism.   If Epictetus
starts from the maxim " Follow Nature," it soon
becomes transformed into the gospel " Follow
God."   As Hatch has put it, " on the higher
plane of his teaching Epictetus expresses moral
philosophy in terms of theology.   Human life
begins and ends in God," and I would refer you
to the cento of passages from the *Discourses* and
Manual by which he supports his statement.[1]

Even in the earlier Stoicism, there is implicit
in its cosmological foundation a mystical emotion,
the force of which it would be a mistake to underestimate.   The contemplation of the stars
affected man in the Eastern Levant with greater
emotion than most of us experience in our more
fuliginous climate.   " From my earliest years,"
the Emperor Julian tells us, " my mind was so
completely swayed by the light which illumines
the heavens that not only did I desire to gaze
intently at the sun, but whenever I walked
abroad in the night season, when the firmament
was clear and cloudless, I abandoned all else
without exception and gave myself up to the
beauties of the heavens ; nor did I understand
what anyone might say to me, nor heed what I
was doing myself.   I was considered to be over-
anxious about these matters and to pay too much
attention to them, and people went so far as to
regard me as an astrologer, when my beard had
only just begun to grow.   And yet, I call heaven

---

1.   Hatch, *op. cit.*, pp. 155 foll.

to witness, never had a book on this subject come into my hands, nor did I as yet even know what that science was."[1] " 'When shall I see Athens again, then, and the Acropolis ? ' Unhappy man, are you not content with what you see day by day ? Can you set eyes on anything better or greater than the sun, the moon, the stars, the whole earth, the ocean ? And if you really understand Him, that governs the universe, and if you carry Him about within you, do you still long for a paltry stone and pretty rock ? " [2]

The contemplation of the vast, orderly movements of the heavens, so Cicero tells us, will necessarily fill the wise man's soul with pleasure. By the perpetual reflection and study of the universe his mind is brought to the true knowledge of itself and so to the inexhaustible joy of the realisation of its essential oneness with the Divine Mind.[3]

We too, perhaps, are not insensitive to the beauty of the starry heavens, but I doubt whether their splendour and majesty make an impression

---

1. Julian, *Hymn to King Helios*, 130D.

2. Epictetus, *Disc.*, ii, 16, 32. Cf. utinam quidem quemadmodum uniuersa mundi facies in conspectu uenit, ita philosophia tota nobis posset occurrere simillimum mundo spectaculum. Profecto enim omnes mortales in admirationem sui raperet, relictis iis quae nunc magna magnorum ignorantia credimus, Seneca, *Ep.*, lxxxix, 1.

3. Cicero, *Tusc.*, v., 24, 69-25, 70 : quo tandem igitur gaudio adfici necesse est sapientis animum cum his habitantem pernoctantemque curis ! ut cum totius mundi motus conuersionesque perspexerit sideraque uiderit innumerabilia coelo inhaerentia cum eius ipsius motu congruere certis infixa sedibus . . . haec tractanti animo et noctes et dies cogitanti exsistit illa a deo Delphis praecepta cognitio, ut ipsa se mens agnoscat coniunctamque cum diuina mente se sentiat, ex quo insatiabili gaudio compleatur. The same ideas find similar expression in Cicero, *de leg.*, i, 23.

upon us at all comparable to that which they evidently made upon the ancients. This I have emphasised, because it explains the extraordinary readiness and completeness with which Hellenistic civilisation made Babylonian cosmography its own.   It explains the ideas to us, or at any rate to me, so strange in conception, that man was originally made to walk upright in order that he might regard the heavens [1] or that the perfection of bliss would be realised by the spirits of the great and good in the eternal contemplation of the regular movements of the heavenly bodies. [2]

In any case that a genuine and mystical emotion was, in fact, evoked by the sensitiveness of the ancients to the great spectacle of the firmament cannot be doubted.   " I know that I am a mortal, a creature of a day ; but when I search into the multitudinous, revolving spirals of the stars, my feet no longer rest on earth, but, standing by Zeus himself, I take my fill of ambrosia, the food of the gods." [3]   Those are the feelings of the Greek man of science. This aesthetic emotion was touched to the issues of religion. A sense of mystic rapture in the contemplation of the perfect and orderly movement of the starry heavens, which present so noble a contrast to the instability and accidents of terrestrial life, [4] again

---

1. Cicero, *de leg.*, i, 9, 26, Ovid, *Met.*, i, 84.   Seneca, *Ep.* xcii, 30. Of primitive man he tells us, in another passage, " libebat intueri signa ex media coeli parte uergentia, rursus ex occulto alia surgentia.   Quidni iuuaret uagari inter tam late sparsa miracula ? *Ep.* xc, 42.

2. E.g. Seneca, *Cons. ad Marciam*, xviii, 2 from Posidonius, and see below, p. 225

3. Ptolemy, *Anth. Pal.* ix, 577 (trans. Paton).

4. See for example Manilius, i, 463-519.

and again finds its expression in Stoic literature. Here is the true hope of escape from the chances and changes of this mortal life.

> Felix qui potuit rerum cognoscere causas,
> Atque metus omnis et inexorabile Fatum
> Subiecit pedibus, strepitumque Acherontis auari.[1]

---

1. " Happy he who was able to apprehend the causes of things and subdued beneath his feet all fears and inexorable Fate and the roar of greedy Acheron." Vergil, *Georgic*, ii, 489. Upon this passage see the comment of Cumont, *After Life*, p. 210. Such knowledge is only possible because the universe is one and God is immanent in it and in man. Quis coelum possit, nisi coeli munere, nosse/ et reperire deum, nisi qui pars ipse Dei est ? Manilius, ii, 113.

LECTURE VI

THE DECLINE OF RATIONALISM.

" The medical remedies which the gods prescribe are the very most opposite of what one would expect, and indeed just the very things which one would naturally most avoid."

Aristides, (Keil), xxxvi, 124. cf. xlii, 8.

" Modern works of religious art are to be admired for their curious craftsmanship, but they have less of the glory of God " (than the rough idols of antiquity).

Porphyry, de abst. ii, 18.

" Just as the Gods have made the goods of sense common to all but those of intellect only to the wise, so the myths state the existence of Gods to all, but who and what they are only to those who can understand."
Sallustius, <i>de diis et mundo</i> iii (trans. G. Murray, <i>Five Stages of Greek Religion</i>, p. 243).

THAT during the early centuries of the Christian era there was a progressive decline in scientific rationalism will scarcely be denied, and that the temper of medieval science, which lies at the far end of them, is markedly distinct from that of Greek science, which preceded them, hardly needs assertion. Nor is it a matter of dispute that in scientific temper the philosophy and science of Plato, Aristotle, and the earlier Alexandrians, has the advantage over medieval learning. But, though I fancy that it is very generally supposed that Christianity is the main and primary cause of this decline, an examination of the facts will hardly warrant this inequitable assignment of responsibility. The decline of rationalism, as we shall see, is a general and continuous process, which began before Christianity had been preached, and affected the whole of Græco-Roman civilisation, pagan as well as Christian. Christian thought shared, but it did not impose, the intellectual limitations of the period.

The course of this movement of the intellectual outlook from a position of critical rationalism to one of superstitious credulity, I will attempt very briefly to describe; but before beginning our survey, there is just one matter which it may be well to clear out of the way. It is sometimes thought, and it can be maintained as a thesis, that Christianity decried or denounced secular learning as such. It is, indeed, true that the new religion had first been preached by the peasant apostles to peasants. The message of its Founder was addressed to the simple and unlettered. It lacked that intellectual attitude towards ethics, which is fundamental to Greek philosophy. It accused the Greek teachers of intellectual arrogance, while it was itself repugnant to many pagan thinkers because it appeared to make its appeal to an ignorant emotionalism. It is further true that this tradition was to some extent followed by, what may be called, the Cynic wing of the Christian movement, and there did exist a school of thought which held that the revelation of the Scriptures made secular learning superfluous.[1]

---

1. See Wendland, *op. cit.*, pp. 226-7.

But, first of all, we may notice that this attitude is not confined to Christians. It corresponds, as I have suggested, to the extreme Cynic assertion of the unimportance of learning and culture in relation to the paramount importance of morals. Secondly, it would be ridiculous to assert that this Puritan wing in Christianity, any more than the Cynics in Paganism, succeeded in effecting a wholesale conversion to the extreme view, and in inspiring a general contempt for learning. Thirdly, it is well to be careful in handling passages, which seem at first sight to support such a view. For example, Arnobius tells us that science is a vain pursuit : knowledge of God is the one essential.   What business is it of man to enquire about the origin of souls or to speculate whether the sun is larger than the earth ?   Leave those things to God. Knowledge of Him is more urgent, for Hell is upon us if we are ignorant of Him.[1] But we must not force unduly a passage where a preacher is overstating his own position in the earnestness of the moment and from his desire to drive home the supreme importance of religion. Patently Arnobius himself does not absolutely despise learning ; he is even erudite.

The same idea will be found not dissimilarly expressed in pagan thought, for example in the passage quoted by Seneca from Demetrius the Cynic,[2] or finding expression in a passionate impatience with the arid intellectualism of philo-

---

1. Arnobius, *adv. Gentes*, ii, 60 foll. I have summarised, not quoted.
2. Seneca, *de Ben.*, vii, " Licet nescias, quae ratio Oceanum effundat ac reuocet," etc.

sophical debate, when men's souls are at stake.
"What is the good to me of your making up those
miserable games ? It is no time for playing at
cross-word puzzles : you are summoned to the
help of men in distress."[1] This outburst is
primarily inspired by the unreality and triviality of
much of the mental gymnastic and scholastic
pedantry of the philosophical schools, but it
touches a deeper issue, that upon which the
Cynics, up to a point, were right, to wit, the
relative importance of the spiritual and intellectual
needs of mankind and the urgency of the former
necessities at that particular moment. But no
one who knows Seneca, would suppose that,
because he can express himself thus with complete
sincerity, he was a consistent enemy of learning
or considered knowledge to be worthless. Many
of the Christian utterances of a similar character
must be similarly regarded. It is not generally
true of the Fathers that they were enemies of
learning or science ; they were themselves, for
the most part, among the learned men of their
day. If a Puritan wing of Christianity in extreme
reaction against intellectualism preached the
complete worthlessness of secular scientific knowledge, an extreme party among the Pagans
did much the same. In either case the attitude
was prompted by a genuine sense of the spiritual
needs of contemporary life and their paramount

---

1. Quid mihi ista lusoria componis ? Non est iocandi locus : ad miseros
aduocatus es. Seneca, *Ep.* xlviii, foll. It is the same feeling which prompts
the thankfulness of Marcus Aurelius : ὅπως τε ἐπεθύμησα φιλοσοφίας, μὴ
ἐμπεσεῖν εἴς τινα σοφιστήν, μηδὲ ἀποκαθίσαι ἐπὶ τοὺς συγγραφεῖς ἢ
συλλογισμοὺς ἀναλύειν ἢ περὶ τὰ μετεωρολογικὰ καταγίνεσθαι, Marcus
Aurelius, i, 8.

importance, which lent a real force to their preaching. The perception of this no doubt affected, and legitimately affected, the occasional utterances of the more philosophic preachers, both Pagan and Christian, but it finds expression in impatient overstatements of the moment rather than forms part of the consistent structure of their thought.

At least it is no truer a picture of Christianity than it is of Stoicism, to represent it as placing an embargo upon secular science in the spirit of the Caliph who destroyed the Alexandrian Library, on the grounds that what was recorded already in the Koran was superfluous, while what was not so recorded was pernicious. Indeed, rightly to apprehend the nature and the causes of that change of intellectual temper, which we have called the decline of rationalism, we must direct our regard not to Christianity but to Græco-Roman civilisation as a whole, and our enquiry must begin before the Christian era.

I have summarised elsewhere the history of the development of Roman religion from the early agricultural religion of Numa to the worship of anthropomorphic gods derived from Greece.[1] From Greece, besides mythology, had come literature and philosophy. The latter, at the time of its first influence upon Rome, was essentially a destructive force, for both the two elder schools of Greek thought, the Academy and the Peripatetics, after the deaths of Plato and

---

1. *History of Roman Religion from Numa to Augustus.*

Aristotle, had moved in the direction of scepticism. Of individuals, Carneades, a member of the Academy, who visited Rome in 156 B.C., created most impression and exercised the greatest influence. He was, in fact, banished from Italy, because of the destructive influence of his teaching.

Again, the doctrines of Euhemerus were translated and popularised by the first great Roman poet, Ennius. His theory represented the counterpart to the Hellenistic doctrine of the divinity of kings, in as much as it explained that the gods of Greek mythology had been human monarchs, who had been paid divine honours after their death, in gratitude for the benefits which they had conferred upon their subjects. All these influences naturally exercised a destructive influence upon the old religion. In the first century B.C., Quintus Mucius Scaevola, the most learned of Roman pontiffs, the official head of the state religion,[1] laid it down that religion might be divided into three kinds (1) the purely ornamental fictions of the poets; (2) philosophy; (3) the religion of the state, which was merely an instrument of statecraft to be used in keeping the lower orders under control.

This dictum very fairly indicates the religious attitude of the educated classes in the last century before Christ, which was essentially a sceptical period. True, the emotional religions of the east which had been brought to the cosmopolitan

---

1. Cf. Cotta the pontifex in Cicero's *De Natura Deorum*, who is the protagonist of the agnostic point of view.

capital of the world, were beginning to gain ground, notably among the newly emancipated women, and one, the worship of the Great Goddess of Asia Minor, had been officially adopted by the state in the closing years of the Second Punic War. But taking society as a whole, the dominant note was scepticism and irreligion, accompanied, as is not seldom the case, by crude and irrational superstition.

Then the pendulum swings from scepticism in the direction of credulity. The turn is marked by the activity of Posidonius, who was born at Apamea in Syria about 135 B.C., and after extensive travels opened a school at Rhodes, where Cicero was among his hearers. Posidonius, whose writings survive only in the works of others, does not seem to have been a great original or creative philosopher, but he possessed encyclopædic knowledge and, evidently, considerable powers of exposition. His influence was immense, partly, no doubt, because he systematised the ideas towards which his age was already inarticulately moving. It seems to have been Posidonius who gave its new direction to Stoicism, by adapting it to harmonise with ideas of Neo-Pythagorism, and by incorporating in it the religious views attaching to Babylonian cosmography. His predecessor, Panætius, the friend of the Younger Scipio and the first considerable Stoic missionary in the Roman world, had been sceptical about immortality ; henceforward the astral immortality of the soul was a usual, though not a necessary, tenet of Stoicism, and the Stoic philosophy gave a whole-hearted sanction to the efficacy of astrology and divination.

In a sense the career of Posidonius marks the turning of the tide, and henceforward, as it seems to me, thought and science move steadily and inevitably in the direction of the medieval attitude of mind. Cicero is characteristically in the slack water between the tides. Eclectic, in an age of syncretism, his earlier thought inclined to Carneades and the scepticism of the Academy. As he grew older, partly the current contemporary influences, in particular perhaps his intimacy with Nigidius Figulus, the Neo-Pythagorean senator, and magical adept, partly the disappointments of life and the longing for the religious hope and consolation which scepticism denied, and partly the great sorrow occasioned by the loss of his beloved daughter Tullia, brought about a change. In his later philosophical writings, in the *Hortensius* and *Tusculans* for example, he inclines to believe, where he had before been sceptical.

It is certain, at any rate, that after Posidonius a new and more emotional note is sounded in Stoicism. The new Stoicism of Seneca and Epictetus we have seen to be as much a religion as a philosophy. An increasing emphasis is laid upon the idea of communion, or at least of our community, with God, and also upon the social duties of kindness, forbearance and goodness in relation to our fellow men. Of the tendency to speak of the Divine Principle in terms which are really applicable, not to a tenuous rational and fiery substance which pervades the universe, but to a just and benevolent, personal God, we have already noticed examples.

In the essential point as to the nature of God, Stoicism, it is true, had not made terms with Neo-Pythagorism and Platonism, for while the former regarded God as immanent and material, the latter maintained that he was transcendent and immaterial. The distinction is of course philosophically fundamental, but in practice it loomed less largely than in theory, for philosophy in the early centuries after Christ was mainly interested in its application to life, *i.e.*, in conduct. By the great majority of adherents the metaphysical background, no doubt, was taken for granted. Naturally, the professional philosophers maintained their distinctions and their differences, and the irony of Lucian has drawn a merciless picture of their unending and tumultuous wrangling,[1] but, nevertheless, there was a body of thought common to them all, a general direction towards which the ideas of the day were moving.[2]

The philosophic systems, like the religions of the day, maintained distinctions and rival claims, but the various systems shade into one another,

---

1. Cf. facilius inter philosophos quam inter horologia conueniet, Seneca, *Apocol.*, 2, 1.

2. The kindly Plutarch, as a good Platonist, is even a venomous critic of the Stoics, but it would not be difficult to show that he himself owes much to them and shares much with them. Cf. soleo enim in aliena castra transire, non tanquam transfuga, sed tanquam explorator, Seneca, ii, 6; cf. ix, 20; Perseuerabo Epicurum tibi ingerere ut isti, qui in verba uiuant, nec quid dicatur aestimant, sed a quo, sciant quae optima sunt, esse communia, xii, 11. Has uoces non est quod Epicuri esse audias, publicae sunt, *Ep.* xxi, 9: cf. xxix, 11, xxxiii, 2. Thus Clerc with justice remarks of Celsus, " Platon n'est pas son seul inspirateur. . . . Celse est un digne représentant du syncritisme de l'époque," Clerc, *Les théories relatives au culte des images*, p. 189.

and in philosophy, as in religion, the average adherent was eclectic. The direction of the intellectual movement of the day was definitely towards, what I may call, credulity. From Lucian alone it is evident that, at the end of the second century, Epicureanism was going under ; sceptics ceased to be popular in a world of believers in the miraculous.[1] The Stoic in the *Philopseudes* is equally credulous with the Platonist. In the third century Stoicism, too, began to take a secondary place to Neo-Platonism, though it continued no less than the latter to influence the form of much Christian thought. The cause of its decline is really that the growth of the mystical element, to which we have drawn attention, allowed it to lose its identity. In the words of Dill, " the later Stoicism melts into the revived Platonism."

Both the social conditions and the intellectual tendencies of the first two centuries after Christ promoted the belief in the marvellous and stimulated the appetite for wonders. The growth of superstition is an almost inevitable revenge of imaginations which have been starved by a crude and sceptical materialism. Trimalchio's table is just the place where we should expect to hear the affirmation of the existence of witches and witness a round-eyed acceptance of old wives' tales.[2]

---

1. Indeed Lucian and Sextus Empiricius represent the last flash in the pan. Already Julian can say μήτε 'Επικούρειος εἰσίτω λόγος μήτε Πυρρώνειος· ἤδη μὲν γὰρ καλῶς ποιοῦντες οἱ θεοὶ καὶ ἀνηρήκασιν, ὥστε ἐπιλείπειν καὶ τὰ πλεῖστα τῶν βιβλίων, *Letter to Priest*, 301c.

2. Petronius, 61 foll. In more refined circles tales of wonder were a staple of after dinner conversation. Thus Pliny came across the story of the wonderful tame dolphin of Hippo "at the dinner-table, while the guests were telling various marvellous tales ", *Ep.*, ix, 33.

It is quite in character, again, that the old scoundrel Marcus Regulus who possessed the sharpest wits at the Roman bar, a pitiless informer, completely devoid of moral scruple, should be intensely superstitious.[1]

Again, part cause and part effect was the general acceptance of the theory of intermediate daemonic agents, who intervene in terrestrial affairs. This doctrine had been developed from Platonism by the Neo-Pythagoreans, and it became later an integral part of Neo-Platonism. In alliance with Neo-Pythagorism, Platonism had turned from the scepticism of the Academy of Carneades back to Plato. In contrast to the Stoic monism, the metaphysic of Platonism had a dualistic basis. In Plato's system God was absolute, immaterial, and transcendent. The phenomena of this world are but imperfect copies of the absolute " ideas," which constitute reality. The embodiment of " ideas " in matter is the source of imperfection or unreality. This dualism accounts, by the imperfection of matter, for the existence of evil; but if it solves the moral problem of reconciling the goodness of God with the existence of an evil world, it raises a difficulty that is not more easy of solution. If God is absolute and transcendent, how is he to be brought into relation at all with the imperfect world of

---

1. Pliny, *Ep.* ii, 20, vi, 2. Regulus was the son of one of Nero's victims. Exceedingly able, ambitious and unscrupulous he retrieved the exile and ruin of his youth by becoming an indispensable agent of tyranny. He prudently retired into obscurity under Vespasian, but under Domitian he became the leader of the Roman bar. His success Pliny attributed to his industry and his power of concentration. Saepe tibi dico inesse uim Regulo. mirum est quam efficiat in quod incubuit, *Ep.* iv, 7.

mutability ? Epicurus had admitted the trans-
cendence of God, but had drawn from it the
conclusion that nothing, consequently, could be
postulated about him, not even that He exists.
To bridge the great gulf thus fixed,[1] the ideas,
which Plato had expressed in the *Timaeus*, had
been developed in the direction of supposing that
the phenomenal world was the actual creation of
subordinate and intermediate spiritual agents or
daemons, who are ordained to take care of Nature
in generation and corruption.[2]

To Platonists, like Plutarch, the materialism
of the Stoic conception of God, and the Stoic
transformation of the gods of mythology into
allegories of natural processes or objects, were
alike anathema.[3] With the Stoics, of course, they
agreed in the essential unity of God. Their
solution of how to reconcile polytheistic practice

---

1. "It seems to me, on the other hand, that those who have inserted the
class of daemons between Gods and men, to draw and knit together the fellowship of the two orders after a fashion, have cleared away more perplexities
and greater" (even than Plato did). Plutarch, *de def. orac.* 10, 415A
(Prickard, p. 126).

2. Plutarch, *de EI apud Delph.*, 21, 393D foll., where this view of polytheism is contrasted with the Stoic explanation.

3. "Before they are aware they change and dissolve the divine beings
into blasts of wind, streams of water, sowings of corn, ploughings of land,
accidents of earth, and changes of seasons; as those who make Dionysus to
be wine and Hephaestus to be flame. . . . For these men seem to me to
be nothing wiser than such as would take the sails, the cables and the anchor
of a ship for the pilot; the yarn and the web for the weaver; and the bowl
or the mead or the physic for the doctor. And they, over and above, produce in men most dangerous and atheistical opinions, while they give the
names of gods to those natures and things that have in them neither soul
nor sense, and that are necessarily destroyed by men who need them and
use them." Plutarch, *Isis and Osiris*, 66, 377D–E. Cf. *de def. orac.*
29, 426, where he says that the Stoics "enclose the gods within matter
and that in so strict a manner as to make them liable to all the changes,
alterations and decays of it."

with philosophical monotheism was to identify
the gods of popular polytheism with daemons.
But further than this, it was admitted that
daemons, all of whom, though incorporeal, shared
the imperfections necessarily resulting from contact with the world of mutability, were both good
and bad.[1]   Here was a rival explanation to Stoic
allegory for the crudities of mythology, for
historical instances where an oracular god had
been proved to lie, and also for savage or revolting
forms of primitive ritual.   " I will never think
those done on any of the gods' account," says
Plutarch, " but rather to avert, mollify, and
appease the wrath and fury of some bad demons."[2]

It will at once be noticed, with what a weapon
Plutarch has presented Christian polemic.[3]   He
has admitted not only that pagan gods are
daemons, but that the rites paid in some cults
are offerings to bad daemons.   The belief in the
constant miraculous intervention in human affairs
of spiritual agencies both good and evil, angels
and devils, was not, in fact, a failing peculiar to
Christians, but formed part of the common
intellectual background of the time.

Another   disastrous   influence   upon   the
intellectual life of the time was the use of allegory,
in which the Stoics had set the example.   Allegorical interpretations, which, in religious matters,
enabled conservatism to retain myths and ritual
which now offended a more civilised taste, had

---

1.   Plutarch, *de fac. in orb lun.* 30, 944D, *Is. et Os.*, 25-26, 360D-361C,
Porphyry, *de abst.* ii, 36-43.
2.   Plutarch, *de def. orac.*, 14, 417C.   Cf. *de Is. et Os.*, 20, 358E.
3.   *E.g.* Tertullian, *Apol.*, 22.

become general.[1] Not only mythology, but literature, was interpreted in an esoteric sense, and the extraction of the hidden meanings of Homer, at which already Cicero had poked fun,[2] in such works as the treatise of the Pseudo-Plutarch *On the Life and Poetry of Homer*, reached the point of making Homer the founder of science, history, philosophy, politics, music, rhetoric, siege-works, astronomy, medicine, gymnastics, surgery and painting.[3]

The application of this allegorical method to religion and the increasing tendency to avoid facing intellectual difficulties by seeking a plausible way round them, is rather well illustrated in the attitude of the Greeks and Romans towards the animal gods of Egypt. The Greek attitude in the third century B.C. is frankly scornful of

---

1. *E.g.* " But why have they put in the myths stories of adultery, robbery, father-binding, and all the other absurdity ? Is not that perhaps a thing worthy of admiration, done so that by means of the visible absurdity the soul may immediately feel that the words are veils and believe the truth to be a mystery ? " Sallustius, *de diis et mundo*, iii, (trans. G. G. A. Murray, *Five Stages*, p. 243).

2. ut etiam ueterrimi poetae, qui haec ne suspicati quidem sint, Stoici fuisse uideantur, Cicero, *de nat. deor.*, i, 15, 41, cf. Seneca, *Ep.* lxxxviii, 5.

3. [Plutarch], *de uit. et poes. Hom.*, 148, 162, 182, 192, 216. On the study of Homer as a general authority upon everything see Strabo, i, 2, 3, 16 foll., and Wendland, *op. cit*, p. 113. Plutarch himself, though he is ready to chaff others (*e.g. de def. orac.*, 3, 410D), is not guiltless. A good example of how Homer can be " explained " is Porphyry, *de antro nympharum* ; similarly the hidden philosophical meaning of the wanderings of *Ulysses* is extracted by Thomas Taylor, the Neo-Platonist, in an appendix to his translation of Porphyry (1823). Hatch mentions a work by G. Croesus, entitled Ομηρος Εβραιος *siue historia Hebraeorum ab Homero Hebraicis nominibus ac sententiis conscripta in Odyssea et Iliade* (Dordrecht, 1704), which shows that the conquest of Canaan is the topic of the Iliad and that the Odyssey recounts in fact the wanderings of the Children of Israel. But the champions of the theory that the Britisn are the descendants of the " Lost Tribes," still hold crowded public meetings ; we cannot claim to be better than our fathers.

so irrational a proceeding as the worship of
animals as divine. " I could not be your ally,
for our ways and laws do not agree at all, but differ
far from one another. You adore the ox, but I
sacrifice it to the gods. You think the eel the
greatest spiritual power, but we consider it by
far the greatest of delicacies. You don't eat
pork, but I especially enjoy it. You worship the
dog, but I beat him when I catch him thieving
in the larder."[1]   This scornful attitude remains a
part of the classical tradition as late as Juvenal's
sixteenth satire. Thus Cicero shares the contempt for the animal gods of Egypt, but, even in
Cicero, we notice an inclination to find a way
round. The old familiar genius of superstition is
whispering his hoary catch-word, " after all, there
must be something in it." The first, and not
very effective, line of justification is upon
Euhemerist lines. The Egyptians have deified
specific animal kinds because of the benefits which
they have conferred upon men, killing vermin and
so forth.[2]   Then we come to Plutarch, and the
dear old man, so intelligent and yet so pious, is
clearly somewhat distressed. But piety wins in
the end. Of course, the literal worship of
animals as divine beings is absurd, but first of all
may not it just be a way of symbolising characters
of gods, not unlike the association of certain

---

1. Anaxandrides, *Poleis*, Kock, *Comic. Att. Frag.* ii, p. 150, Frag. 39 from
Athenaeus, vii, 297 f.

2. Cicero, *Tusculans*, v, 27, 78, *de nat. deor.* iii, 15, 39.   For usefulness see
de nat. deor., i, 36, 101. This extends to theriomorphic gods the explanation
which Euhemerus offered for anthropomorphism : οὕτω δὲ καὶ τῶν θεῶν
ἕνα ἕκαστον, τῶν χρησίμων τινὸς εὑρετὴν γενόμενον, τιμᾶσθαι, Strabo,
i, 2, 15, 24.

animals with Greek gods—in fact, a cruder form
of the same thing ?   Besides, he goes on, certain
kinds of animals have performed invaluable
services to mankind, i.e., the Euhemeristic argument again.   But finally, and this is the theory
which was destined ultimately to be victorious,
the apparent absurdity surely hides a deep and
mystical esoteric meaning ; its very irrationality
is a benevolent spur to the religious mind to
grope for the hidden spiritual significance.[1]
On these lines Porphyry is a whole-hearted
champion of Egyptian animal gods,[2] and this was
the view which ultimately prevailed in the pagan
world.

That the method of explanation by allegory,
though reprobated by them in the Stoics, was
adopted by the Christians to explain difficulties
in Holy Writ, in particular those raised by the
Old Testament, we have already remarked.   It
formed part indeed of the common intellectual
stock of the age.   But as such it was a powerful
agent in inducing an unscientific attitude of
mind, preferring, as it did, to reject obvious
meanings in favour of some far-fetched esoteric
explanation.   Indeed, we may say that it put a
premium on the fantastic, or even the irrational,
as opposed to straightforward common sense.

Indeed, throughout the period, the appetite
for the marvellous steadily increased, and it has
left its mark upon every department of life.

---

1. Plutarch, *de Is. et Os.* 71, 379 D foll.   With the idolatry analogy cf.
Maximus Tyrius quoted above p. 7.   Arnobius (iii, 15) inverts the
argument.   You pagans laugh at Egyptian animal worship, but your
idolatry is not dissimilar.

2. Porphyry, *de abst.* iv, 9. foll.   Cf. Celsus in Origen, *c. Cels.* iii 19.

The belief in miracles and in demoniac possession, or the foolish absurdities which are to be found in the Pseudo-Clementines, the Apocryphal Acts of the Apostles, and in the Lives of the Saints, belong to the age not specifically to early Christianity. To an average individual of the third century after Christ it seemed more probable that the cause of any given phenomenon was supernatural or miraculous, than that it should be the inevitable result of some natural cause, working in accordance with a rational law of nature. This lamentable attitude of mind, for which a basis was provided by the universal acceptance of the doctrine of daemonic agents, naturally cut away the foundation of true scientific speculation. The more strange a phenomenon, the more convincing was the illusory but final answer, that it was the result of the action of some miraculous agency. Curiosity was thus allowed neither the impulse nor the freedom to investigate further.

The practice of magic and witchcraft steadily increased. The magical papyri belong mainly to the third and fourth centuries after Christ. Beside the tales which are told at Trimalchio's table, may be placed the witches of Apuleius' *Golden Ass*. That here literature faithfully reflects contemporary life is shown by the elaborate *Apology* of Apuleius, which is an authentic and serious defence against an actual charge of magical malpractices.[1]

The literary taste of the day betrays the same

1. Upon the whole matter of magic in this period consult Abt, *Die Apologie von Apuleius von Madaura und die antike Zauberei*

bias. Problems like the cause of oracular inspiration particularly interest the intellectuals, and the popularity of discussions of the nature of the daemon of Socrates is a sign of the times. On a less philosophical plane, the pseudo-scientific, are wonder-books, like that of Hadrian's freedman Phlegon, *de mirabilibus*, or the Pseudo-Plutarch's tract *On Rivers*, of which a vast literature was in circulation. To take more ambitious works of science, think of the rubbish embalmed in the erudition of the Elder Pliny in the first century, or in the third century of the works of Aelian, a blend of nonsense with natural history, which was destined to be used as a model and a source by Byzantine and mediaeval learning.

Akin on the one hand to the Hellenistic romance, and on the other to these works of pseudo-science, is the pseudo-biographical litera-ture, often with a religious bias—the aretalogy, which narrates the miraculous acts of some thaumaturge, and thereby supplies both enter-tainment and edification to the credulous. Of literature of this type we possess not only the parodies of Lucian, but the complete romance of Apollonius of Tyana written by Philostratus.[1]

The hero of this most unhistorical romance was a teacher born at Tyana in the reign of Tiberius, who professed the Neo-Pythagorean rule and achieved a local reputation in Asia Minor.

---

1. On aretalogies see Reitzenstein, *Hellenistische Wundererzäblungen*. For Philostratus see the introduction in Phillimore, *Philostratus, In honour of Apollonius* and my *Folklore Studies Ancient and Modern* pp. 156 foll.

It is improbable that his renown was widely spread outside Asia before his sanctity was advertised by the patronage of the empress Julia Domna, at whose orders Philostratus composed his work. Apollonius is not mentioned by any writer before Dio Cassius and Lucian, and the silence of his contemporaries as to his alleged intervention in affairs of importance in Alexandria, Athens and Rome, brands the details of the romance as completely unhistorical. *The Life of Apollonius* has, in fact, precisely the same kind of historical value as the Apocryphal Acts of the Apostles and much of later Christian hagiology. Here, once more, we find that the Christians were men of their time.

After the appearance of the book, it is true, Apollonius had a great vogue as the pattern of the Neo-Pythagorean miracle-worker and saint. His statue stood beside those of Christ, Abraham, and Orpheus in the private shrine of the eclectic emperor Severus Alexander, and at the very beginning of the fourth century, Hierocles, "a chief instigator" of the persecution of the Christians under Diocletian, published a work upon *A Comparison between Apollonius and Christ.* Indeed, the figure of Apollonius became a rallying point for the waning forces of paganism, and the tradition of the great sage and magician, Apollonius, passed on into the Middle Ages. With Plato, Hippocrates, Aristotle, and Alexander he became, for Moslems, one of the great legendary wonder-workers of antiquity, a maker of magical talismans such as could still be seen to exist in the surviving Greek monuments at Constantinople, though they had lost their magical force at the birth of the Prophet.[1]

The details of the romance of Apollonius are unhistorical, but the wandering miracle-worker was actually a feature of contemporary society. The travelling philosopher with a mission to the world was often regarded, and sometimes regarded himself, as not only possessed of miraculous powers of exorcism and the like, but as in some sense divine. Epicureans and unbelievers might call him *goes*, a miracle-working charlatan ; to his followers he was *philosophos*, a sage, or even θεῖος, divine.[2] The class of such persons ranged in practice from the crudest forms of imposture for gain, like those conjurers of the market-place with whom Celsus compares Christ,[3] to teachers who, however mistaken, were undoubtedly sincere.

The belief in the divine preacher found a certain support in the religious philosophy of the day. Temporary possession had always been admitted as a source of inspiration. For example, the Pythia at Delphi, at the moment of giving the responses, was held to be actually possessed by the god. The physical condition of religious

---

1. Upon this aspect of the Apollonius tradition, see R. M. Dawkins, in *Folk-Lore*, xxxv, 1924, pp. 230-236.

2. Upon ἄνθρωποι θεῖοι see Reitzenstein, *Hell. Myst. Rel.*, p. 99. It should be unnecessary to stress an obvious difference between the conception of man becoming God and that of God becoming man, though it may be well to state it, to avoid a possible misunderstanding. The character of the sage was sometimes sadly misunderstood by those who were not his followers ; thus the hierophant at Eleusis refused Apollonius " access to the holy things, saying that he would never admit a charlatan (γόητα), nor open Eleusis to a man of impure theology (μὴ καθαρῷ τὰ δαιμόνια)," Philostratus, *Vit. Apoll.*, iv, 18, 138.

3. Origen, *c. Cels*, ii, 14, ii, 49, iii, 50.

ecstasy, in which inspired prophets and prophet-
esses delivered utterance, the high excitement,
the gasping for breath, the rigidity of the body,
and the subsequent exhaustion were recognised
as outward and visible signs of the temporary
presence of the god in the mortal envelope of his
servant. The genuineness of such possession
early Christians did not for a moment doubt,
any more than they questioned the inspiration
of Homer or Hesiod. Their contention was not
to deny possession, but to affirm that the spiritual
agents were evil spirits.[1]

Again the divine and immortal character of
the soul was generally accepted. Characteristic
of certain contemporary mystery cults were the
ideas that it was possible to purify and
disencumber this divine element by ritual and
moral discipline, and that the reward of such
purification was oneness with the divinity. The
object of much religious and magical ritual was
to achieve an immediate union with God, a
temporary foretaste of eternal union in a life to
come. Nor was the conception of a divine man

---

1. A curious and perhaps dangerous analogy is used by Arnobius, i, 62,
where he is comparing the incarnation with the case of the prophetess. " If
the Sibyl, when she was uttering and pouring forth her prophecies and oracular
responses, was filled, as you say, with Apollo's power, had been cut down and
slain by impious robbers, would Apollo be said to have been slain in her ? "
No; it therefore follows that Christ was not slain on the Cross. Origen,
c. Cels. iii, 25, rightly distinguishes between the entry of Apollo into the
Pythia and the Incarnation because Christ became incarnate in a body of
his own. For the poets, cf. Theophilos, ad Autolycum, ii, 10, 87C.
ἤτοι γὰρ οἱ ποιηταί, Ὅμηρος δὴ καὶ Ἡσίοδος, ὥς φασιν, ὑπὸ Μουσῶν
ἐμπνευσθέντες φαντασίᾳ καὶ πλάνῃ ἐλάλησαν, καὶ οὐ καθαρῷ πνεύματι
ἀλλὰ πλάνῳ· ἐκ τούτου δὲ σαφῶς δείκνυται εἰ καὶ οἱ δαιμονῶντες
ἐνίοτε καὶ μέχρι τοῦ δεῦρο ἐξορκίζονται κατὰ τοῦ ὀνόματος τοῦ ὄντως
θεοῦ καὶ ὁμολογεῖ αὐτὰ τὰ πλάνα πνεύματα εἶναι δαίμονες οἱ καὶ τότε
εἰς ἐκείνους ἐνεργήσαντες.

inconsistent with another line of argument. If
kings or emperors were divine in virtue of their
omnipotence as compared with the ordinary
man, were there not other spheres of a value
fully equal in importance to that of temporal
power—the spheres, for example, of art, intellect,
or holiness ? Might not pre-eminence in these
equally justify the ascription of divinity ? [1] This
line of thought, which we find strongly developed
in the mystic sects, may be traced back beyond
the Christian era. " Divine Homer " meant a
little more than the expression of admiration for
poetic skill, in fact very much what Vergil means
by saying of Augustus *deus nobis haec otia fecit.*
Similarly Lucretius had spoken of Epicurus as
deus, and so did Cicero of Plato.

Human nature being what it is, we should
expect to find that the opportunity for exploiting
credulity for gain was not neglected. A pagan
counterpart to Simon Magus is the charlatan
Alexander of Aboutoneichos, of whom Lucian
has described at length the sham epiphanies and
the faked miracles. Even a Roman senator of
high official standing was not only an ardent
believer in the divinity of the impostor, but was
proud to be privileged to marry his bastard
daughter, the offspring it was alleged of an amour
of this pinchbeck magician with the Moon. But
if we are inclined to feel that we are superior
persons belonging to a more enlightened age, we

---

1. E.g. Hermes Trismegistus, Stobaeus, *Ecl.,* i, 49, 69 (Wachsmith, i,
p. 466). πολλαὶ γάρ εἰσι βασιλεῖαι· αἰ μὲν γὰρ εἰσι ψυχῶν, αἰ δὲ
σωμάτων, αἰ δὲ τέχνης, αἰ δὲ ἐπιστήμης, αἰ δὲ αὖ τῶν καὶ τῶν.
See Cumont, *After Life,* p. 114.

may perhaps recall, with profit to our modesty, the achievements in our own time of Rawson, the prayer-healer, both in America and in this country.

It would, however, be a mistake to suppose that all the pagan professors of a divine mission were, equally with Alexander, cynical and insincere. Just as among the more intellectual philosophers of the time if there were many whose learning was prostituted for hire, there were others like Dio Chrysostom who obeyed a vocation higher than that of professional ambition or worldly gain, so among these religious preachers, if I may call them so, there were many who, however mistakenly, were themselves sincerely convinced of the genuineness of their powers and of their mission.[1] An example of these is the Cynic Peregrinus, who crowned his career by seeking a voluntary apotheosis in the flames of a pyre erected at the Olympic festival. In this action I am inclined to see a curious example of the passion for martyrdom in itself, like that which becomes characteristic of certain phases of early Christianity, and a psychological phenomenon characteristic of the time.[2] It is not the least interesting thing about Peregrinus that he was

---

[1]. For " vocation " see Epictetus, *Disc.*, iii, 22 ; compare Seneca, *Ep.*, xlviii.

[2]. The rhetoric and overemphasis of Latin literature of the Silver Age reflects, I think, a genuine psychological characteristic of the time. The almost hysterical theatricality of temperament, of which Nero is the most conspicuous example, comes out in the lives, as well as in the literary style, of Lucan, Petronius or Seneca. In part, no doubt, it is the product of the nervous strain of court life lived under terrible conditions. But mental poise seems to have been shaken, life and death to have become a matter of gestures. The very strong phrase, libido moriendi, Seneca, *Ep.* xxiv, 25, as well as the mere necessity of preaching against self-destruction for trivial

at one time a prominent member of a Christian community.

Lucian handles Peregrinus with a merciless savagery. His self-immolation he represents as prompted solely by a passion for notoriety and self-advertisement. But, whatever we may think of the Cynic's common sense, it would be unjust with Lucian to impugn his sincerity.

The travelling prophet or moralist brings us to the topic of education. Here the second century was marked by a great development. Education was no longer the privilege of a few, who could afford a tutor. It was, indeed, very widely diffused; grammar-schools were springing up in the smaller provincial towns, often, like that founded at Como by the Younger Pliny, as the result of private munificence; universities in which there were Regius chairs, thanks to the facilities of communication, were widely patronised. Educational theory was seriously considered and was highly developed. Quintilian's views upon such matters as the rival merits of school and tutor, the valuable stimulus of competition, the formative influence of games upon character, the defects of a system of corporal punishment in the class-room, the ability of young boys to attack a wide and varied curriculum

---

reasons, may illustrate this psychological condition. For Christians, Clement censures those " who have rushed on death " and " banish themselves without being martyrs, even though they are punished publicly," (*Strom.*, iv, 4), and readers of Gibbon will remember the passage in Tertullian, *ad Scap.*, 5. " When Arrius Antoninus was driving things hard in Asia, the whole Christians of the province, in one united band, presented themselves before his judgment-seat : on which, ordering a few to be led forth to execution, he said to the rest, ' Oh, miserable men, if you wish to die, you have precipices or halters '."

with profit, have a value independent of their age.[1]
The main basis of the higher education was
Greek literature, an important factor in that
Hellenisation of the culture of the empire, which
we have discussed. If, in the remotest East, the
citizens of Borysthena all knew Homer by heart,
in the extreme West, Greek as well as Latin
rhetoric was being taught in Britain.[2] It is
remarkable that Apuleius, by birth an African
who, no doubt, spoke Punic in the home, learned
Greek at school, but did not master Latin until
he went to Rome as an adult.[3]

In addition to the provision made for school

---

1. For schools, the model of which was found in the Hellenistic East
(Wendland, *op. cit.*, p 73), see Pliny, *Ep.* iv, 13. There were schools for the
children of the miners at Vipasca in Spain where the schoolmasters enjoyed
immunity from rates (Reid, *op. cit.*, p. 324 : the text of the *lex Met. Vip.*
will be found in Bruns, *Fontes Juris Rom.*, 6th ed., p. 266,) Vespasian started
the endowment of rhetoricians from state funds at Rome. Hadrian, followed
by Antoninus Pius, made similar payments to professors at Athens. Marcus
Aurelius endowed two Regius chairs, as we should call them, in each of the
four great philosophical schools at Athens and created two of rhetoric (literary
and forensic). An interesting paper by Hahn, " Ueber das Verhältnis von
Staat und Schule in der römischen Kaiserzeit," *Philologus*, 76, 1920, pp.
176-191, maintains that the patronage of the universities by the Antonines
was a piece of statecraft, designed to enlist upon the side of the imperial
system what had been its most serious opponent under the Julio-Claudians.
That this was the result is doubtless true, but the deliberateness of
political motive seems to me to be overstated. For educational theory
see Quintilian, *Inst. Or.* i, which is best consulted in the recent
admirable edition of F. H. Colson, Cambridge Press, 1924.

2. καὶ τἄλλα οὐκέτι σαφῶς ἑλληνίζοντες διὰ τὸ ἐν μέσοις οἰκεῖν τοῖς
βαρβάροις ὅμως τὴν γε ᾿Ιλιάδα ὀλίγου πάντες ἴσασιν ἀπὸ στόματος,
Dio Chrys, xxxvi, 9. Nunc totus Graias nostrasque habet orbis Athenas/
Gallia causidicos docuit facunda Britannos,/ de conducendo loquitur iam
rhetore Thule, Juvenal, xv, 110.

3. " There in my boyhood's first campaigns did I win for my possession
the speech of Athens. Thereafter in the Latin city I came to studies that
were strange to me, and with grievous toil and never a master to teach
me, set myself diligently to learn the native speech of the Quirites," Apuleius,
Met., i, 1. Substitute Polish for Punic, French for Greek, and English
for Latin, and the curiously exact analogy between the circumstances of
the authors of the *Metamorphoses* and of *Almayer's Folly* is obvious.

and university education, we may further notice the very general establishment of public libraries. Again Pliny's munificence to his native Como provides us with an illustration, and quite frequently the municipal library was founded by the generosity of some private donor (e.g., at Volsinii, Ephesus and Timgad), whose benefaction often included a sum for the upkeep of the building and for the purchase of new books. The structures consisted essentially of two parts, the reading room and the place for the storage of the books, which was organised, of course, under subject headings. The reading room was generally ornamented by busts of distinguished authors and contained *armaria* in which a certain number of books were kept for immediate reference. A stone bench usually ran round the room, but for the most part, no doubt, the readers sat upon portable chairs or stools.[1]

Education then was widely diffused ; there was the same general desire for its advantages as in our own day, if there was the same tendency in some quarters to expect from it, not so much an equipment for life, as a means of livelihood. There was also a certain shallowness, which is perhaps an inevitable concomitant of wide diffusion, and we hear complaints which strike a sadly familiar note. Too often his pupils came to Epictetus for a mere veneer of education, to acquire a few philosophic catchwords for display

---

1. All the available material is brought together and discussed by Cagnat, " Les Bibliothèques Municipales dans l'Empire Romain," *Mém. Acad. Inscr. et Belles Lettres*, xxxviii (1909), pp. 1-26. Pliny's gift to Como, *Ep.* i, 8. For the busts see the Elder Pliny, *Nat. Hist.*, xxxv, 2, (2), 9 : at certe ex aere in bibliothecis dicantur illis, quorum immortales animae in locis iisdem locuntur, quin immo etiam quae non sunt finguntur, pariuntque desideria non traditos uultus, sicut in Homero euenit.

in public. "Sheep," he reminds them, "do not bring grass to their shepherds and show them how much they have eaten, but they digest their fodder and then produce it in the form of wool and milk" (*Manual*, 46). Dio, too, protests against the false idea that education consists in a process of acquiring literary information rather than a training for life, with the result that the plain man, looking at its product, rounds on higher education and mistakenly brands it as worthless. "There are two kinds of education, the one divine, the other human; the divine is great and powerful and easy; the human is mean and weak, and has many dangers and no small deceitfulness. The mass of people call it education (παιδείαν) as being, I suppose, an amusement (παιδίαν), and think that a man who knows most literature—Persian and Greek and Syrian and Phoenician—is the wisest and best educated man; and then, on the other hand, when they find a man of this sort to be vicious and cowardly and fond of money, they think the education to be as worthless as the man himself."[1]

It is a commonplace that the rhetorical bent of classical antiquity had a deleterious effect upon literature and thought. It may be admitted that

---

1. Dio Chrys., iv, 1.   I have borrowed Hatch's rendering.   For protests against regarding education as a memorising of points of literary history, see Epictetus, *Discourse*, iii, 21 (on the teacher's qualifications. "Those who have learnt precepts and nothing more are anxious to give them out at once, just as men with weak stomachs vomit food."); *Manual*, 49 (philosophy is more than a study of the writings of dead philosophers or "I am turned into a grammarian, except that I interpret Chrysippus in place of Homer"); *Discourse*, i, 4 (philosophy has to do with life and conduct, it is a training of the will; "if all the student's efforts are turned to the study of books, if on this he spends his labour, and for this has gone abroad, then I bid him go straight home.")

our depreciatory use of the word "rhetoric" conveys an unfair implication, and that the study of rhetoric as laid down by Quintilian is an arduous and satisfactory scheme of general education. Nevertheless, it is true that the rhetorical form of training has disadvantages.   Long ago Aristophanes had pilloried its moral dangers, in the controversy between the Just and the Unjust Arguments in the *Clouds*.   But more subtly and generally operative was the lack of proportion in its emphasis upon style as opposed to matter, on " the rhetoric and poetry and foppery of speech " from which Rusticus had rescued Marcus Aurelius to higher things.   Under the empire, the loss of political freedom had deprived it of the intimate contact with public life, which, under conditions of the city state, had given it reality.   Rhetoric as employed for purposes of education had become purely literary ; divorce from life had enmeshed it in the trammels of affected archaism and scholastic erudition.[1]

---

1.   Marcus Aurelius i, 7.   On Quintilian's scheme of general education see Colson, *op. cit.*   For the futility of dialectic see Seneca, *Ep.*, xlv, xlviii, xlix, lxxi, 6.   Non est philosophia populare artificium nec ostentationi paratum.   Non in verbis, sed in rebus est.   Nec in hoc adhibetur, ut cum aliqua oblectatione consumatur dies, ut dematur otio nausia.   Animum format et fabricat, uitam disponit, actiones regit, agenda et omittenda demonstrat, sedet ad gubernaculum et per ancipita fluctuantium dirigit cursum, *Ep.*, xvi, 3.   Mere note-book knowledge is quite useless, *Ep.* xxxiii, 7.   Epictetus, *Disc.* ii, 19 insists that philosophy should teach a way of life not a literary history of philosophers.   Was it Ambrose who said " non in dialectica complacuit Deo saluum facere populum suum ? "   For a scathing attack upon the pedantic scholasticism of the rhetorical schools see Lucian, *rhetorum praeceptor*, 16 foll.   We may, perhaps, recall the favourite medieval *exemplum* of the master Sella who, after being visited by the ghost of one of his students which was clad entirely in parchment covered with the *curiositates* upon which he had wasted his life, abandoned logic for the Cistercian rule, remarking in execrable verse,

Linquo coax ranis, cra coruis, uanaque uanis ;
ad logicam pergo, que mortis non timet ergo.

Crane, *Exempla of Jacques de Vitry*, No. xxxi, pp. 12 and 146.

It was, further, an educational disadvantage of this literary rhetoric that its exercises, often upon ridiculous and artificial themes, encouraged the habit of mind which pays little attention to intrinsic reality.

" I believe," says Petronius (i, 1), " that college makes complete fools of our young men, because they see and hear nothing of ordinary life there. It is pirates standing in chains on the beach, tyrants pen in hand ordering sons to cut off their father's heads, oracles in times of pestilence demanding the blood of three virgins or more, honey-balls of phrases, every word and act besprinkled with poppy-seed and sesame. People who are fed on this diet, can no more be sensible than people who live in the kitchen can be savoury."

Even art suffered from the divorce from facts. The dexterity of its great exponents must command admiration ; in the subtle skill of literary nuance the Philostrati eclipse Stevenson, but theirs is an art without the inspiration of a compelling theme, a skill which searches desperately for subjects to decorate. This divorce of education, literature and art from direct contact with objective fact had inevitably a profound moral and intellectual influence, which was to bear fruit in the medieval attitude of mind.

In the meantime, one result of the widespread diffusion of education and the rhetorical character of literary study was a craze for listening to lectures, which has not been surpassed in our own day. People flocked to remote Nicopolis to

listen to the discourses of the famous Epictetus.
Everywhere the travelling philosopher or sophist
was assured of a welcome and a livelihood.
Distinguished exponents of the art of rhetorical
display became the spoiled darlings of the
educated public, the friends of emperors, and
persons of political influence. Through their
representations their native cities acquired the
grant of privileges or the benefits of imperial
munificence. Prusa gained much, though it had
hoped for more, from the good offices of Dio
with Trajan, and Aristides was called the second
founder of Smyrna (ii, 9, 582). In the *Lives of
the Sophists*, by their admirer Philostratus,
ostentation, vanity and that " artistic temperament," which is popularly associated with prima
donnas, are abundantly in evidence. The culti-
vation of personal peculiarities for purposes of
advertisement may be suspected ; the wealth of
Herodes (ii, 1, 547), the gorgeous equipages of
Polemon (1, 25, 532) or Adrian (ii, 10, 587), the
devotion to physical exercises of Rufus of Perinthus
(ii, 17, 598), the quarrelsomeness of Philagrus
(ii, 8, 578), the strong head of Chrestus (ii, 11, 591)
remind us of the personal paragraphs in which the
modern public eagerly studies the irrelevant peculiarities of its favourites of the stage or film. Even
the tragedy of the infant prodigy is supplied by
Hermogenes, whose fame at fifteen induced the
emperor Marcus Aurelius to make a journey to
hear him declaim, but whose talent subsequently
declined and left him to endure an old age
rendered the more ignoble by memories of the
illusory promise of his early youth (ii, 7, 577).

Never were professors at such a premium.
Rhetorical competitions were a regular feature in
the programme of the festivals of Greek Asia ;
the people of Athens were not peculiar in their
passion for hearing new theses expounded. You
will remember the familiar scene. " So he
reasoned in the synagogue with the Jews and
devout persons, and in the market-place every
day with them that met him. And certain also
of the Epicureans and Stoic philosophers
encountered him . . . And they took hold of him
and brought him into the Areopagus, saying,
' May we know what this new teaching is that
is spoken by thee ? ' "

New teaching, however, in any real sense, was
rare indeed. In general the novelty consisted
at best in a fresh treatment of some threadbare
theme, which was often itself trivial or fantastic
in character. Favourable specimens of this art
have survived among the works of Lucian.
Fantastic topics might serve as material for the
sophists' fancy to embroider ; Lucian composed
an eulogy of the fly, and Dio sang the praises of
the mosquito or the parrot. Set historical
subjects were frequent, like that proposed by
Marcus to test the skill of Adrian : " Hyperides,
when Philip is at Elatea, pays heed only to the
counsels of Demosthenes " (ii, 10, 589). More
fantastic was the theme suggested by Megistias
to Hippodromus for an extempore oration ;
" the magician who wished to die because he was
unable to kill another magician, an adulterer "
(ii, 27, 619). Nevertheless proficiency in the
oratorical treatment of such foolish essays was

admired by the educated public with an enthusiasm which it is difficult for us to comprehend.
In Rome, if we are to believe Philostratus
(ii, 10, 589), the news that Adrian was declaiming
would empty the music hall, and the whole
audience would leave the dancers and rush post
haste to the lecture room. The public indeed
were nice critics of professional skill, for both
philosophical dialectic and rhetoric were games
conducted strictly in accordance with recognised
rules. The greatest of entertainments was provided when the opportunity arose to pit two
famous exponents of the art against each other
in public debate.[1]

The rank and file of these professors, whether
philosophers or rhetoricians, were professionals,
who had adopted this means of getting a livelihood. That their lot, whether as peripatetic
lecturers or as domestic chaplains, was not always
easy, will be clear to any reader of Lucian's
tract *upon those who give their society for hire.*
Lucian had reason to know. In some, no doubt,
an affected austerity served as a cloak to vice. It
was the stock argument of the Philistine to urge
from individual and notorious examples that
philosophers were but whited sepulchres and
moral philosophy a sham. The philosopher,
like the parson in the days of the so-called

---

1. The references above are to Philostratus, *Lives of the Sophists.* For
the history of the "second sophistic" see Boulanger, *Aelius Aristide et la
sophistique dans la province d'Asie au 11e siècle de notre ère* (Paris, 1924), and
von Arnim, *Leben und Werke des Dion von Prusa* (Berlin, 1908). The section,
in the latter book, upon the Bithynian speeches gives an extremely interesting
picture of social and political conditions in a Greek town of Asia Minor in
the second century.

" Bohemian journalists," was the conventional
butt for stale jesting. Some, again, if guiltless
of gross immorality, were pretentious humbugs
or soulless professionals. Such had no vocation
other than to give the public what it wanted—
for pay. But there were great exceptions, such
as Dio Chrysostom, who travelled through all
parts of the empire preaching against materialism
and shallow learning. With regard to the rank
and file, Seneca and Epictetus admit, as they
were bound to do, the existence of charlatans
or of philosophers whose conduct was grossly
unworthy of their profession, though Epictetus
points out that the conspicuousness of the cloth
draws attention to every erring philosopher, where
a layman's peccadilloes would pass unheeded. But
they rightly insist that the existence of a worthless
or immoral philosopher does not prove that philosophy in itself is either immoral or worthless, a line
of argument which is similarly employed by Tertullian to urge that Christianity is not to be condemned because of the existence of bad Christians.[1]

---

1.   Sham philosophers, a favourite butt of Lucian, come under Juvenal's
lash in his second satire : circulatores, qui philosophiam honestius neglexissent,
quam uendunt, Seneca, *Ep*. xxix, 7.   Damnum quidem fecisse philosophiam
non erit dubium, postquam prostituta est.   Sed potest in penetralibus
suis ostendi, si modo non institorem sed antistitem nancta est, *ibid.*, lii, 15.
[Marcellinus] scrutabitur scholas nostras et obiiciet philosophis congiaria,
amicas, gulam.   Ostendet mihi alium in adulterio, alium in popina, alium in
aula, *ibid.*, xxix, 5.   The " immoral parson " joke in Persius, i, 132, uafer,
multum gaudere paratus/ si cynico barbam petulans nonanaria uellat.   " As
it is, when you think that he is behaving ill, when your own conduct is
discreet, you say ' Look at the philosopher ! ' as though it were fitting to
call a man who acts so a philosopher, and again ' There's your philosopher ! '
But you do not say ' Look at the carpenter ! ' or ' Look at the musician ! '
when you discover one of that class in adultery or see him eating greedily."
Epictetus, *Disc.*, iv, 8, 13.   The existence of individual bad Christians
does not prove Christianity bad, Tertullian, *ad Nat.*, i, 5.

Dio was a master of cultivated eloquence. There were other missionaries abroad, the product of a popular reaction against the worship of wealth and also against the fopperies of learning. These were the Cynics, the mendicant friars of antiquity, as they have been called. Like the Christians, they were essentially missionaries of a popular movement, and, like them, they tended to be despised by the educated classes on account of their violent ignorance, uncouthness, and humble social status. Lucian does not spare them on that account, though he has more sympathy with them than with most of his victims ; for he, too, is constantly harping upon their main theme, the vanity of riches and of the standard of values professed by the world of Trimalchio. The movement was indeed a violent, crude, and even vulgar protest against the materialism and artificiality of civilisation. The Cynic in his person abjured refinement and even cleanliness. With his staff, scrip, rough cloak, and shaggy populated beard, he claimed to be self-sufficient in his virtuous rags. Education, literary skill, social position or wealth—all these were matters for contempt, and his honesty was sometimes apt to take the form of insolent rudeness. In all such movements individual frauds are likely to be found, but, as a whole, this great Puritan protest against society was genuine and sincere. In spite of his squalor and ignorance, the Cynic's stand for righteousness must command admiration. " The earnestness was of the essence, the squalor was

accidental."[1]   It was a remarkable sign of the
times, and in more than one respect these rebels
against the false standards of society have
obvious affinities with Christians.[2] Peregrinus,
as we have seen, had at one period of his life
been a member of a Christian community.

Very briefly we have summarised some of the
intellectual tendencies of the period. It is
marked, we have seen, by a gradual but steady
decline of rationalism—a sterilisation, as it has
been called, of the human intellect. There is
nowadays, perhaps, a tendency to rate the
intellectual achievements of the Middle Ages
more favourably than was formerly the rule.
Here I can only give the impression of a very
superficial acquaintance. But characteristic, it
seems to me, of medieval learning is its erudition
and its misdirection of energy. Not only the
great range of learning, but the sheer intellectual
power of the medieval masters must evoke
admiration, but their great force so often spends
itself along futile channels. A lamentable feature
of their erudition is a kind of fatal genius for
selecting for perpetuation the more worthless
items in their predecessors' store.[3] This tendency

---

1. Hatch, *op. cit.*, p. 143. A good example of the notorious bad manners
of the Cynic will be found in Plutarch, *de. def. orac.* 7, 413 foll. (Prickard,
pp. 122 foll.).

2. For Cynics and Christians see Wendland, *op. cit.*, pp. 92–93. The
obvious analogy did not escape the notice of their common enemy Julian.
Πάλαι μὲν οὖν ὑμῖν ἐθέμην ἐγὼ τοῦτο τὸ ὄνομα, νυνὶ δὲ αὐτὸ ἔοικα καὶ
γράψειν. ἀποτακτιστάς τινας ὀνομάζουσιν οἱ δυσσεβεῖς Γαλιλαῖοι, Julian,
Or. vii, 224B.

3. Thus it is characteristic that the scientific method of Aristotle's biology
and many of its individual discoveries (*e.g.* how sharks breed) were thrown
overboard, and had to be rediscovered in the nineteenth century, while his
mistaken *a priori* notions of physiology and physics were perpetuated as axioms.

is already noticeable in the late classical period. *The Natural History* of the Elder Pliny is the first great book of medieval science in its industrious erudition and its lack of discrimination. Typical of our period is the *Oneirocritica* of Artemidorus,[1] upon which most of the dream-books of medieval and modern Europe are founded. The whole business is fundamentally silly, but granted the premisses, enormous trouble, industry and care have been taken in creating the systematic pseudo-science of dreams.   To collect his material Artemidorus travelled all over the world and made careful, if uncritical, personal examination of his data. His book is indeed a triumph of " scientific method," and illustrates rather well the dangers, to which present-day research might well pay a little attention, of " method " when not directed by common sense.

The opinions, for that is what " dogmata " in the first instance means,[2] of Chrysippus or of other great philosophers came to be memorised from the textbook and to be regarded as convictions, not relatively, but absolutely   true. Respect for authority, which too often meant authority misunderstood, completely shackled criticism, which is the life-blood of free investigation.

An interesting corollary of the dominance of

---

1. With the *Oneirocritica* may perhaps be mentioned a similar work, Pseudo-Melampus, Περὶ Παλμῶν from which the similar modern books of European superstition are mainly derived. See Diels, " Beiträge zur Zuckungsliteratur des Oksidents und Orients," *Abhl. d. königl. Akad. d. Wiss.* (Berlin, 1908, 1909).

2. On the instructive history of the word " dogma " see Hatch, *op. cit.,* pp. 119 foll.

uncritical reverence for authority is the rank
growth of apocryphal literature which is
characteristic both of the later paganism and of
the Middle Ages. For the motive of such
fraudulent ascriptions of forgeries to great names
is, of course, precisely derived from the un-
questioning faith which the authority of such
names inspired.

Learning, indeed, as literature had done,
became more and more widely separated from
reality and common sense. If in this regrettable
divorce the indirect influence of rhetoric had its
share, much of the responsibility must be laid
upon the increasing use of allegory in the interpretation of the literature of the past, and the
consequent habit of mind which gave to the
fantastic or the picturesque the preference over
the obvious. The presupposition that a plain
statement of fact must mean something other
than it appeared to mean induced a lack of
precision and, if we may so express it, a woolliness
of mind, which the mystical tendencies of the
contemporary religious movement, pagan as well
as Christian, did not diminish.

The allegorical method itself in part arose as the
result of a respect for tradition and the consequent
need of explaining away religious survivals, which,
if literally interpreted, offended the reason or the
conscience of a more civilised age. Reinterpretation was the necessary price of the retention,
which the authority of their antiquity commended.
But in the intellectual professions, too, the
respect for authority had become general, and
with it the habit of copying out uncritically the

dogmata of previous investigators. The beginnings of the tendency go back to Alexandrian science with its immense erudition, considerable specialisation, and great output of activity. Learning was to some extent, as indeed it is to-day, swamped by its material. The polymath is despised by the severer specialist, and an Eratosthenes, the last of the great all-round scholars of Alexandria, was unkindly nicknamed B as being a Jack of all trades and a master of none. Intense specialisation upon a considerable scale inevitably breeds dogmatism. No man can hope to keep up with the rapid and intricate developments in other fields than those upon which his own studies trench. At the same time there developed a great popular interest in learning, science, and education. The result was the production of a mass of handbooks and popularising compendia to meet the need.

He would be a bold man who would claim to have discovered to-day the secret whereby the successful wholesale diffusion of education might be accomplished, without a simultaneous lowering of the intellectual standard. Perhaps that is an unavoidable price, which must be paid ; whether it is worth it, opinions will differ ; for my own view is not that which is likely to be popular. But whatever may be true of present conditions, there can be little doubt that the over-specialisation of science and the development of popular education in the Hellenistic age led to the decline of mental activity, the cult of information-mongering, education by textbook and erudition by index. The " source book," to use our modern name for

the atrocity, began to supersede the works of
great authors, and the use of compendia, handbooks, epitomes, and other illusory short cuts to
knowledge had taken disastrously firm root
before the time of Pliny and Plutarch.   For this,
though leading Stoics are always protesting
against its demoralising results, the popular
teaching of Stoicism had no little responsibility.[1]

While emphasising this tendency of respect for
authority to strangle free investigation, we may
notice a current supposition to the detriment of
Christianity, which I believe to be unfounded.
It is, I fancy, very commonly believed that the
acceptance by Christianity of the doctrine of the
Creation was one of the principal agents in
retarding speculation in natural science.   Now it
is undeniable that the earlier Greek philosophers
were fortunate in being unhampered by any
religious doctrine of how the world came into
being, which was in any sense an article of faith.
But, although Christianity did take over the Old
Testament, it is very difficult to maintain that
the narrative of Genesis seriously fettered science
during the early centuries of our era ; and that for
the simple reason that the choice between a
literal or allegorical interpretation of the Old
Testament was an open one.   Origen, for example,
declares that the Scriptures " have a meaning,

---

1. On the growth of the use of handbooks and the popularisation of
knowledge in the Hellenistic Age see Wendland, *op. cit.*, p. 61.   On the
summarium or *breuiarium*, Seneca, *Ep.* xxxix.   " Quare depone istam spem,
posse te summatim degustare ingenia maximorum uirorum; tota tibi
inspicienda sunt, tota tractanda, *Ep.* xxxiii, 5.   Apart from the dressing
the substance of the poems of Juvenal and Persius are little more than tags
from the Stoic handbook done into verse.

not such only as is apparent at first sight, but also another, which escapes the notice of most : for the things which are written are the forms of certain mysteries, and the images of divine things." Thus he proceeds to apply the Stoic method of Cornutus to the story of the Creation. "What man of sense will suppose that the first and the second and the third day and the evening and the morning existed without a sun, or moon and stars ? Who is so foolish as to believe that God, like a husbandman, planted a garden in Eden and placed in it a tree of life, that might be seen and touched, so that one who tasted of the fruit by his bodily lips obtained life ? " All these stories are not literally true : they are allegories. Similarly Tertullian declares that the meaning of Adam's fig-leaves is esoteric : sed arcana ista nec omnium nosse.[1] I am myself convinced that the supposedly restrictive influence of the doctrine of the Creation upon the science of the period with which we are dealing, is, at the least, highly exaggerated. The contrary supposition, no doubt, is attributable to false analogy from the part which the Book of Genesis did actually play in the theological controversies of the last century.

Though the current charge against Christianity in this respect breaks down, it is, perhaps, true that, what may be called, a theological attitude towards scientific investigation had become general and inevitably hampered free thought during our period. But neither in its origin nor

---

1. Hatch, *op. cit.* pp. 76 foll., Origen, *de princip.*, iv, i, 7-16, Tertullian, *de pall.*, 3.

in its operation was it specifically Christian. It may be traced rather to the oriental element in Hellenistic culture; for in the East science had developed under sacerdotal influences, and learning had been a monopoly of the priesthood. Again, we are led back to the founder of the new Stoicism, for Cumont has drawn attention to "the dangerous idea that knowledge is the reward of piety," implicit in the attack of Posidonius upon the cosmographical shortcomings of Epicurus.[1]

The most profoundly disastrous influence, however, which more than any other single agent was responsible for the retrogression of the natural sciences, was the dead hand of astrology. Once this Babylonian superstition had obtained a firm hold on Western civilisation, it dominated to its detriment every branch of scientific thought. To each planet was attached a plant, a metal, a stone; each presided over a period of life, a portion of the body and a faculty of the soul; each possessed a colour and a taste, and corresponded to one of the vowels. No department indeed of human knowledge or of human activity escaped the baleful influence of sidereal pseudo-science, the presuppositions of which diverted every enquiry at the outset from the path of rational investigation into the fantastic and hopeless morass of fatalistic superstition. Its plausible appearance of being a rational and intelligible system depended in reality upon the acceptance of a geo-centric theory of physics. The pretensions of astrology to provide

---

1. Cumont, *Astrology and Religion*, p. 151, referring to Cleomedes, *de mot. circ.*, ii, 87.

an axiomatic presupposition of all scientific investigation, were doomed by the discoveries of Galileo and Copernicus.   But that its hold endured so long is due to a curious and unhappy accident, *viz.*, that the whole cosmological system of Stoicism happened to be based upon a theory of the nature of the universe as a finite and geo-centric whole.   The true hypothesis that the earth revolved round the sun was actually put forward by Aristarchus of Samos in the third century B.C., and his work was subsequently followed up by Seleucus of Seleucia, who explained that the universe was heliocentric, that the earth revolved round the sun and rotated upon its axis.[1]   The responsibility for rejecting the hypothesis of Aristarchus lies partly with the savants of Alexandria, but mainly with the Stoics, who directed against it a vigorous polemic inspired by, what it is not unfair to call, theological prejudice.   It is true that Aristarchus did not, like Galileo, suffer personal persecution, but it was none the less the hostility of Cleanthes and his followers, which finally decided the fate of the true theory and thereby shackled scientific enquiry for centuries to a fundamental error. Here, indeed, is an unhappy instance of a victory of the theological over the scientific spirit, but the responsibility cannot be laid to the account of Christianity, which inevitably accepted the errors of astrology together with the rest of the intellectual equipment of contemporary culture.

---

1. Plutarch, *de fac. in orb. lunae*, 6, 922 F (Prickard, p 264). Heath, *Aristarchus of Samos*, pp. 301 foll., Cumont, *Astrology and Religion*, pp. 67-8.

LECTURE VII

UNION WITH GOD AND THE IMMORTALITY OF THE SOUL.

"Our souls will not have reason to rejoice in their lot until, freed from the darkness in which they grope, they have not merely caught a glimpse of the brightness with feeble vision, but have absorbed the full light of day and have been restored to their place in the sky—until, indeed, they have regained the place, which they held at the allotment of their birth. The soul is summoned upwards by its very origin, and it will reach that goal even before it is released from its prison below, as soon as it has cast off sin and, in purity and lightness, has leaped up into celestial realms of thought."

Seneca, Ep., lxxix, 12.

"Since I, a mortal, born of a mortal womb, but made better by all powerful strength and the right hand of incorruption, I am to-day to behold with immortal eyes and with immortal spirit the immortal Aeon and the Lord of the Fiery Diadems, inasmuch as I am purified with pure purifications and held up for a little by the pure strength of my man's soul, which I shall once more receive again after this present bitter necessity, which now oppresses me with the burden of sin, I, N, the son of my mother N., by the irrevocable decree of God ευηιαεηια ωειαυιυαιεω, since it is not attainable for me, who am of mortal birth, to mount on high with the golden flashing rays of immortal Light ωηυ αεω ηυα εωη υαε ωιαε. Stay still, perishable mortal nature, and immediately release me in accord with inexorable and urgent need."[1]

Parisian Magical Papyrus, Dieterich, *Eine Mithrasliturgie*, p. 4.

THESE two quotations are of very different

---

1. The use of the mother's name not the patronymic is the rule in magical documents. "It is a wise child which knows its own father," but about the mother there can be no physical doubt. When the mother's name is un-

origin. The first is from the writings of a Stoic philosopher, the second is part of a magical rigmarole which belongs to what is intellectually the most degraded stratum of the religious thought of the period which we are discussing. Yet, in both, a fundamental similarity of idea and aspiration leaps to the eye. Indeed the great religious movement of the time may manifest itself in very different forms in philosophy, in the mystery cults, and in magic, but throughout these variations, from the highest to the lowest, there runs an essential unity. The character of the reactions may vary with the intellectual and emotional equipment of individuals, but it is to the same stimulus of human need that they respond.

Let us first consider philosophy. Here we may notice at once that in all the forms of universal philosophy which dominated the Graeco-Roman world, what I may call the element of other-worldliness had become increasingly characteristic. Even Epicureanism, a sceptical but waning force, rejected in its purer forms the common standard of values. The prizes of this world are not worth having ;

---

known, that of Earth, the mother of all, may be used, *e.g.*, " bind every limb and sinew of Victoricus, whom Earth, the Mother of all living things, bare, the Blue charioteer " (*C.I.L.*, viii, 13511).

The names of power (ὄνομα θεσπέσιον ἢ ῥῆσιν βαρβαρικήν, Lucian, *Philops.* 9) are a mixture of all sorts of eastern gods ; the Jewish Iahwe, El, Sabaoth, Adonai, etc., are very common. Many of the magic names are gibberish, either due to corruptions of foreign words, or to arbitrary combinations of divine names or simply to arbitrary combinations of letters.

Combinations of the vowels, as here, are very usual. Orphic and Gnostic wisdom had followed Pythagorean mysticism in identifying the seven vowels with the seven planets. See Hippolytus, vi, 43, and for a discussion of the matter Dieterich, *op. cit.*, pp. 32 foll.

pleasures necessarily accompanied by pains are Dead-Sea fruit. A crude but not wholly false generalisation might put it that the Epicureans met the resulting difficulties of life by attempting to run away from them. They offered a negative, not a positive, solution to the problem raised by the falsity of this world's standards.

Platonism had always maintained the immortality of the soul, the essential reality of another world than this, and not merely the unreliability of sense perception, but the unreality of all material things. Even its sceptical phase was essentially based upon the unreality of this world of matter ; it was less concerned with disproving the existence of reality than with proving the impossibility of human knowledge of it. Platonism had then become associated with Pythagorism, with its Orphic catchword *sôma sêma*, the body is the tomb of the soul, and in its later manifestations it made definitely the same alliance with religious mysticism, which had been a feature of Pythagorean teaching from the time of its founder.

The *sôma sêma* doctrine had indeed become part of the common stock of philosophical thought and had profoundly affected the neo-Stoicism[1]. Even the older Stoicism, however, involved not merely the Epicurean contradiction of mundane values, but the assertion of other and more real values than those of this transitory world of accident and of the flesh. The Stoic's

---

1. For the adoption of the *sôma sêma* doctrine by neo-Stoicism, see Bevan, *Stoics and Sceptics*, p. 100.

philosophy is indeed applied philosophy, in the sense that it is less concerned with speculation than with the practical problems of how to live rightly, but the reference of its maxims for conduct is to the standard of spiritual ideals, to πνευματικά not to ψυχικά nor to σαρκικά.[1]

It is the divine spark within man, the God whom he carries in him, that justifies, nay demands, moral effort. This is the basis of the self-respect,[2] which will keep him from unworthy action. " But you are a principal work," says Epictetus, " a fragment of God Himself, you have in yourself a part of Him. Why then are you ignorant of your high birth ? . . . Do you not know that it is God you are nourishing or training ? You bear God about with you, poor wretch, and know it not. Do you think I speak of some external god of silver and gold ? No, you bear Him about within you and are unaware that you are defiling Him with unclean thoughts and foul actions."[3]

The Divine Element in us is our real self ; the material body and the environment of this world crib, cabin and confine it. The new Stoicism admits that evil is innate in man and

---

1. " Dedit tibi illa quae si non deserueris, par deo surges. Parem autem te deo pecunia non faciet ; deus nihil habet. Praetexta non faciet ; deus nudus est," etc. Seneca, *Ep.* xxxi, 9-10. " Scit, inquam, aliubi positas esse diuitias quam quo congeruntur ; animum impleri debere, non arcam." Seneca, *Ep.* xcii, 31.

2. The soldiers swear to respect no man above Caesar, but we respect ourselves first of all, Epictetus, *Disc.* i, 14, 17.

3. Epictetus, *Disc.* ii, 8, 11-14. For the Divine in us cf. i, 1. We should always be proudly conscious that we are children of God (i, 2, i, 9) and we should bear with one another as children of one Father (i, 13). With the language of the passage quoted in the text compare *I Corinthians*, iii, 17, vi, 13.

is conscious of a sense of sin.[1]　A recognition of
our weakness is indeed the beginning of
philosophy,[2] but the study of philosophy, or
rather, as both Seneca and Epictetus would
agree, the study *and practice* of philosophy, will
subdue the sinful element, which is not something
external, but is within us,[3] and it will develop
the divine self to be a companion, not a suppliant,
of God,[4] nay to return to its Heavenly Home
and be at one with God.

　　" ' Is this the path to the stars ? '

　　" For that is exactly what philosophy promises
to me, that I shall be made equal with God.
For this I have been summoned, for this purpose
have I come.　Philosophy keep your promise." [5]

　　" ' He in whose body virtue dwells and spirit
　　　' E'er present,'
" he is equal to the gods ;　mindful of his origin,
he strives to return thither.　No man does wrong
in attempting to regain the heights from which
he once came down.　And why should you not
believe that something of divinity exists in one
who is a part of God ?　All this universe which

1.　This dualism of soul and body came into Stoicism with Posidonius,
who here grafted Platonic dualism upon Stoic monism.　See Bevan, *Stoics
and Sceptics*, pp. 192 foll.

2.　Epictetus, *Disc.* ii, 11.

3.　" Quid nos decipimus ?　Non est extrinsecus malum nostrum ; intra
nos est, in uisceribus ipsis sedet, et ideo difficulter ad sanitatem peruenimus
quia nos aegrotare nescimus."　It is the consciousness of sin which is the
necessary beginning of progress.　Seneca, *Ep.* l, 4, cf. *Ep.* vi, 1, liii, 7-8.　We
make things more difficult because we are always leading each other into
sin.　Sed hanc difficilem facit communis insania : in uitia alter alterum
trudimus, Seneca, *Ep.* xli, 9.

4.　" Hoc est summum bonum.　Quod si occupas, incipis deorum socium
esse, non supplex."　Seneca, *Ep.* xxxi, 8.

5.　Seneca, *Ep.* xlviii, 11, quoting Vergil, *Aen.* ix, 641.

encompasses us is one, and it is God; we are associates of God; we are members of Him." [1]

In such passages, you will notice the presence of ideas which recur again and again in Seneca and Epictetus, the sense of sin and the great objective of moral struggle, oneness with God. We may notice further that the language of conversion, that idea of a rebirth into a new life, which we shall find to be a characteristic promise of the mystery religions, also affects philosophic vocabulary. Once roused by the sense of sin and weakness to the consciousness of our high calling, we undergo a real change of character and become new men reborn to a new life. [2]

How then is sin to be overcome and the divine element to be developed? By incessant and deliberate concentration upon real values and by training of the will. Here we may perhaps notice that philosophy realised the value and also the dangers of two aids to the spiritual life, the use and, it must be added, the abuse of which is a familiar phenomenon in the history of all religions. As an experienced moral teacher, Epictetus repeatedly insists upon the practical value of the formation of good habits. Training, *askesis*, if rightly used, is a valuable subsidiary means towards the great end. Ascetic exercises, abstinence from food and drink, etc., are to be

---

1. Seneca, *Ep.* xcii, 29-30, quoting Vergil, *Aen.* v, 363.
2. Intellego, Lucili, non emendari me tantum sed transfigurari, Seneca, *Ep.* vi, 1. Philosophy shakes off the unreal nightmare of the sinful life and wakes us into the life of reality, *Ep.*, liii, 8. Nondum sapiens est nisi in ea quae didicit, animus eius transfiguratus est, *Ep.*, xciv, 48. τοῦτο πάθε, καὶ ὀρθὸς εἶ, ἀναβιῶναί σοι ἔξεστιν· ἴδε πάλιν τὰ πράγματα ὡς ἑώρας· ἐν τούτῳ γὰρ τὸ ἀναβιῶναι, Marcus Aurelius, vii, 2.

recommended for self discipline, but, as Epictetus is careful to point out, they are not to be ostentatiously practised in order to win admiration or to gratify hysterical vanity.[1] The warning was necessary, and their dangers led some philosophers entirely to condemn the ascetic practices, which had become a feature of the religious life of the day. For, as always, the instruments of self discipline tended to be abused, and we even hear of persons dying under the severity of self inflicted tortures.[2]

The need for retreat from the world was also widely felt, but again the spiritual dangers, as well as the spiritual possibilities, were clearly grasped by the philosophers. The withdrawal from the distraction of worldly interests must not be ostentatious, but should be the unadvertised response to a need which is genuinely felt, and it must be a real withdrawal to a stable concentration, not a restless wandering about. Such is the moral of Seneca's advice to Lucilius.[3] The whole matter forms the subject of one of Dio Chrysostom's orations. A mere change of scene, he points out, is futile, and a mere shirking of public duty is wrong. It is true that thought is facilitated by quiet isolation, but solitude in

---

1. Epictetus, *Manual*, 47, *Disc.* iii, 13, 20-23, iii, 14, 4-6. In his youth Seneca abstained from animal food for a year, but relinquished the " rule " in deference to his father's wishes, *Ep.*, cviii, 22. He recommends proper use of ascetic practices in *Ep.* xviii, 7, which also alludes to the practice of millionaires to seek relief from the tedium of luxury in an artificial simple life, cf. Martial, iii, 48. A rule of living had always been a feature of Pythagorism from its earliest days. Its prevalence in the religious life of the second century was probably in part a Pythagorean contribution to the common stock.

2. Lucian, *Nigrinus*, 27-28, 67-68.

3. Seneca, *Ep.*, xviii, lxix.

the desert has its real dangers. The imagination easily runs away with a man under such conditions, and hallucinations or worse are a probable result. The true retreat, he concludes, consists in real concentration, like that of a hound upon a scent. The counsel of perfection is retreat into yourself (ἡ εἰς αὐτὸν ἀναχώρησις); whether you are in Babylon or in Athens, makes no real difference then.[1]

But let us return from the means to the great end, union with God. This, as we shall see, is the ultimate goal of the mystery religions, and in them this eternal bliss is foreshadowed by the temporary achievement of mystic ecstasy which may be attained, according to circumstances, by ritual action, the possession of secret knowledge, or by spiritual *gnosis*, or by these in varying degrees of combination. In the magic of the day, which may almost be regarded as a parody of mystical religion, ritual action and the knowledge of magical formulae are thought to achieve the temporary identification of the magician with the power which he invokes, thereby enabling him to direct its supernatural energy to accomplish his own human ends.[2] Though neither so completely nor yet so transitorily, and with an opposite intention to that of the magician, the Stoic, too, aims at the present identification of his higher self with God. As

---

1. Dio Chrys., *Or.* xx. περὶ ἀναχωρήσεως. The same phrase is used by Marcus Aurelius, iv, 3. Cf. *ibid.*, vii, 28, and Seneca, *Ep.*, vii, 8, recede in te ipsum, *ibid.*, lvi.

2. For the identification of the magician with the god or spirit invoked as the essential process in late classical magic, see Reitzenstein, *Poimandres*, p. 236.

the training of the will progresses, as the Divine in us becomes strengthened, perfect surrender of the will to God becomes easier. This thought recurs again and again in Epictetus, and it is this complete and unconditional surrender of the will to God, upon which is based the genuine, secure, and unmistakable happiness which inspires his teaching.

" When you have a Leader such as this and identify your will with His, you need never fear failure any more. But, once make a gift to poverty and wealth of your will to get and your will to avoid, and you will fail and be unfortunate. Give them to health and you will be unhappy ; or to office, honour, country, friends, children— in a word, if you give them to anything beyond your will's control. But give them to Zeus and the other gods ; hand them to their keeping, let them control them and command them, and you can never be miserable any more." [1]

Once this surrender of the will has been achieved, we shall join in the perpetual hymn of praise to which, in a famous passage, he invites us. " What else can a lame old man as I am do but chant the praise of God ? If indeed, I were a nightingale, I should sing like a nightingale, if a swan, as a swan : but as I am a rational creature, I must praise God. This is my task and I do it : and I will not abandon this duty, so long as it is given me ; and I invite you all to join in this same song." [2]

---

1. Epictetus, *Disc.* ii, 17, 23-25, cf. ii, 16.
2. Epictetus, *Disc.* 16, 20-21.

This complete identification of the will with the will of God is the secret of Epictetus' happiness; it is this, too, which explains his attitude towards suicide. True, in a well-known passage he speaks of death as a door of escape which is always open,[1] but he is far more cautious than Seneca in justifying its use. It is not lightly to be undertaken out of mere pride in divine kinship or as a short cut to felicity. We are soldiers of God and must serve with uncomplaining obedience. We may not lightly abandon the post which He has allotted to us; we must await His signal to depart.

It is the teacher's duty " to prevent young men from arising of the type who, discovering their kinship with the gods and seeing that we have these fetters attached to us in the shape of the body and its possessions . . . may desire to fling all these away as vexatious and useless burdens and so depart to the gods their kindred. . . . Men as you are, wait upon God. When He gives the signal and releases you from this service, then you shall depart to Him; but for the present be content to dwell in this country, wherein He appointed you to dwell." [2]

---

1. " To sum up remember that the door is open. Do not be a greater coward than the children, but do as they do. Children when things do not please them, say, 'I will not play any more'; so, when things seem to you to reach that point just say, 'I will not play any more,' and so depart, instead of staying to make moan." Epictetus, *Disc.*, i, 24, 20.

2. Epictetus, *Disc.*, i, 9, 10-19, cf. *Disc.*, iii, 24. Seneca, too, finds it necessary to utter a warning against suicide upon frivolous pretext. uir fortis ac sapiens non fugere debet e uita, sed exire. et ante omnia ille quoque uitetur affectus, qui multos occupauit, libido moriendi, *Ep.*, xxiv, 25.

Death itself is more than a release. " When He sounds the recall, He opens the door and says, ' Come.' ' Where ? ' ' To nothing you need fear, but to that whence you were born, to your friends and kindred, the elements. So much of you as was fire shall pass into fire, what was earth shall pass into earth, the air into air, the water into water. There is no Hades nor Acheron, nor Cocytus, nor Puriphlegethon, but all is full of God and divine beings. When one has this to think upon, and when he beholds the sun and moon and stars and enjoys land and sea, he is not forlorn any more than he is destitute of help." [1]

At that last solemn moment he will not be afraid to render his account to God—you will notice once more how ethical conviction has translated a physical theory into the language of deep, religious emotion. " If death finds me thus occupied, I am content if I can lift up my hands to God and say, ' I have not neglected the faculties which I received from Thee, to enable me to understand Thy governance and follow it, I have not dishonoured Thee so far as in me lay. See how I have dealt with my senses, see how I have dealt with my primary notions. Did I ever complain of Thee, did I ever show discontent with anything that happened to any-one or wish it to happen otherwise, did I offend

---

1. Epictetus, *Disc.*, iii, 13, 14.   I have ventured to modify Mr. Matheson's translation of " spirit into spirit."   Although the Greek words are ambiguous, there can be little doubt that the airy element is the meaning. Compare Marcus Aurelius, iv, 4, or the epitaph quoted below, p. 226, note (a).

in my relations towards others ?   In that Thou
didst beget me I am grateful for Thy gifts :
in so far as I have used what Thou gavest me, I
am satisfied.   Take Thy gifts back again and
place them where Thou wilt : for they were all
Thine, Thou gavest them to me ! '   Are you not
content to leave the world in this state of mind ?
Nay what life is better or more seemly than
his who is so minded, and what end can be more
happy ? " [1]

The message is authentically from the heights,
but the mountain is hard indeed to climb by
Epictetus' road.   Perfect identification of the
will with the working of an abstract Providence
is not easy of attainment, nor is the goal, *viz.*,
the absorption of the rational element in the
parent mass which permeates the universe, one
which will completely satisfy the average human
longing for personal survival after death !   The
eloquent and perfectly sincere conviction of
Epictetus blinds us for a moment to the cold
impersonality of absorption in the cosmic
process.

But an assurance of immortality was
that for which men were athirst.   It had
been generally agreed that the fabled terrors
of mythology were an idle tale ; learned
men had even given considered reasons

---

1. Epictetus, *Disc.*, iv, 10, 14-17. Compare *Disc.*, iii, 5, 7-11, where a
similar rendering of account to God concludes with thanksgiving. " Did I
ever come before Thee but with a cheerful face, ready for any commands
or orders that Thou mightest give ? Now it is Thy will for me to
leave the festival. I go, giving all thanks to Thee, that Thou did'st deign
to let me share Thy festival, and see Thy works, and understand Thy
government."

why a subterranean Hades was a physical impossibility.[1]

The Epicureans had accepted annihilation. " Suns can set and rise again," wrote Catullus (v. 4), " but we, when our brief day is set, must sleep for an eternal night." Numerous epitaphs express this hopeless creed. " I was once composed of earth, water and airy breath, but I perished and here I rest having rendered all to the All. Such is each man's lot. What of it ? There whence my body came, did it return, when it was dissolved."

Marcus Aurelius expresses agnostic doubt, which admits extinction as an alternative probability, but maintains that at worst death ensures eternal rest. " If it be for another life, there is nothing even there which is void of gods ; but if to complete unconsciousness (ἀναισθησία), you will be released from the bonds of pleasures and of pains " (iii, 3). This melancholy comfort of a respite from the ills of life is also the frequent doctrine of the epitaphs. " I have fled the ills

---

1. " No one is so childish as to fear Cerberus, or the dark shadows, or the spectral garb of those who are held together by naught but their unfleshed bones. Death either annihilates us or strips us bare. If we are then released, there remains the better part, after the burden has been withdrawn ; if we are annihilated, nothing remains ; good and bad are alike removed," Seneca, *Ep.* xxiv, 18. In a well-known passage Juvenal (ii, 149), as so often, is giving us an extract from Stoic commonplace.

> Esse aliquos manes et subterranea regna
> et contum et Stygio ranas in gurgite nigras,
> atque una transire uadum tot milia cymba
> nec pueri credunt, nisi qui nondum aere lauantur.

Cf. Cicero, *Tusc.*, i, 4, 48 ; i, 6, 10. *Nat. Deor.* ii, 21.

Posidonius argued that, as the earth was solid, a subterranean Hades was impossible, Serv., *Aen.*, vi, 127. The Elder Pliny suggests that if there were a subterranean Hell, miners would by now have broken through to it. Pliny, *Nat. Hist.*, ii, 63 (63), 158.

of disease and the greatest evils of life ; I am tormented no longer ; I enjoy quiet peace."

Scepticism, however, for vulgar minds easily degenerates into materialism, which in many epitaphs finds even a crudely jocular expression. N.F., F., N.S., N.C. " I was not, I was, I am not, I do not care." " Eat, drink, play, come hither." " While I lived I drank with a will ; drink ye who are alive." " What remains of man, my bones rest sweetly here. I am no longer worried as to whether I shall suddenly starve ; I have no gout, my body is no longer pledged for my rent ; I enjoy free and perpetual hospitality." " Baths, wine and love corrupt our bodies, but life is made up of baths, wine and love." [1]

But the very bravado of many of these epitaphs betrays uneasiness of soul, and the universal practice of making permanent record in stone of even the details of the life of the deceased, is witness to a pathetic hankering for some sort of survival beyond the grave.[2] " What is it like below, Charidas ? "—" Very dark."—" And what about return ? "—" All lies."—" And Pluto "— " A myth."—" I am done for." This epigram of Callimachus (*Anth. Pal.* vii, 523) is, of course, deliberate comedy, but it is a Scotch humour deriving its piquancy from a grim and real fear.

---

1. Compare Seneca's summary of the weary round of the materialist's life. Cogita, quamdiu iam idem facias ; cibus, somnus, libido, per hunc circulum curritur, Seneca, *Ep.*, lxxvii, 6.

2. ἡ γὰρ στήλη καὶ τὸ ἐπίγραμμα καὶ τὸ χαλκοῦν ἑστάναι μέγα δοκεῖ τοῖς γενναίοις ἀνδράσι καὶ μισθὸς οὗτος ἄξιος τῆς ἀρετῆς τὸ μὴ μετὰ τοῦ σώματος ἀνῃρῆσθαι τὸ ὄνομα μηδ᾽ εἰς ἴσον καταστῆναι τοῖς μὴ γενομένοις, ἀλλ᾽ ἴχνος τι λιπέσθαι καὶ σημεῖον, ὡς ἂν εἴποι τις τῆς ἀνδραγαθίας, Dio, xxxi, 20, (von Arnim, i, p. 224).

Though Hell may be a myth, the fear of annihilation is no less formidable. Aeque enim timent, ne apud inferos sint, quam ne usquam.[1]

Even a grave and thoughtful agnosticism hopes at least for a survival in the memories of mankind. " If there is any dwelling-place for the spirits of the just, if, as the wise believe, noble souls do not perish with the body, rest thou in peace ; and call us, thy family, from weak regrets and womanish laments to the contemplation of thy virtues, for which we must not weep nor beat the breast. . . . Whatever we loved, whatever we admired in Agricola, survives and will survive in the hearts of men, in the succession of the ages, in the fame that waits on noble deeds. Over many indeed, of those who have gone before, as over the inglorious and the ignoble, the waves of oblivion will roll ; Agricola, made known to posterity by history and tradition, will live for ever." [2]

Stoicism, as we have seen, held that the soul returns to the sky from whence it came. " If it makes use of its powers and stretches upward into its proper region, it is by no alien path that it struggles towards the heights. It would be a great task to journey heavenwards ; the soul but returns thither. Magnus erat labor ire in caelum ; redit." [3]

Belief in this astral immortality had indeed become the common presupposition of the various

---

1. Seneca, *Ep.*, lxxxii, 16.
2. Tacitus, *Agricola*, 46 (translated by Church and Brodribb). With the opening phrase compare the epitaphs referred to in p. 226, note (d).
3. Seneca, *Ep.*, xcii, 30-31.

religions and philosophies of the time. Variations
in the map of the celestial regions at different
times, or for different schools or sects, are
matters of detail which need not here detain
us.[1]

For our purpose it is sufficient to notice that
it became a generally accepted belief that the
soul at death sought its home in the stars, and
that, at least, the good and great became stars,
enjoying that to us so strange felicity, the eternal
contemplation of the orderly movements of the
heavenly bodies. Thus the soul of the Stoic
may mount to be absorbed in the Divine Fire,
which is not seldom typified by the sun, or the
spirit of the Platonist may rise above the seven
planetary spheres to freedom from the inexorable
control of Destiny (εἱμαρμένη) and the Lords of
the Universe (κοσμοκράτορες) to the Ogdoad, or
world of " ideas " beyond. Common again was
the notion that in the course of its ascent
the soul progressively shed the weight of its
imperfections. Posidonius, indeed, had taught
that souls, of which the divine fire had not been
nourished and developed, were unable to soar,
and suffered a speedy rebirth as punishment for
their impurity. Hell was, in fact, another life
upon earth.[2]

" Among the dead," says an epitaph, " there
are two companies : one moves upon Earth, the
other in the ether among the choruses of the
stars. I belong to the latter, for I have obtained

---

1. A good general account will be found in Cumont, *After Life in Roman Paganism*, especially chapters ii, iii, and vi.
2. Diels, *Doxographici Graeci*, p. 614.

a god for my guide." [1]   Again, " Hermes of the winged feet, taking thee by the hand, has conducted thee to Olympus and made thee to shine among the stars." Or " Weep not ; for of what use is weeping. Rather venerate me, for I am now a divine star, which shows itself at sunset." [2]   Indeed the theory of the descent and ascent of the soul through the seven planetary spheres, like the physical conception of a finite

---

1. The idea of the divine guide of the soul goes back to Plato, *Phaedo*, 107D, 108B. It plays, of course, a great part in Neo-Platonism, Gnosticism, the mystery religions and magic. Hermes, in ancient Greek cult the *psychopompos*, was an obvious claimant to this rôle. Hence his importance in the mystic lore of the period and in the Hermetic philosophy. See further Cumont, *op. cit.*, p. 163.

2. The illustrations of epitaphs I have filched mainly from Cumont, *op. cit.* A few references to specimen examples may be given, unless otherwise stated to numbers in Bücheler, *Carmina Latina Epigraphica.* Those which have been quoted in the text are printed in italics.

(a) *Death is annihilation : Arch.-epigr. Mitt. aus Oestereich*, vi, 1882, p. 30.

ἐξ ὕδατος καὶ γῆς καὶ πνεύματος ἦα πάροιδεν
ἀλλὰ θανὼν κεῖμαι πᾶσι(ν) τὰ πάντ' ἀποδούς.
πᾶσιν τοῦτο μένει· τί δὲ τὸ πλεόν ; ὁππόθεν ἦλθον
ⲓⲥ τοῦτ' <αὖτ'> ἐλύθη σῶμα μαραινόμενον.

(Cf. the language of Epictetus quoted above, p. 220. The tone of the epitaph, however, is more acidly negative.) B. No. 1495.

(b) *Death as rest from ills of life : morborum uitia et uitae mala maxima fugi nunc careo poenis, pace fruor placida, No. 1274,* cf. Nos. 507, 573.

(c) *Jocular scepticism :* Dessau Nos. 8162 foll., B.Nos. *1500, 1247, 1499,* 182-191, 244.

(d) *Agnostic doubt :* (cf. Tacitus, *Agricola*) sei quicquam sapiunt inferi, No. 180, si quid Manes sapiunt, No. 1147, si tamen at Manes credimus esse aliquit, No. 1190, si quis post funera sensus, No. 1339. With the Tacitean passage compare mors terribilis est iis quorum cum uita omnia exstinguuntur ; non iis quorum laus emori non potest, Cicero, *Paradox. Stoic.* ii, 18.

(e) *Astral immortality :* Kaibel, *Epigr. Graec. 650, Revue philol.* xxxiii, *1909, p. 6, I.G.,* xii, *7, 123,*

non ego Tartareas penetrabo tristis ad undas . . .
nam me sancta Venus sedes non nosse silentem
iussit et in coeli lucida templa tulit,

No. 1109. Hence Timarchus sees the souls as stars, Plutarch, *de gen Socr.* 22, 591D, and Cicero can say totum prope coelum nonne humano genere completum est ? *Tusc.* i, 12, 28.

universe upon which it is based, forms a common background to the philosophical, religious, and magical beliefs of the day. Even the various theories as to the manner and means by which the soul made its journey find their counter-parts in the magical papyri, and without doubt, if our information was more complete, we should find them no less prominent in the esoteric ritual of the mystery religions.

At the bottom of the religious movement of the day is this craving for immortality, the desire for escape from the hard circumstance of life with its unjust and unreal values, from the caprice of Fortune and from the inexorability of a mechanical Destiny, and a longing for being made one with God. Epictetus has shown us one way to attain the goal, but it is a hard way, and not for all to tread. Apart from the difficulties of conforming in practice to an unfaltering standard of detached excellence, a difficulty which is in some degree common to all ethical philosophies and religions which refuse to compromise with the second best, its basis is intellectual. But though all men may be capable of reason, then, as now, but comparatively few are capable of sustained intellectual effort. Nor if the appeal is made to reason, can they take the premisses of the philosophers on trust! The philosophers are at war among themselves. If the men of wisdom disagree, how is the plain man to decide which is the true path to follow ? By writing out the names of the various schools and drawing one of them from an urn ?[1]   Lucian's

---

1. Lucian, *Hermotimus*, 57, 798.

Hermotimus, of which this is the conclusion, betrays the pathetic wistfulness of the agnostic. After all, it is conviction not reason which has the last word in these matters. It is impossible not to feel the tragedy of the poor old seeker after salvation, whose fragile bubble of hope is so ruthlessly pricked by the sceptic's rapier, and beneath his raillery the uneasiness of soul of the iconoclast himself.

Conviction, that was what men wanted. The fracas of philosophical dispute left them bewildered and unsatisfied. In Hatch's words, "men were sick of theories; they wanted certainty." [1] This is what religion offered, certainty—a certainty based ultimately upon an appeal not to logic, but to faith. This is essentially true not only of Christianity, but also of the contemporary mystery religions, and Celsus, when he voices the intellectual's antipathy to the substitution of another arbiter for reason, is here perfectly right to include pagan mysteries in his censure. Here the prophets of the worship of Mithras, Sabazios and Hecate are indeed comparable to the preachers of Christianity in their exhortations "Do not examine, but believe," and "Your faith will save you." [2]

We have, indeed, noticed another voice than that of reason intruding itself into philosophy,

---

1. Hatch, *op. cit.*, p. 312.
2. Origen, *c. Cels*, i, 9. Origen's counter is interesting. Partly owing to the necessities of life and partly owing to the differing grades of intelligence, it is impossible for every one to think things out and become a philosopher, and indeed only a few can do so. Christianity here admits the facts, but attributes to irrational belief a virtue which pagan philosophy denied. We are, indeed, in contact with the fundamental difference of outlook indicated above, p. 136.

and the essentially religious emotions of a consciousness of sin and of reliance upon Divine
assistance in the upward struggle, are making
themselves heard. This note sounds most strongly
in Seneca, perhaps because of his unique
experience of the sombre tragedy of life. The
longing for immortality and for a happiness
transcending the disappointments and emptiness
of this world's goods, the sense of weakness and
the difficulties of unaided release, the comfort
and assurance of resting in union with a more
than mortal Saviour, these are the needs to
which the mystery religions were a response.
To the believer they gave assurance of
immortality, not primarily through the effort of
an intellectual process, but through faith in the
Saviour god, and by obedience to the terms of
that holy service in which, by initiation, he had
become enrolled. Through the guidance and
help of his god, his soul after death could
successfully triumph over the difficulties of the
way of return. Of the ultimate felicity of
perpetual union with God, the worshipper
through purification and mystic ritual enjoyed
a foretaste in the ecstasy of direct communion
and identification with the object of his worship.
" I am Thou and Thou art I. Thy name is
also my name, for I am the double of Thee."
Such is the constant refrain of liturgy and magic.

Indeed, as we suggested at the beginning of
the lecture, the philosophy, religion and magic
of the period may well be regarded as parts of
the same great movement. If philosophy and
magic represent the opposite poles, what lies

between them is continuous. Magic shades
into religion ; religion shades into philosophy.
There are no sharp edges to define their respective
fields with accuracy. Philosophy itself becomes
steadily more religious and even more magical in
temper with the dominance of that Neo-
Platonism, in which it is becoming the fashion
to discern such notable merit.

A broad distinction between the three, of
course, there necessarily remained. The basis
of philosophy is intellectual and its final appeal is
to reason. Reason it never avowedly jettisoned ;
rather it clapped it under hatches in a sad
obscurity, hidden beneath an alien cargo of
mystic emotionalism and magical theurgy. The
appeal of religion was primarily to the emotions,
to a sense of unworthiness, and to a faith in a
beneficent God, powerful to save. Its practice
and its precepts were capable of lofty spiritual
interpretation and, as such, did in fact afford
satisfaction to the spiritual needs of men who
were undoubtedly moral, high-minded, and
devout. Its ritual forms, however, were sub-
stantially the same as those employed in magic,[1]
and, as is the tendency in all religions, with
the less intelligent or spiritual of its adherents the
letter counted for more than the spirit. Such
attributed to its rites a literal, not a symbolical,
efficacy, which was in no sense dependent upon
the intention or the spiritual condition of the
participant.

Here, surely, we have already crossed the

---

1. See de Jong, *Das Antike Mysterienwesen*, 2nd ed., pp. 163 foll.

border-line into magic. For, without trenching
upon that once hotly debated problem of
the original relation or respective priority of
magic and religion, a practical distinction of
what we broadly mean by the two words in
relation to the period which we are discussing,
is surely not difficult to attain. Both in method
and purpose there is a distinction. Religion,
at least in its higher forms, approaches a
beneficent and powerful God with a humble
spirit and a contrite heart. It may make subsidiary use of ritual forms and disciplinary
exercises, and even attach the greatest importance
to their observance, but they are not held to be
per se effective. The hope of the worshipper
depends in part upon the spiritual condition, to
which these symbols or this training may help
him to attain, but ultimately its fulfilment
depends upon the grace of his God. The
magician is less humbly minded. For him the
ceremonial has itself an efficacy, which the knowledge of it and its due performance will enable
him to direct for his own, in Black Magic, anti-
social purposes. Formulae or names of power
are in themselves forces which their fortunate
possessor may employ at will. Exact knowledge
of course, is necessary, and blunders indeed are
highly dangerous; for his is a completely logical
formalism. For example, as Origen tells us,[1]

---

1. Origen, *c. Cels.*, v, 45. For Christian belief in magical nominalism
we may compare the curious theory of Tertullian about the Roman *indigita-*
menta, Cardea, Forculus and the like. "Of course we know that though
names be empty and feigned, yet when they are being drawn down into
superstition, demons and every unclean spirit seize them for themselves
through the bond of consecration," *de idol.*, 15.

Hebrew or other foreign names of power may not be translated into the native tongue of the magician, for in that event their efficacy would disappear with the change of form.

From the belief in the efficacy inherent in magical rites and formulae in themselves, it follows that the magician, who is master of them, is master also of the power which is attached to them. The most usual form which is taken by magical procedure in our period, is for the practitioner by the knowledge and use of such conjurations to identify with himself the particular god or spirit concerned and thereby to compel it to carry out his wishes.

Alike in the philosophy, the religion and the magic of this period, the idea of union with God plays a fundamental part. Both in the later Stoicism and in the higher teaching of the mystery religions this union is an end ; in magic it is a means. For Epictetus such union, we saw to be partially realised in this life by the deliberate subordination of the will of the individual to the will of God ; after death it will be more completely consummated in the absorption of the rational element or soul in the Divine Principle, which is the soul of the cosmic process. In the mystery religions, too, a temporary foretaste of perpetual union after death with the Saviour God may be achieved on earth through mystic ecstasy, but, as compared with philosophy, the matter, both as regards here and as regards hereafter, is more emotionally envisaged, and the conception of God is more warmly invested with personality. In magic the union is temporary and its purpose is not to realise the will of God but the will of the magician. It is not so much a matter of the absorption of the human soul by the Divine Spirit of the universe, as of an absorption of the god or spirit by the wonder-worker, who thereby controls it for his own ends.

Such is the nature of the real distinctions, which remained in some degree permanently valid, but it is a characteristic feature of the time that the less intelligent influences tended to become increasingly dominant. The magical element became more and more prominent in religion, and this, in turn, affected philosophy, between which and religion the bond, already close in the latter forms of Stoicism, became yet more intimate. Finally, in Neo-Platonism, in which mystical apprehension supplemented or even supplanted rational perception, philosophy was to claim a perilous kinship with theosophy and theurgy.

The disastrous consequences are sufficiently indicated by the continuous succession of the turn of the third and fourth centuries. Plotinus, Porphyry, Iamblichus, Maximus : how swift and abysmal a descent !

LECTURE VIII

THE MYSTERY RELIGIONS.

" For many glorious and divine things as your Athens
seems to me to have produced and to have brought into
human life, yet none of them is better than those
mysteries, by which we have been educated out of a
boorish and savage life into humanity and have been
made civilised. From them we have learned the
rudiments (*initia*) as they are called, which are in fact
the fundamental principles (*principia*) of living, and
thereby have received a rule not only of happy living
but of dying with a better hope."

Cicero, de leg. ii, 14, 36.

" O happy is he to whom the blessedness is given to
know the mysteries of the gods, who is pure in his life
and keeps holy revel in his soul, being made a Bacchos
in the mountains with holy purifications."

Euripides, Bacchae, 73.

" And at first we ourselves, having fallen from heaven
and living with the Nymph, are in despondency and
abstain from corn and all rich and unclean food, for
both are hostile to the soul. Then comes the cutting
of the tree and the fast, as though we also were cutting
off the further process of generation. After that the
feeding on milk, as though we were being born again ;
after which come rejoicings and garlands and, as it
were, a return up to the Gods."

Sallustius, de diis et mundo, 4, (trans. G. Murray, Five Stages,
p. 246).

" For ' many,' as they say in the mysteries, ' are the
thyrsus-bearers, but few are the Bacchoi '—meaning, as
I interpret the words, the true philosophers."

Plato, Phaedo, 69 c.

THE conquest of the Graeco-Roman world by

the oriental religions was irresistible, and long before the battle of Actium, whatever might be their technical and legal status, their actual hold upon Rome and Italy was too secure to be shaken by any temporary measure of attempted suppression. The number of their adherents was by no means restricted to the foreign immigrants from their native homes who were now resident in the seaports of the West or in the cosmopolitan centres of commerce ; it included large numbers of Romans, and in particular a considerable proportion of the emancipated women of the upper class. Their vogue steadily increased under the Empire. Augustus might attempt to discountenance them by his expressed disapproval of alien cults ; his individual successors might take sporadic action against this or that particular cult ; but, in fact, the oriental religions had come to stay. It was, indeed, not long before Isis obtained an official status equal to that which Cybele had long enjoyed, and the various divinities of the East became rivals for the patronage of imperial favour.[1]

A process indeed was repeated upon a larger scale, very similar to that which can be traced in the religious history of Athens even before Alexander. There, for example, we find the worship of the Phrygian goddess entering Attica as a reflex consequence of the expansion of Athenian commerce in the fifth century B.C. The repul-

---

[1]. The failure of repeated attempts at repression by the State and the influence of imperial predilections in religion is rather well illustrated in the history of the cult of Isis at Rome, for a detailed account of which see Lafaye, *Culte des divinités d'Alexandrie*, pp. 38-63.

sive barbarities of its ritual profoundly shocked the populace, who, according to tradition, put one too zealous propagandist to death. Complaints as to its subversive influence upon feminine morals show us that, nevertheless, it made steady way, partly through its appeal to the emotionalism of the feminine temperament.

The nervous tension of a great war, no doubt, abetted the propagation of oriental cults. The worship of Adonis, as we may be reminded by the famous omen of disaster to the armada setting sail for Sicily, was a considerable public ceremony before the fifth century had ended. In the fourth century active professional participation in such cults was still despised, and Demosthenes can employ the religious activities of Aeschines and his mother effectively to prejudice an Athenian jury. No Greek city, it is true, is known to have admitted the cult of Cybele to the same official status as did Rome, until imperial times, but the records of the association for the worship of the Great Mother at Piraeus during the fourth and third centuries B.C. show us a considerable and flourishing religious community the existence of which was authorised by the State.[1]

---

1. See Graillot, *op. cit.*, pp. 21-24. For the story, which may not be true, of the execution of a propagandist, Suidas and Photius s.v. Μητραγύρτης, Schol. Aristoph. *Plut.*, 431. Self mutilation on the altar of the twelve gods at Athens, Plutarch, *Nicias*, 13. Influence on feminine morals, Aristophanes, *Birds*, 876 and scholia, compare Phintys *ap.* Stobaeus, *Florilegium* (Meineke), iii, p. 63, and law of Eresos, *Classical Review*, xvi, 1902, p. 290. For the parody of initiation into a private mystery cult in Aristophanes' *Clouds* see Dieterich, *Kleine Schriften*, pp 117-124. The mourning for Adonis, Plutarch, *Alcibiades*, 18, *Nicias*, 13; cf. Aristophanes, *Peace*, 420, *Lysistrata*, 387. Aeschines in Demosthenes, *de cor.*, 259. For the community in Piraeus see Foucart, *Ass. rel. en Grèce*, pp. 85-109.

If in Athens of the fifth century B.C., where the civic cults of the state were by no means in the moribund condition of the Roman state-religion at the time when the oriental cults reached Italy, and where the generally high intellectual and aesthetic temper was even less disposed than Roman *dignitas* to look with favour upon crude and repulsive barbarities of ritual, the oriental religions, nevertheless, made steady and invincible progress, it is not surprising that their conquest of the cosmopolitan society of the Roman Empire was rapid and complete. Even their repulsive or intellectually degraded features lent them a certain fascination, and, as we have already noticed, the incomprehensible itself challenges esoteric interpretation. Actions obviously so indefensible by common sense or by decent feeling as the public self-emasculation of the Galli inevitably provoked an idea that they must necessarily have some hidden and mystical justification.

The general causes for the victory of the oriental religions in the Graeco-Roman world are not difficult to discern. The value of, what we may call, the city-state religion had naturally disappeared with the particular form of small political community, out of the needs of which it had grown, and the needs of which it had satisfied. The cults of the city-state had been, in the main, expressions of civic or corporate religious duty, restricted in their horizon to the welfare of a particular race or community, or to that of its essential social or political sub-divisions. The participation of the individual in acts of worship was primarily conditioned by his membership of the community, *i.e.* his status as a citizen or his position as the head of a household. But the conditions favourable to the continued existence of political life organised upon the small scale of the city-state were already passing in Greece at the beginning of the fifth century, and it was a necessary consequence that the form of religion, which was an integral part of the structure of that particular type of social organisation, should decline before the rival attractions of other forms which were adapted to what was quite a different view of life and the world. I emphasise this point, at the risk of irrelevance, for I cannot help thinking that it is not always appreciated how early those religious influences, the results of which we see fully developed under the Roman Empire, began to be effectively operative in the Mediterranean world.

Unlike the cults of the city-state, the oriental religions were at once cosmopolitan and individualistic. Their message was not restricted to any particular political, racial, or social group, and their concern was with the relation of the individual soul to its God. Their ritual, too, differed essentially from the glad, sociable feasts presided over by a secular, civic magistrate, which, upon the whole, are typical of the older worship of the Olympian gods. From their Eastern homes the new cults had brought with them the appeal of sensuous pageantry and of solemn emotional ritual performed by, or under the direction of an official and consecrated, professional priesthood.

The impressive external features of their public ritual appealed to popular imagination, and lent them dignity and importance. The daily services at definite times of day produced the psychological effects of regular reiteration, and helped to establish them as a solemn but integral part of the recurring daily round. The members of the sacerdotal hierarchy were distinguished from laymen by the majestic garb of their calling, and in things spiritual they were vested with an authority which no layman, whatever his rank or worldly status, could challenge. Again, the great processional pageantry of popular festivals, like that of the carnival of the Hilaria on March 25th in honour of the Great Mother, or the Isiac " Launching of the Ships," which has been so vividly described by Apuleius, deeply impressed the popular imagination.[1]

Not less impressive were the ritual surroundings and the character of the rites themselves in the esoteric services of the initiated members. The ascending grades of initiation established a disciplined hierarchy of holiness, of which the higher grades were reached by stages of progressive trial and revelation, and the meetings for sacramental communion with God conducted in some subterranean church, like the basilica recently discovered in Rome, the symbolic paintings on the walls of which heightened through the sense of sight the excitement which was evoked by instrumental music, met and stimulated a lively religious emotion.

---

1.   For the *Hilaria* see Graillot, *op. cit.*, pp. 131-136.   For the *Ploiaphesia*, Apuleius, *Met.*, xi, 8 foll.

The doctrines of these oriental religions were, further, not without an intellectual attraction. They offered an apparently rational and complete account of the universe, which served as an adequate explanation for such questionings as to Why and How as were likely to perplex the ordinary man. With them from the East had come the tradition of learning as a sacerdotal prerogative, and the comfortable doctrine of respect for the authority of spiritual pastors, whose infallible wisdom was based upon the unchallengeable claim of access to those super-natural sources of information, which are open to holiness alone. From the East, too, had come the note of self-abasement, the deep consciousness of sin and the conception of holiness, which are characteristic of these cults.[1]

Purification both ritual and spiritual played a dominant rôle among the means to grace. Indeed the sense of sin and the gratification of self-abasement not seldom found their expression in penance and self-torture. You will remember the unfortunate devotee of Isis crawling in mid-winter on her bleeding knees to break the ice and then to immerse herself three times in the Tiber, whom Juvenal, rather characteristically, includes amongst his examples of feminine depravity.[2]

The central action of the ritual of many of the mysteries consisted in the mourning of the dying god, *e.g.*, Adonis, Attis or Osiris, followed by the ecstatic celebration of his resurrection.

---

1. On the appeal offered by the oriental religions see Cumont, *Les Rel. Orientales*, pp. 45–69.
2. Juvenal, *Sat.* vi, 522.

As in the Roman Catholic and Orthodox celebrations of the Passion and Easter, the dying god
was often represented in effigy. The scene must
indeed have been extraordinarily like that to be
witnessed to-day in any church in Greece at Easter.
The crowd of worshippers joined with passionate
emotion in the lamentations over the death of
their god, and burst into no less ecstatic joy,
when the still small voice (*lento susurru*) of the
officiating priest announced the glad tidings
of his resurrection.

> " Be of good cheer, ye initiates, for the
>   god is saved.
> For he shall be to you a Salvation from
>   ills."

" We have found him ! We rejoice together "
was the jubilant cry which was raised at the
culminating point of the ritual of the mysteries
of Osiris.[1]

Like the Eleusinian mysteries of the loss and
rediscovery of Persephone by Demeter, this
ritual was originally founded upon a primitive
vegetation magic, the purpose of which was to
celebrate and to ensure the rebirth of nature in
spring after the death of winter. For this type
of ceremony, Sir James Frazer has collected a
vast number of analogies from all stages of culture
and from all parts of the world.[2] But the

---

1. For the εἴδωλον τοῦ μειρακίου see Diodorus, iii, 59, 7, cf. ἔστρωσεν δὲ
καὶ κλίνην εἰς ἀμφότερα τὰ Ἀττίδεια, *I.G.*, ii, 1, No. 622. The description
of the Attis (Adonis ?) service is paraphrased from Firmicus Maternus,
de err. prof. rel. (Ziegler), xxii. For passages describing the burial service
see further Hepding, *Attis*, p. 131. A convenient collection of the liturgical
fragments of the mystery cults, which have survived, will be found at the
end of the second edition of Dieterich, *Eine Mithrasliturgie.*

2. Frazer, *Golden Bough*, 3rd edition, *Attis, Adonis and Osiris.*

promise of Nature's resurrection had early come to be interpreted in terms of the individual worshipper.[1] At any rate the quotation, which has been given above, from the liturgy of Attis or Adonis clearly shows that, at the period with which we are dealing, the resurrection of the god was held to be a guarantee of the resurrection of his worshipper. Thus, upon his tombstone, a wife records her gratitude to the husband who brought her to religion and thereby redeemed her from the lot of death and made her the handmaid of the gods.

> tu me, marite, disciplinarum bono
> puram ac pudicam sorte mortis eximens
> in templa ducis ac famulam diuis dicas.[2]

The idea of death and rebirth, an echo of which we have noticed in the terminology of the philosophers, runs right through the mystery religions. " Deaths, too, and vanishings, do they construct, passages out of life and new births, all riddles and tales to match the changes mentioned."[3] Initiation was itself regarded as a death to sin and a rebirth to righteousness ; the carnal man was buried, the spiritual man was born.

At death, we are told, the soul undergoes an

---

1. First explicitly expressed by Pindar, *Frag.* 137a (102), (Bergk-Schroeder), ὄλβιος ὅστις ἰδὼν κεῖν' εἶσ' ὑπὸ χθόν'· οἶδε μὲν βίου τελευτάν, οἶδεν δὲ διόσδοτον ἀρχάν. For the idea of a new life is a little different from the promise of preferential treatment in another world made in the Homeric Hymn to Demeter.

2. *C.I.L.* vi, 1179d, ll. 22 foll.

3. καὶ φθοράς τινας καὶ ἀφανισμοὺς, τὰς ἀποβιώσεις καὶ παλιγγενεσίας, οἰκεῖα ταῖς εἰρημέναις μεταβολαῖς αἰνίγματα καὶ μυθεύματα περαίνουσι, Plutarch, *de EI ap. Delph.* 9, 389A (Prickard, p. 67).

experience analogous to that of celebrants at the mysteries. There is a real connection both verbal and substantive between death (τελευτᾶν) and initiation (τελεῖσθαι).[1] Thus, inversely, the candidate for initiation is termed by Firmicus Maternus " the man who is about to die," homo moriturus.[2] It is possible that in some initiatory rites this process may even have been dramatically represented. Proclus, for instance, mentions an Orphic rite in which the candidate was buried in the earth up to the neck.[3] A portion of the initiatory ceremony in the mysteries of Cybele was technically called the κατάβασις, and I am inclined to agree with Hepding that the very frequent use of subterranean chapels was in part connected with the symbolism of a descent into the grave.[4] A qualification, it is true, is necessary because in particular cases there were special reasons or justifications which might be put forward. In some of the Neo-Pythagorean

---

1. Themistius or possibly Plutarch (see below p. 272) *ap.* Stobaeus, *Flor.*, 120, 28 (Meineke iv, p. 107). διὸ καὶ τὸ ῥῆμα τῷ ῥήματι καὶ τὸ ἔργον τῷ ἔργῳ τοῦ τελευτᾶν καὶ τελεῖσθαι προσέοικεν, Cf. Plutarch, *de fac. in orb. lun.*, 28, 943. ὃν δ᾽ ἀποθνήσκομεν θάνατον, ὁ μὲν ἐκ τριῶν δύο ποιεῖ τὸν ἄνθρωπον, ὁ δ᾽ ἐκ δυεῖν, καὶ ὁ μὲν ἐστιν ἐν τῇ τῆς Δήμητρος . . . ἐν αὐτῇ τελεῖν, καὶ τοὺς νεκροὺς Ἀθηναῖοι Δημητρείους ὠνόμαζον τὸ παλαιόν. I cannot help thinking that the saying (Proclus, *in Alcib.*, ed. Creuzer, i, p. 40) οὐ γὰρ χρῆ κείνους (sc. θεοὺς) σε βλέπειν πρὶν σῶμα τελεσθῇς has ambiguous associations.

2. Firm. Mat., *de err. prof. rel.* xviii, i, c. " In quodam templo, ut in interioribus partibus homo moriturus possit admitti, dicit : ‘de tympano manducaui, de cymbalo bibi et religionis secreta perdidici.’ This passage Hepding, *op. cit.*, p. 194, rightly connects with the passage of Apuleius discussed below, p. 256. For the connection of apocalyptic visions with initiation see below, p. 259. For analogies of ritual death in initiation ceremonies in the Lower Culture, see de Jong, *op. cit.*, pp. 253 foll.

3. Dieterich, *Eine Mithrasliturgie*, p. 163.

4. Macrobius, *Sat.* i, 217, ritu eorum catabasi ; Hepding, *op. cit.*, p. 194.

sects it is probable that Plato's cave would have been given as the obvious model,[1] and there was a special fitness, as will become apparent, for the performance of Mithraic ceremonies in a cave, similar to that celebrated in Mithraic mythology. But, although these individual reasons might be advanced in special cases, I cannot help thinking that behind them all was a common symbolical congruity with the doctrines of death and rebirth.

The performance of an actual ceremony of rebirth seems almost certainly to be the explanation of a liturgical fragment preserved by Hippolytus, which announces that the goddess has borne a holy son.[2]

This doctrine of rebirth to immortality is indeed cardinal to the pagan as to the Christian, religious thought of the time. As an example, let me quote the conclusion of the Parisian magical papyrus, the very confused and difficult expression of which is also characteristic of the confused, indefinite, and often incoherent mystical thought of the time. " Lord, being born again I perish in that I am being exalted, and having been exalted I die ; from a life-giving birth being born into death I was thus

---

1. For the mystical meaning of subterranean chapels or caves and its connection with the descent and ascent of souls see Porphyry, *de antro nymph.*, 2-3.

2. Hippolytus, *Ref. omn. haer.*, v, 8, 164, 62ff. ἱερὸν ἔτεκε πότνια κοῦρον βριμὼ βριμόν. Hippolytus gives this as Eleusinian, but this is probably a mistake on his part, see Farnell, *Cults of the Greek States*, iii, pp. 177, 183, with whom I agree as against Foucart, that the whole of this passage is very poor evidence for *Eleusinian* practice. For our purposes, however, it matters little whether the ascription to this particular cult is correct.

freed and go the way which Thou hast founded,
as Thou hast ordained and hast made the
mystery." [1]

I have been speaking of the pagan mystery
religions as though they formed a single
undifferentiated whole. Actually, pagan religion
had passed through much the same kind of
development as philosophy. The same passage
through syncretism to a monotheistic basis and
the same development of a large body of doctrine
which was shared in common by all the various
schools, which we saw to be characteristic of
philosophy, is characteristic also of the development of religion in Hellenistic times. All its
various forms made an universal appeal to
mankind at large, and all, whatever the particular
name which was employed in their invocations,
claimed to worship the Great Supreme and
Divine Power in the universe. " I think," said
Celsus, " that it makes no difference whether you
call the Highest Being Zeus or Zen or Adonis
or Sabaoth, or Ammoun like the Egyptians, or
Pappaeus like the Scythians." [2]

Men may attribute different functions to
different gods, and think of godhead as divided.
That is a mistake due to the limitations of human
thought and its expression. The nature of God
is one, though the names of God are many,
just as there is only one sea, though we call
different parts of it by different names, the

---

1. κύριε, πάλιν γενόμενος ἀπογίγνομαι αὐξόμενος καὶ αὐξηθεὶς τελευτῶ,
ἀπὸ γενέσεως ζωογόνου γενόμενος εἰς ἀπογενεσίαν ἀναλυθεὶς πορεύομαι,
ὡς σὺ ἔκτισας, ὡς σὺ ἐνομοθέτησας καὶ ἐποίησας μυστήριον.

2. Origen, c. Cels., v, 41., cf. Maximus Tyrius xvii, 4-5.

Ægean, the Ionian, the Myrtoan Sea, and so on.[1]
In a sense the various cults were rivals rather
than enemies. All were proselytising, and, as
Reitzenstein has remarked, the extension of their
claims to embrace the world helped in each case
to blur their outlines and to lessen the degree of
their original or peculiar individuality.[2]

Each particular deity came to be regarded as a
special form, the authentic form its worshippers
would claim, of the single great deity of Nature,
who inevitably tended to assume a pantheistic
guise. Such formulae as *Hermes omnia solus et ter
unus* or *Isis una quae es omnia* are characteristic
of the time.[3] "Lo, Lucius, I am come moved
by thy supplication," says Isis in the *Metamorphoses* of Apuleius, "I, nature's mother, mistress
of all the elements, the first-begotten offspring of
the ages, of deities mightiest, queen of the dead,
first of heaven's denizens, in whose aspect are
blent the aspects of all gods and goddesses. With

---

1. Ἀγνοοῦσιν γάρ οἶμαι, ὡς θεοῖς πᾶσιν εἷς νόμος καὶ βίος καὶ
τρόπος, οὐ διῃρημένος, οὐδὲ στασιωτικός· ἄρχοντες πάντες, ἡλικιῶται
πάντες, σωτῆρες πάντες, ἰσοτιμίᾳ καὶ ἰσηγορίᾳ συνόντες τὸν πάντα
χρόνον· ὧν μία μὲν ἡ φύσις, πολλὰ δὲ τὰ ὀνόματα. ὑπὸ γὰρ ἀμαθίας
αὐτῶν τὰς ὠφελείας τὰς ἑαυτῶν ἕκαστοι ἐπονομάζομεν ἄλλος ἄλλῃ
κλήσει θεοῦ. καθάπερ καὶ τὰ μέρη τῆς θαλάττης Αἰγαῖον τοῦτο, Ἰώνιον
ἐκεῖνο, Μυρτῶον ἄλλο, Κρησαῖον ἄλλο· ἡ δ' ἐστὶν μία, ὁμογενής, καὶ
ὁμοπαθής, καὶ συγκεκραμένη. οὕτω καὶ τ' ἀγαθόν, ἓν ὂν καὶ ὅμοιον αὐτῷ
καὶ ἴσον πάντοθεν, ὑπὸ ἀσθενείας τῆς πρὸς αὐτὸ καὶ ἀγνωσίας ταῖς
δόξαις, διαιρούμεθα. Maximus Tyrius, xxxix, 5. Cf. Plutarch, *de Is. et
Os.* 67, 377F.

2. Reitzenstein, *Hell. Myst. Rel.*, p. 6. Oxyrhyncus Papyrus 1380 contains a list of the cult sites of Isis in the whole world. On the back of the
same papyrus is the claim of the worshipper of an obscure sect which inevitably
reminds Reitzenstein (p. 70) of *Philippians* ii, 11. Ἑλληνὶς δὲ πᾶσα
γλῶσσα τὴν σὴν λαλήσει ἱστορίαν καὶ πᾶς Ἕλλην ἀνὴρ τὸν τοῦ Φθᾶ
σεβήσεται Ἰμούθην. For Imouthes son of Ptah possibly originally an
historical person Imhotp, Reitzenstein, *Poimandres*, pp. 120 foll.

3. See Reitzenstein, *Hell. Myst. Rel.*, pp. 15 foll.

my rod I rule the shining heights of heaven, the
health-giving breezes of the sea, the mournful
silence of the underworld." [1]

Just as in philosophy, so in religion, the average
man was eclectic.[2] While the sects, like the
schools, might jealously maintain distinctions, all
were in essentials similar and shaded into each
other. It was not at all uncommon for an
individual to undergo initiation into a number of
various sects, a phenomenon which I have somewhere read to have been characteristic also of
German mysticism of the sixteenth century.
Thus Plutarch's friend, Clea, to whom the tract
on *Isis and Osiris* was addressed, was head of the
college of Thyiads at Delphi and was also an
initiate in the Egyptian cult. The inscriptions,
indeed, provide many examples of an individual
reaching the highest grade in more than one
religious community. Thus a man who dedicates
an altar to the Great Gods, the Mother of the
Gods and Attis, was at once Pater Patrum Dei
Solis inuicti Mithrae, Hierofanta Hecates, Dei
Liberi Archibucolus, taurobolio criobolioque in
aeternum renatus.[3]

A claim to precedence was sometimes made by
a particular cult upon the grounds that the parti-

1. Apuleius, *Met.*, xi, 5. Compare the hymn of praise in xi, 25.
2. Apuleius, *Apology*, 55, declares " pleraque initia in Graecia participaui
. . . at ego ut dixi, multiiuga sacra et plurimos ritus et uarias caerimonias
studio ueri et officio erga deos didici." Cf. *C.I.L.* vi, 1179d, ll. 15 and 25.
diuumque numen multiplex doctus coles . . . te teste cunctis imbuor
mysteriis. Hence it was held that the great master Pythagoras had been
initiated into all the religious mysteries of all countries. See Julian, *Or.*
vii, 237a, Iamblichus, *Vita Pyth.*, 3, 14 and 4, 18.
3. Plutarch, *de Is. et Os.*, 35, 364E; *C.I.L.*, vi., 510. Cf. *ibid.* Nos.
504, 507, 509, 1778. See further Dieterich *Eine Mithrasliturgie*, p. 210.

cular name of God employed by its members
was that under which aboriginal man had worshipped Him, and that, therefore, this was alone
the true and authentic name.   Thus in Apuleius,
Isis declares " the whole earth worships my
godhead, one and individual, under many a
changing shape, with varied rites and by many
divine names.   There the Phrygians, first-born
of men, call me the Mother of the Gods that
dwells at Pessinus ; there the Athenians sprung
from the soil they till, know me as Cecropian
Minerva," and so on.   The catalogue concludes,
" the Egyptians, mighty in ancient lore, honour
me with my peculiar rites and call me by my
true name, Isis the Queen." [1]   This tendency to
base a peculiar claim upon the antiquity of the
cult as being the genuine and original *Urreligion*
was, of course, strengthened by the importance
given to names by the current nominalism of
religion and magic, and also by that increasing
respect for traditional authority and the wisdom
of the remote past, which has been discussed
above.   This attitude of mind again explains
the pains at which the Fathers put themselves to
maintain the priority of the Old Testament
dispensation to the Greek poets and sages, e.g.,
that Moses antedated Homer.[2]

---

1. Apuleius, *Met.* xi, 5.   Cf. the invocation quoted by Hippolytus, v, 4.
Again, " as for Isis, all mankind have her and are well acquainted with her
and the other gods about her : and although they had not anciently learned
to call some of them by their Egyptian names, yet they, from the very first,
both knew and honoured the power which belongs to every one of them,"
Plutarch, *de Is. et Os.*, 66, 377D.

2. This matter constantly recurs in Christian apologetics, e.g. Tertullian,
Apol. 19, *ib.* 47.   Much of the " borrowing " controversy in the Fathers
really turns upon it.

Characteristic of the organisation of these
missionary mystic cults was the formation of
comparatively small associations of members
devoted to the service of a particular deity,
similar in their nature and purpose to the Orphic
brotherhoods. The head of such an association
was the spiritual father of those whom he
instructed and initiated, while the members
were brothers in a spiritual family. For this
conception of the community as a spiritual family
was by no means confined to the Mithraic
associations, which are discussed in the next
chapter.[1] In matters of this kind, it does not
seem to me at all improbable that more than one
converging influence may have helped to bring
about the result. I find no difficulty in agreeing
with Hepding,[2] that initiation into a fraternity of
a cosmopolitan cult is in a sense analogous to,
and may be a survival from, initiation into the
religious ceremonies of a restricted primitive
social or political group. Under the conditions
of cosmopolitan systems of religion, the religious
world had been, so to say, cut off from the secular
world. Initiation is still initiation into a limited
society, though the group now belongs exclusively
to the religious sphere, and not to that of social
or political organisation. But I should no less
agree with Reitzenstein,[3] that the relationship

---

1. For examples see Hepding, *Attis*, pp. 178, 187, and Nock, *Classical
Review*, xxxviii, pp. 105 foll. Origen denies that it was true of any Christian
sect, as Celsus had alleged, that " he who impresses the seal is called father
and he who is sealed is called young man and son," *c. Cels.*, vi, 27.

2. Hepding, *Attis*, pp. 186 foll.

3. Reitzenstein, *Hell. Myst. Rel.*, pp. 27, 117, quoting Diodorus, i, 73, 5,
and ii, 29, 4.

between priest and initiate was at least in part
an inheritance from the genuinely hereditary
priesthoods of the ancient East, in which the
sacred lore was handed down from father to
son. This spiritual relationship, whatever its
origin, was close and, perhaps inevitably, proved
capable of mystic extensions and difficult con-
foundings of persons. The Mithraic initiate, for
example, is the son of the Pater Patrum of the
association into which he has been admitted by
him; he is also a son of Mithras, though by
acts of worship he may be made one with
Mithras. Similarly Helios may be regarded as
a son of Mithras, but yet Helios-Mithras are
mystically one; yet again Mithras is an intermediary between men and his Father, God, with
whom he is also mystically identical.[1]

The general tendency towards the formation
of small religious associations of this type, the
members of which stand in a close spiritual
relationship to its head, was almost inevitably
bound to affect the organisation of the new
religion of Christianity. It is interesting to find
the danger already serious in the Apostolic age.
For the type of fraternity, which we have been
discussing, was clearly the model which was
followed by the Corinthians, who thereby, as
St. Paul clearly perceived, at once threatened
the unity of Christianity and imperilled the

---

1. For this *unio mystica* see below, p. 294. The relation of the divine
bringer of *Gnosis* to the intermediary instructor, or his to the human pupil,
is again habitually expressed in these terms in Hermetic writings, e.g.,
αἴνιγμά μοι λέγεις, ὦ πάτερ, καὶ οὐχ ὡς πατὴρ υἱῷ διαλέγῃ—τοῦτο
τὸ γένος, ὦ τέκνον, οὐ διδάσκεται, ἀλλ', ὅταν θέλῃ, ὑπὸ τοῦ θεοῦ
ἀναμιμνήσκεται, *Corpus Herm.* xiii (xiv) 2, Reitzenstein, *Poimandres*, p. 340.

unrivalled authority of its Founder. "Now this I mean, that each one of you saith, I am of Paul ; and I of Apollos ; and I of Cephas ; and I of Christ. Is Christ divided ? Was Paul crucified for you ? Or were ye baptised into the name of Paul ? I thank God that I baptised none of you save Crispus and Gaius, lest any man should say that ye were baptised into my name." [1] Indeed, the more one becomes familiar with the pagan religious thought of the day, the more evident is the real danger of what may be loosely called the Gnostic tendencies to the continued existence of Christianity. The doctrinal danger is evident enough. Even in a writer like Clement one is continually struck with how dim, at points, becomes the dividing line between Christian Platonism and pagan religious philosophy. But, further, supremely dangerous from the point of view of the Church as an institution struggling not only to maintain the individuality of its doctrines but also its corporate entity in opposition to a pagan world, was the inevitable tendency of cults organised in this way to multiply by subdivision into independent groups, each of which followed its own line of development in the direction determined by the personal idiosyncrasies of its "Father." However much the consequent loss of spiritual values may be regretted, the hardening of the conception of orthodoxy and the stern imposition of doctrinal

---

1. *I Corinthians*, i, 12 foll. With the sects of Apollos and of Cephas compare the titles of Rhodian pagan religious societies, Παναθαναϊσταν Λινδιασταν των συν Γαϊωι . . . . . Ἀγαθοδαιμονιασταν Φιλωνείων, *I.G.* xii, 1, No. 161, Διοσαταβυριασταν Εὐφρανορίων των συν Ἀθηναίω Κνιδίω, *I.G.* xii, 1, No. 937.

discipline was an absolute necessity to which, in fact, there could have been no practical alternative. Had it not been achieved, Christianity would have become a mere aggregate of small sects united but by the vaguest common denominator.

For, like the other *collegia*, which we briefly considered in an earlier lecture, the pagan religious fraternities were normally of small size, and they were not interconnected in a single all-embracing organisation.[1] We may also notice that as in the other *collegia*, the social distinctions of the outside world had no meaning within the doors of the religious meeting place. The slave member left his slavery outside; inside was a world of completely different values and of distinctions which were determined not by worldly rank, but by religious attainment. It was a new world into which the initiate was reborn.

Not a little of the religious feeling, which was aroused and satisfied by initiation, may be recaptured from the eleventh book of the *Metamorphoses* of Apuleius. As this is the only relatively complete continuous account of such an initiation which we possess, I will venture to summarise it. Fortunately the full narrative is very easily accessible, even to those who would find the Latin of Apuleius difficult, in the excellent translation of Professor H. E. Butler, of which I have made free use.

You will remember that an incautious experi-

---

1. For the more apparent than real exception in the cult of Cybele see above, p. 58, note.

ment with magical ointments had ended in an unfortunate mistake, by which Lucius, the hero of the novel, instead of growing wings was turned into an ass.   In this shape, he undergoes a series of comical and tragical misadventures, until at length, after purification in the sea, he invokes the goddess Isis.   In response to his invocation, she manifests herself to the ass, and tells him how to pluck the roses which will be carried in her procession, and promises that by eating them he will regain his human shape.   " But thou must remember surely and keep hidden in thine inmost soul this—that the rest of thy life's course to the term of thy last breath is dedicate to me " (cap. 6).   The great procession is then described ; the ass successfully attains the roses, and Lucius recovers his human shape.   Then one of the priests becomes filled with the goddess and prophesies.   I will quote the conclusion of his utterance, which illustrates ideas which we have already noticed, the edification of the faithful by miracles, which become the subject matter of a *hieros logos* or *aretalogy* of the god,[1] the release through a saviour deity from the control of Fortune, and once more the vocation to enrolment in the army of the goddess.   " Let those behold that are not of the faith, let them behold and know their error.   Lo ! Lucius, freed from his former woes by the providence of mighty Isis, triumphs rejoicing over Fortune his foe.

But that thou mayest be the safer and the more perfectly armed, enrol thy name in this sacred

---

1. Upon this see Reitzenstein, *Hell. Wundererzählungen.*

soldiery [1]—for 'tis but a little while since thou wast summoned to take the solemn oath—and dedicate thyself to the ministry of our faith and take upon thee the voluntary yoke of service. For when thou hast begun to be the servant of the goddess, then shalt thou perceive more fully the greatness of thy liberty " (cap. 15).

Lucius then takes up his abode in the temple precincts, and lives with the priests. He receives visions summoning him to serve the goddess; " but I, though my desire for initiation burned strong, was held back by a certain religious awe and terror, for I had often been told that the service of the faith was hard, that the laws of chastity and abstinence were not easy to obey " (cap. 19). In spite of these fears, however, his longing for initiation increases, and he urgently entreats the high priest, who insists upon the necessity of divine vocation; only those whom the goddess summons may be initiated.[2] But he " with kindly and gentle words, such as parents use to check the precocious desires of their children, put off my insistence." The language is of course appropriate to their spiritual relationship of father and son. " There are none," he said, " of all the order of priests of Isis so abandoned in spirit or so given over to death as to venture rashly and sacrilegiously to undertake the service of the goddess without her express

---

1. On the *militia sacra* see below, p. 302.
2. Cf. Pausanias, x, 32, 3. The temple of Isis at Tithorea and the healing sanctuary of the nether gods in the cities on the Maeander may only be entered by persons divinely warned to do so in a dream. Isis seems to have been peculiarly fond of sending messages to her worshippers in dreams, see Juvenal, vi, 530.

command and thus to contract mortal guilt
. . . the very act of dedication is regarded as a
voluntary death and an imperilling of life,
inasmuch as the goddess is wont to select those
whose term of life is near to its close, and who
stand on the threshold of the night, and are
moreover men to whom the mighty mysteries
of the goddess may be safely committed.
These men the goddess by her providence brings
to new birth and places once more at the start of
a new race of life." You will notice in this
speech the strong influence of the idea that
initiation consists in a death and rebirth.

Eventually the goddess reveals both to Lucius
and to her high priest Mithras, whose name
suggests a syncretism of cults, that the initiation
is to take place. After morning service the
priest " brought forth from the hidden places
of the shrine certain books with titles written in
undecipherable letters." Lucius is then taken
to the baths which are ordained for neophytes
and is baptised. " After he had first prayed to
the gods to be gracious to me, the priest
besprinkled me with purest water and cleansed
me." This ceremony took up the greater part
of the morning ; the candidate then returned to
the temple and was seated at the feet of the
goddess and instructed in certain secrets which
must not be revealed.[1] This instruction con-

---

1. The *sacramentum* or oath of fealty taken by candidates at such initiations normally included the promise not to reveal the mystical secrets about
to be imparted to any save the initiated. καὶ τότε δοκιμάσαντες δέσμιον
εἶναι τῆς ἁμαρτίας μυοῦσι τὸ τέλειον τῶν κακῶν δήσαντες μήτε ἐξειπεῖν
μήτε τῷ τυχόντι μεταδοῦναι, εἰ μὴ ὁμοίως δουλωθείη, Hippolytus, *Ref.
proem*, 2, 9. Cf. tu pius mystes sacris/teletis reperta mentis arcano premis,
C.I.L. vi, 1779d, 13. See further below, p. 302.

cluded with an injunction to abstain for ten days
from all pleasures of the table, to eat no living
thing, and to drink no wine.

At sunset of the tenth day of this probationary
ascetic purification, the ceremonies of the
initiation proper commenced. The candidate
first received the encouragement of a full congregation of the faithful. " On all sides crowds of
the holy initiates flocked round me, each after the
ancient rite honouring me with diverse gifts."
Then all the uninitiated were excluded; a
new linen robe, which had not hitherto been
worn by man, was placed upon the candidate
and he was led by the high priest into the very
heart of the holy place.

The actual ceremonies which took place during
that night, Apuleius is not at liberty to describe
in plain terms. " I drew nigh," says Lucius, " to
the confines of death, and having trodden the
threshold of Proserpine, I was borne through all
the elements and returned to earth again; I
saw the sun gleaming with bright splendour at
dead of night; I approached the gods above and
the gods below, and worshipped them face to
face. Behold I have told thee things of which,
though thou hast heard them, thou must yet
know naught."

Inevitably this veiled statement has provoked
much speculation.[1] The general character, however, of the experience seems to be clear enough,

---

1. The passage is elaborately discussed by de Jong clause by clause. A
good deal of the material which he has collected from modern spiritualism
and psychical research, interesting though it may be in itself, would
appear of doubtful relevance.

and harmonises, as we shall presently see, with the allusions which pagan writers permit themselves to make to similar experiences. The opening reminds us of the *homo moriturus* and the doctrine of the ritual death of the carnal man. Now the testimony is unanimous that the earlier stages of the initiatory ceremony consisted of terrifying experiences causing shock and consternation (κατάπληξις). Thus Celsus compared the Christian's preaching of the eternal punishment of unbelievers to the apparitions and terrors (φάσματα καὶ δείματα) of Dionysiac initiation ceremonies.[1] Consternation (κατάπληξις) was produced " partly by what was said and partly by what was shown," and " symbols of certain underworld spirits were displayed, and visions which violently disturbed those who were being initiated." [2]

That some kind of vision was produced I have, for my own part, no doubt whatever. But since Lobeck's very proper exposition of the fantastic follies of Sainte Croix, many scholars have adopted an extremely sceptical attitude towards the performance at all of any dramatic ritual to impress the initiates. It is also true that the result of the excavations at Eleusis has shown that anything in the nature of subterranean machinery or of elaborate theatrical properties in the Eleusinian mysteries is out of the question. I should, nevertheless, agree with Maass and Foucart that scepticism may be pushed too far.

---

1. διόπερ ἐξομοιοῖ ἡμᾶς τοῖς ἐν ταῖς Βακχικαῖς τελεταῖς τὰ φάσματα καὶ δείματα προεισάγουσιν. Origen, c. Cels., iv, 10, cf. viii, 48.
2. See passages from Proclus quoted below, p. 271.

The negative evidence of the omission of payment
for stage properties in the accounts has been
overstated by Farnell, for as Foucart has pointed
out the inscription is not complete, and the
possible general arrangement of the Hall of
Initiation as suggested by Foucart, though
necessarily purely hypothetical is at least plausible.
As to the means employed to produce illusion
we are really guessing in the dark, but that an
illusion was produced it seems to me impossible
to doubt. The passage in Philostratus which
indicates the use of a theatre for cult purposes,
is not necessarily relevant to the discussion of
initiation ; but Dio's reference to " some mystic
inner room of marvellous beauty and size, where
he sees many spectacles (θεάματα) and hears many
voices of like character, and ten thousand other
things happen to him in an alternation of light
and darkness," is surely explicit. Perhaps the
marvellous size of the room is rhetorical exaggeration or possibly the result of an illusion produced
by the ceremony with its alternation of light and
darkness upon the highly-strung and nervous
initiate. If there was no palatial staging at
Eleusis, there was certainly no grandiose
machinery in the comparatively small chapels of
Mithras. But to admit that is not to concede
the sceptic's contention. If for a moment we
consider how little dependent is great tragic
art upon stage realism for producing its
effect, or even how the illusion and consequent
emotion in the spectator is not heightened
but destroyed by the distraction of elaborate
theatrical machinery, we shall surely feel

that much of the sceptic's argument is irrelevant.[1]

The terrible sights, which so affected the initiate, appear to have included a revelation of the Lower World. A passage in Lucian would seem to support this view. In the *Cataplus*, it will be remembered, Charon lands his passengers on the farther shore, and the souls are turned over to Hermes. It is pitch dark but Micyllus and Cyniscus remain undaunted and irreverent. "Very good," says Micyllus, "give me your hand— I suppose you have been admitted to the mysteries of Eleusis ? That must have been something like this, I should think ? " " Pretty much," replies Cyniscus. " Look, here comes a torch- bearer : a grim and forbidding dame. A Fury, perhaps ? " Like Lucius, Cyniscus when being initiated had descended to Hades and had drawn nigh to the confines of death. I am further inclined to agree with the suggestion of de Jong that the apocalyptic visions in philosophic myth, of which Plato's *Republic* provides the great prototype, are, as it were, literary analogues to the sights witnessed by the initiate in the mysteries. To the examples mentioned by de Jong I would add the vision of Timarchus, when

---

1. Ernst Maass, *Orpheus*, pp. 84, 93, Philostratus, *Vit. Apoll.* iv, 21, 140, Dio. Chrys., xii, 33 (von Arnim i, p. 163). Criticism of Farnell, Foucart, *Mystères d' Eleusis*, p. 404. Possible, though I hesitate to write probable, arrangement of *telesterion*, Foucart, *op. cit.*, p. 413. I cannot agree with Foucart's main theory of the Egyptian origin of the Eleusinian mysteries, and in the main Farnell's account of Eleusis (*Cults of the Greek States*, iii, pp 180 foll.) is in my opinion much the sounder. Indeed, with particular statements of Farnell I should find it difficult to quarrel, but the general impression conveyed by his discussion of the problem of the dramatic element is, perhaps, over-sceptical though I may exaggerate the difference, which is one mainly of degree, between our respective views.

he visited the oracle of Trophonius, as narrated by Plutarch. It is, however, the story of Thespesius, which shows most similarity in detail to mystery doctrine. The oracle that " he will live better, when he has died " (563D), the change of name from Aridaeus to Thespesius (564C) and the corresponding change of character as the result of his experience (563D), the gracious and familiar spiritual guide and the lonely isolation in which he faces the terrors of witnessing the place of torment (567A), the sudden appearance of a bright light from which the divine voice announces that the soul of Nero has performed its allotted punishment (567F), all these seem to be echoes of an initiate's experiences.[1]

After treading the threshold of Proserpine, Lucius was borne through all the elements and returned to earth again : et calcato Proserpinae limine, per omnia uectus elementa remeaui. This rite has been explained by Graillot, upon the basis of practices in the cult of Cybele, as consisting of successive baptisms or purifications by water, mud, and fire.[2] But the actual words of Apuleius are surely a remarkable way, even making allowance for mystical obscurity, of describing a ceremony of this kind, and I have little doubt that this explanation is mistaken. Far more probably, what Lucian seeks to convey, is an enactment by the neophyte of the journey of the soul through the planetary spheres. Of

---

1. Lucian, *Cataplus*, 22, 644 ; de Jong, *op. cit.*, pp. 300 foll. ; Timarchus in Plutarch, *de genio Socratis* ; Thespesius in Plutarch, *de ser. num. vind.*, 22 foll.

2. Graillot, *op. cit.*, p. 179.

this doctrine of the soul's return we shall have more to say anon, but that at least in Mithraism it was in some way dramatically enacted we have the definite evidence of Origen, who mentions the stage property of the ladder, with gates made of different metals to correspond with the different planets.[1]

Now this performance of the return journey of the soul, it may be pointed out, is really but a reduplication of the eschatological vision of Hades. If I am right in believing that in the fifth century B.C. a vision of the Lower World was a part of the experience of the initiate, and the allusions in Aristophanes' *Frogs*, though they cannot perhaps be called conclusive, seem to me to support this view, what I imagine to have happened is this. Originally in the Greek mysteries a revelation of Hades was an integral part of the ceremonies of initiation. Then the astral theory, as we have seen, came in and dominated Graeco-Roman eschatology. The geography of Hades itself was transferred to the Heavens and the theory of descent and ascent of the soul through the planetary spheres became the commonly received doctrine. In consequence the vision of the new purely astral eschatology was grafted on to the old subterranean eschatology.

1. See below, p. 298. If we accept the view that the return journey of the soul through the astral spheres was enacted also in other than Mithraic mysteries, the appeal of Cicero, *Tusc.*, i, 12, 29 : reminiscere, quoniam es initiatus, quae tradantur mysteriis, though intelligible enough upon either view, perhaps gains in point. The context deals it is true with apotheosis, but rather noticeably with *astral* apotheosis, e.g., a few lines earlier in 12, 28 : totum prope coelum, ne pluris persequar, nonne humano genere completum est ?

The sudden effulgence of a bright light in
Apuleius' account immediately precedes the
meeting of the gods face to face, and this harmonises with our other accounts. To the bright
light from which the Voice announces that
Nero's torment is over, we have alluded above ;
Dio, it will be remembered, spoke of alternations
of light and darkness (σκότους τε καὶ φωτὸς ἐναλλὰξ
αὐτῶι φαινομένων). At least in some Mithraic
mysteries it would appear that the neophytes
were blindfolded during the earlier stages of the
ceremony.[1] The illumination (ἔλλαμψις, compare
the Christian φωτισμός), the sudden bursting of a
great light, occurs at the moment of revelation,
when the consummation of the religious experience is realised in the union with God. " For
to those who make themselves fitted for it," says
Proclus, the neo-Platonist, who is particularly
fond of using the language and analogies of
mysteries to express his philosophical ideas, " there
happens the illumination from God, which is
happiness." [2]   " And as in the most holy initiations
they say that the mystae first of all meet with

---

1. Pseudo-Augustine, *Quaest. uet. et nov. test.*, Migne, *Patr. Lat.*, xxxiv,
p. 2214, see below, p. 300 note.

2. Τοῖς γὰρ ἐπιτηδείους ἑαυτοὺς ποιήσασιν ἡ θεόθεν ἔλλαμψις
παραγίνεται, ἥτις εὐδαιμονία ἐστι, Proclus, *in Alc.* (Creuzer) ii, p. 123.
πᾶν γὰρ τῶν θεῶν γένος τοιοῦτον, ἐν δὲ τοῖς δαίμοσι κατ' οὐσίαν, ἐν δὲ
ταῖς ψυχαῖς κατ' ἔλλαμψιν, *ibid.*, i, p. 65 in a celebrated passage in the
Phaedrus, (250) Plato has in mind the light which signalises the consummation
of the mysteries. ὁλόκληρα δὲ καὶ ἁπλᾶ καὶ ἀτρεμῆ καὶ εὐδαίμονα
φάσματα μυούμενοί τε καὶ ἐποπτεύοντες ἐν αὐγῇ καθαρᾷ, καθαροὶ
ὄντες καὶ ἀσήμαντοι τούτου, ὃ νῦν σῶμα περιφέροντες ὀνομάζομεν,
ὀστρέου τρόπον δεδεσμευμένοι. Compare also Plutarch, *quomodo in uirt.
sent. profect.*, 10, 81E, ὁ δ'ἐντὸς γενόμενος καὶ φῶς μέγα ἰδών, οἷον
ἀνακτόρων ἀνοιγομένων, ἕτερον λαβὼν σχῆμα καὶ σιωπὴν καὶ θάμβος,
ὥσπερ θεῷ τῷ λόγῳ ταπεινὸς ξυνέπεται καὶ κεκοσμημένος.

projections of the gods of many forms and many shapes (πολυειδέσι καὶ πολυμόρφοις τῶν θεῶν προβεβλημένοις γένεσιν ἀπαντᾶν), and then entering fearlessly and protected by the initiations, suddenly they receive into their bosoms the divine illumination itself, and naked—as they would say—are partakers with the divine." [1]

Upon the morning after this nocturnal experience, which we have been compelled to discuss at such length, Lucius was clad in the mystic robe embroidered with the figures of beasts, which is known to the initiates as the cloak of Olympus[2]; then with a flaming torch in his hand and a rayed crown of palm leaves upon his head, he was "set up like to the image of a god," upon a dais beside the image of the goddess. The curtain, behind which this had taken place, was then dropped, [3] and he was revealed to the crowd of worshippers thronging the temple. It is, in fact, an epiphany of the initiate as divine; his recent mystical experience has brought him face to face with god, and has made him one with god.

This enthronement of the initiate (θρόνωσις or θρονισμός), as it was technically called, for

---

1. Proclus quoted by Ernest Maass, *op. cit.*, p. 15, note 17. I have been unable to identify the passage. The concluding words run αὐτὴν τὴν θείαν ἔλλαμψιν ἀκραιφνῶς ἐγκολπίζεσθαι καὶ γυμνῆτας—ὡς ἄν ἐκεῖνοι φαῖεν—τοῦ Θείου μεταλαμβάνειν. Maass' γυμνῆτας for γυμνίτας in the sense *nudos* must be right. In some initiatory ceremonies the first action was to strip the neophyte of his clothes, Aristophanes, *Clouds*, 497 and schol; clearly a *rite de séparation*. For a parallel in early Christian baptismal ritual see Anrich, *op. cit.*, pp. 200 foll.

2. Compare the beast-embroidered robe worn by the Lion grade of Mithraic initiates, Pophyry, *de abst.* iv, 16.

3. Compare the arrangements for a curtain in front of the cult statuary in Mithraic chapels (see below p. 299).

the practice of which Plato supplies the earliest
literary reference, seems to have been a usual
feature of the initiatory rites of more than one
mystery cult. Dio speaks of "what they call
the enthronement in which the officiants seat
those who are being initiated and dance round
them in a circle." Graillot is doubtless right in
explaining that the two thrones which are
mentioned in an inscription from the Piræus,
are intended for use in this rite, one by the goddess,
in this case Cybele, and one by the newly-initiated
candidate, who is placed, like Lucius, beside her.
For the adoration of the person, who by ritual
action has been made one with god, we may
further compare the well-known account by
Prudentius of how the congregation adore the
gory person of one who has undergone the
baptism of bull's blood or *taurobolium*.[1]

Three days of celebration of this spiritual
birthday [2] followed, upon the last of which the
proceedings ended with a solemn breaking of the
initiate's fast. For several days longer Lucius
enjoyed " the ineffable delight of dwelling with
the image of the goddess " and then returned
to Rome. His fortunes there, how he worshipped

---

1. Plato *Euthydemus*, 277D, Dio, xii, 33 (von Arnim, i, p. 163) εἰ
καθάπερ εἰώθασιν ἐν τῶι καλουμένωι θρονισμῶι καθίσαντες τοὺς
μυουμένους οἱ τελοῦντες κύκλωι περιχορεύσειαν. See also Farnell, *Cults*,
iii, p. 301. *C.I.A.*, ii, 1, No. 624, στρωννύειν θρόνους δύο ὡς καλλίστους,
περιτιθέναι δὲ ταῖς φιαληφόροις καὶ ταῖς περὶ τὴν θεὸν οὔσαις ἐν τῷ
ἀγερμῶι κόσμον, discussed Graillot, *op. cit.*, p. 183, whose explanation
seems to me more probable than that of Foucart (*Ass. rel.*, p. 97) that the
second throne was for a cult image of Attis. Nunc inquinatum talibus
contagiis/ tabo recentis sordidum piaculi/ omnes salutant atque adorant
eminus, Prudentius, *Peristeph.*, x, 1048.

2. Similarly the day upon which a man underwent the *taurobolium* became
his spiritual birthday (*natalicium*), see Graillot, *op. cit.*, p. 172.

at the temple of Isis in the Campus Martius, "a stranger it is true to the temple, but no stranger to the faith," and how the call came to him to be initiated in Rome into the mysteries of Osiris, cannot detain us further. But we may perhaps notice before leaving him the prayer of thanksgiving and farewell to the Goddess, which preceded his departure from Corinth. The invocation emphasises the universal character of the goddess' power. Her sway is over life and death; heaven and hell, the earth, the sea, the sky are alike beneath her control. She is the mistress of capricious Fortune and of inexorable Destiny, which men had learned no less to fear. Her saving hand unbinds even the inextricable weft of Fate; she assuages the tempests of Fortune and restrains the baleful orbits of the stars. "My voice is too poor in utterance to tell what I feel concerning Thy majesty. Nay, had I a thousand mouths, a thousand tongues, and everlasting continuance of unwearied speech, it would be all too little. Therefore will I strive to do all that a poor, yet faithful servant may. I will guard the memory of Thy divine countenance and of Thy most holy godhead deep hidden within my heart's inmost shrine, and their image shall be with me for ever."

I have tried to indicate the nature of the external appeal which these mystery religions made to the Græco-Roman world, and something of the character of the initiatory rites and of the ideas which they expressed. What are we to make of it all ? Are these mystery religions just a mixture of silly stories and tinsel mummery, and as such to be incontinently dismissed with contempt ? To adopt such an attitude would be to fall into a serious error. We may remind ourselves that a bald description by a hostile pen of the externals of any religious ceremony is liable to give a quite misleading impression of silliness and triviality. It would not be difficult by this method, while keeping strictly to accuracy of the letter, to make almost any religious rite look foolish. Besides, it must strike us that persons of education did, in fact, feel the spell of these alleged absurdities. The note of sincerity in Apuleius is unmistakable. But Apuleius, you will say, was a superstitious African, a writer of romances and a dabbler in magic. Aristides then : he was a neurotic hypochondriac. But Plutarch, perhaps, is a little more difficult to get over ; for whatever his intellectual shortcomings—and he does, of course, fall short of the standard of genius—no one can read Plutarch and fail to realise that he is in the company of a highly intelligent and cultivated gentleman. In any case there are the yet broader facts. If these religions were purely childish imposture, strange indeed it is that they should have succeeded in hoodwinking so vast an audience, and remarkable that the Fathers should have feared a competition so inept.

That charlatans existed and that the devices of the conjurer were often employed to impress the credulous cannot be doubted. Of that there is proof enough in the history of that unscrupulous quack Alexander of Aboutoneichos as narrated by Lucian, and the curious will find a good deal of interesting detail about conjuring apparatus which was used for producing illusory super-natural phenomena in Hippolytus' *Refutation of all the Heresies* (iv, 28 foll.).

Plutarch was well enough aware that folly and imposture existed and were, indeed, directly responsible for turning men in revulsion into atheists. " Superstition and its ridiculous doings and emotions, words, gestures, juggleries, sorceries, coursings around and beatings of cymbals, purifi-cations which are impure, and cleansings which are filthy, weird illegal punishments and degrada-tions at temples—these give certain persons a pretext for saying that better no Gods than Gods, if Gods accept such things and take pleasure in them." [1] But Plutarch remained a religious man and preached religion to others.

Now it is surely absurd to suppose that persons like Plutarch could be permanently cozened by a conjurer's show, and further, so long as we approach it from the angle of that analogy I am sure that we are looking at the matter awry. The effect which it is the object of mystery ritual to create, is not primarily realistic illusion. The object of its officiants is not that of fraudulent mediums, to convert the sceptical to a dubious hypothesis by the production of apparently

---

1. Plutarch, *de superstitione*, 12, 171B (Prickard, p. 234). Fraudulent parasites of the Great Mother and Serapis, *de Pyth. orac*, 25, 407C (Prickard, p. 107). It is rather amusing to notice that in the novel of Heliodorus the venerable Calasiris, who holds strong views about the difference between the Black Magic of witchcraft and the Holy Science of the Egyptian priesthood (iii, 16 and vi, 14), is not above practising upon the credulity of a layman by a piece of legerdemain (v, 12).

supernatural results ; they are speaking a religious language to convinced believers. Not the art of Maskelyne & Devant, but that of Æschylus or Shakespeare supplies the helpful analogy. Not an optical illusion but an emotional experience, a sensational experience if you will, is what they seek to produce. To the successful result, no doubt the lion's share is contributed by the subjective state of receptivity in the spectator, and in obtaining the effect desired any attempt at realism by means of elaborate mechanical devices, for the absence of which there is considerable evidence, would in fact be more likely to hinder than to help. Such dramatic action or simple stage properties, as may have been employed, can have acted merely as a suggestive stimulus ; the illusion, one must think, was supplied through the imagination rather than solely through the physical senses, and by the initiate himself.[1] That in actual fact a genuine psychological experience, accompanied by a high state of emotional excitement, was undergone, and that this experience might profoundly affect the neophyte in a genuinely religious sense it is difficult to deny.

---

1. Is not this what Proclus has in mind when he writes as follows ? οὐκ ἔξωθεν οὖν παθητικῶς ἡ φωνὴ τοῦ Σωκράτους προσέβαλεν, ἀλλ' ἔνδοθεν διὰ πάσης φοιτήσασα τῆς ψυχῆς, ἡ ἐπίπνοια καὶ μέχρι τῶν αἰσθητῶν ὀργάνων διαδραμοῦσα φωνὴ τελευτῶσα ἐγίνετο, σὺν αἰσθήσει μᾶλλον ἢ αἰσθήσει γνωριζομένη· τοιαῦται γὰρ αἱ τῶν ἀγαθῶν δαιμόνων καὶ τῶν θεῶν ἐλλάμψεις, Proclus, in Alc. (Creuzer) i, p. 80. Initiation was an emotional experience rather than the intellectual mastery of any rational exposition of theological dogma or secret wisdom. Ἀριστοτέλης ἀξιοῖ τοὺς τετελεσμένους οὐ μαθεῖν τι δεῖν, ἀλλὰ παθεῖν καὶ διατεθῆναι, γενομένους δηλόνοτι ἐπιτηδείους, Aristotle, Frag. 45 (Rose), ap Synesius, Orat. 48. " He spoke as a man does in the mystery of an initiation and offered no demonstration or evidence," Plutarch, de def. orac., 22, 422C.

Obviously, in attempting to evaluate the experience of Lucius, we should not underestimate the effect of the preparation and the setting of the drama. There is the long ceremonial prelude, the ten days of isolation and fasting, the accentuation of nervous tension by the secrecy and solemnity of the revelations, the emotional and psychological effect upon the neophyte of being brought from solitary preparation into a crowded atmosphere of religious excitement, of which he is the central figure, and then of being taken alone at night into the secret holy of holies to the unknown test of a supreme revelation of God. When we consider the cumulative effect of all these conditions upon a mind predisposed to believe and fearful yet eager for an awe-inspiring revelation, it is not difficult to believe that the neophyte entered upon his great experience with nerves and emotions keyed up to the last pitch of strain and in a highly " receptive " psychological condition.

The effect of the revelations and ritual actions was evidently to produce a high degree of tension, a period of terror and distress, a feeling of strain and unreality, an hysterical condition of mingled joy and depression, then the crisis, a bright light, a sense of leaving the body and the consummation of union with God. Upon the medical aspects of the experience, a passage in Aristides is the most informing. His sensations are perhaps something analogous to those which are said to be experienced when falling into a trance ; the nearest analogy in my own experience has been provided by the sensation when just " going under " after the administration of an anæsthetic. Aristides is describing one of the most realistic of his frequent experiences of an actual visitation from a god. He compares his condition to the state between sleeping and waking ; it was characterised by a feeling of acute discomfort, anxiety, and an effort to use the senses warring with difficulty in doing so ; his hair stood on end, and he was troubled by fears ; tears were mingled with joy and he felt a sense of mental lightness. " But what human being," he concludes, " could possibly explain it in words ? But anyone who has been initiated will recognise it from experience." [1]

The terrors of the earlier part of the proceedings and the shock which they produce upon the candidate are more than once alluded to by Proclus. In discussing carnal and spiritual love he makes use of the analogy of " the most holy rites of the initiations in which, before the god becomes present, the symbols of certain under-

---

1. Aristeides (Keil), xlviii, 32-34. καὶ γὰρ οἷον ἅπτεσθαι δοκεῖν ἦν καὶ διαισθάνεσθαι ὅτι αὐτὸς ἥκοι, καὶ μέσως ἔχειν ὕπνου καὶ ἐγρηγόρσεως καὶ βούλεσθαι ἐκβλέπειν καὶ ἀγωνιᾶν μὴ προαπαλλαγείη, καὶ ὦτα παραβεβληκέναι καὶ ἀκούειν, τὰ μὲν ὡς ὄναρ, τὰ δε ὡς ὕπαρ, καὶ τρίχες ὀρθαὶ καὶ δάκρυα σὺν χαρᾷ καὶ γνώμης ὄγκος ἀνεπαχθής, καὶ τίς ἀνθρώπων ταῦτά γ᾽ ἐνδείξασθαι λόγῳ δυνατός ; εἰ δέ τις τῶν τετελεσμένων ἐστίν, σύνοιδέν τε καὶ γνωρίζει. The nearest literary parallel known to me is Sappho's description of the physical sensations produced by love.

> ἀλλὰ καμ μὲν γλῶσσα ἔαγε, λέπτον δ᾽
> αὔτικα χρῷ πῦρ ὑπαδεδρόμακεν,
> ὀππάτεσσι δ᾽οὐδὲν ὄρημ᾽, ἐπιρρόμ—
> βεισι δ᾽ ἄκουαι.
> ἀ δὲ μίδρως κακχέεται, τρόμος δὲ
> παῖσαν ἄγρει, χλωροτέρα δὲ ποίας
> ἔμμι, τεθνάκην δ᾽ ὀλίγω 'πιδεύης
> φαίνομαι (ἄλλα). Sappho, Frg. 2.

world (χθονίων) spirits are displayed, and visions which violently disturb those who are being initiated and tear them away from the pure goods and call them out to matter. Wherefore the gods ordain that we must not look upon them before we are fenced about with the powers acquired through the rites of initiation." [1]

Again " now just as in the most sacred rites of initiation certain overwhelming shocks (καταπλήξεις τινες) are produced by the ritual, some by what is said and some by what is shown, which subdue the soul into a favourable disposition towards the divine," so philosophy shocks and stimulates the young and thus brings them to the philosophic life. [2] The function of these ordeals is to purify or to startle by shock into the mental state of " conversion "; they are a necessary prelude to the great experience of God's presence. " In the initiations, purifications and sprinklings and hallowings lead up to the rites which may not be spoken and to the communion with the divine." [3]

Plutarch compares the rites of initiation with the soul's passage through Purgatory to Bliss. The souls of the good must sojourn for a while in the part of the sky which is called " The Meadows of Hades," until the winds have blown away the defilements of the body. " Then they return as from long and distant exile back to their own country ; they taste such joy as men feel here who are initiated, joy mingled with much amazement

---

1. Proclus *Commentary on Plato's Alcibiades* (ed. Creutzer), i, pp. 39-40.
2. *ibid.*, i, p. 61, Cf. p. 142.
3. *ibid*, i. p. 9.

and trouble, yet also with a hope which is each man's own." [1]

Yet clearer is the comparison between initiation and the experience of the soul at the death of the body in the treatise " Upon the Soul." " So with the change and reconstitution of the soul into the whole, we say that it has perished, when it has made its way thither ; while here it does not know this unless at the actual approach of death, when it undergoes such an experience as those do who are initiated into great mysteries. Thus death and initiation closely correspond, word to word, and thing to thing. At first there are wanderings and laborious circuits, and journeyings through the dark, full of misgivings where there is no consummation ; then, before the very end, come terrors of every kind, shivers and trembling, and sweat, and amazement. After this, a wonderful light meets the wanderer ; he is admitted into pure meadow lands, where are voices, and dances, and the majesty of holy sounds and sacred visions. Here the newly initiate, all rites completed, is at large." [2]

Sufficient evidence has perhaps been quoted to illustrate the two points, that the experience of the initiate was intensely felt and that it

---

1. Plutarch, *de fac. in orb. lun.* 28, 943D. (Prickard, p. 304.)
2. The Greek text will be found in Stobaeus (*Florilegium* 120, 28, ed. Meineke, vol. iv, p. 107) where the author is stated to be Themistius, a philosopher of the Fourth Century. Wyttenbach first claimed the fragment for Plutarch and with few dissentients the claim is pretty generally allowed, though, to tell the truth, the attribution rests upon somewhat unsubstantial foundations, see Maass, *op. cit.*, pp. 303–5. Fortunately, however, for English readers, Mr. Prickard has followed the general view and has included the passage in his *Selected Essays of Plutarch*, from p. 215 of which I have quoted.

was capable of a high religious meaning. Did, however, the average worshipper rise to these possibilities ? It may be doubted. In all the higher religions the individual reaps as he has sown ; he gets from his religion a return proportionate to what he puts into it. It was a period, as we have seen, when intelligence was definitely declining, and Plutarch's eloquent tirade has exposed to us the increasing prevalence of superstition. The relative minority of those who were initiates in a real sense would have been frankly admitted by philosophic pagans. Had they been put on their defence, their answer *mutatis mutandis*, would not be so very different from that of Origen to Celsus (see above p. 228), not a very satisfactory answer, but perhaps the only one possible. Proclus would presumably have stressed that the shock of the preparatory rites of terror did sometimes lead to "conversion," and to the ultimate apprehension of spiritual truth, by persons who would otherwise have remained purely carnal men. In one passage he sets about explaining the dual function of the Platonic myth of revealing truth to the man who is nourished upon the inner things, and of startling the man who is sensitive only to external things, by a shock which turns his feet towards the path of knowledge. "But that myths do act upon the many is shown by the rites of initiation. For they, too, use myths in order to shut up in them the truth about the gods, which may not be spoken. Initiations cause the souls to undergo experiences with regard to the ritual actions in a fashion unintelligible to us

and divine, so that some of those who are being
initiated receive a shock being filled with divine
terrors, the others are placed in harmony with
the holy symbols and, completely getting out of
themselves, take up their abode with the gods
and are filled with god (τοὺς δὲ συνδιατίθεσθαι τοῖς ἱεροῖς
συμβόλοις καὶ ἑαυτῶν ἐκστάντας ὅλους ἐνιδρῦσθαι τοῖς θεοῖς
καὶ ἐνθεάζειν).[1]

In the case of the Platonic myth he admits the
existence of souls so dead, the uninitiated, who
are spiritually quite unmoved and remain content
with vulgar meanings.   He equally admits the
existence of low natures which are incapable of
religious profit from the mysteries.   " For who
would not agree that the mysteries and the
initiations lead the souls upward away from this
life of matter and mortality and bring them into
contact with the gods, that they cause to disappear
the disturbance which has crept in from unreason,
by intellectual illumination, and that they eject
the undefined and the darkness from those, who
are being initiated, by the light of the gods ?
But, nevertheless, nothing deters the vulgar from
not suffering all kinds of distortions of these
things and from misusing the benefits and the
powers of them according to their own disposition
towards the worse, whereby they are set aside
from the gods and from the true holy worship,
and are borne into the life of sensation and
unreason." [2]

Something of the same kind of difficulty as we
have encountered with regard to their spiritual

---

1. Proclus, *Commentary on Plato's Republic*, ed. Kroll, vol. ii, p. 108.
2. Proclus, *Commentary on Plato's Republic*, .ed. Kroll, vol. i, p 75.

content attaches to a fair estimation of the ethical value of these religions. It would be a mistake for us, who have not the same excuse as may be allowed to the champions of early Christianity by the heat of battle, to judge pagan religion solely by its worse features. Scandals, of course, there were. We recall the Galli in Apuleius conducting their revival meetings among an ignorant peasantry upon whom they shamelessly prey, while they interlard their religious performances with lustful orgies of the most disgusting kind. Even here we should perhaps be a little cautious in the wholesale dismissal of such persons as completely cynical and insincere. The human animal is a queer creature, and it is a notorious fact of his psychology that opposite extremes are closely intertwined. It is of the sensualists that the ascetics are often made, and "the religious temperament" in all times and places has shown a certain instability, which possesses its own dangers and temptations. Further, this particular kind of moral and emotional instability is perhaps likely to be dangerously encouraged by religions of the mystical type which we have described. Illustrations of similar tendencies would not be difficult to find in the annals of Sufism or of Christian mysticism. Especially as regards sexual morality, cults of this kind are liable to give rise to disorder or even to aberration. One cannot, for instance, read Apuleius without becoming aware of the strong erotic sensualism as well as of the genuinely religious impulses which seem mingled in the man's character.

Accidental offspring resulting from irregularities at orgiastic festivals were not unknown to Greek tragedy, and they figure repeatedly in the plots of the New Comedy.[1] The inevitable moral dangers attaching to nocturnal ceremonies, at which both sexes were present in a high pitch of emotional excitement, may be illustrated by the scandals of the Bacchanalian movement in Italy, which led to its suppression by the Senate. Indeed it may also be inferred from the ready credence which was given to malignant gossip as to the incest and immoralities which took place at meetings of the Christian communities. It is also, perhaps, true that some of the ritual forms in which the idea of union with God was expressed in some of the cults, were dangerously suggestive to weaker vessels or liable to deliberate prostitution by cynical and unworthy celebrants.[2] An example was the incident of the seduction of a Roman lady by a man masquerading as the god Anubis, which led to the banishment of

---

1. *E.g.*, Euripides, *Ion*, 550 foll., Plautus, *Mostellaria*, 156, *cf.* Plautus *Casina*, 979. For the moral temptations of nocturnal celebrations compare the epitaph on Aristion (*Anth. Pal.* vii, 223)

ἐνθάδ᾽ ὑπὸ πτελέαις ἀναπαύεται, οὐκετ᾽ ἔρωτι,
οὐκέτι παννυχίδων τερπομένη καμάτοις.

2. The various forms, in which the idea of union with God finds ritual expression have been well discussed by Dieterich, *Eine Mithrasliturgie*, pp. 96 foll. In the main they are spiritualisations of primitive ideas of a crudely physical kind, the magic of the openings of the body (for this in the Lower Culture see Preuss, "Der Ursprung der Religion und Kunst," *Globus*, lxxxvi). In particular the imagery of sexual union, a familiar form of religious expression in many stages of culture, obviously lends itself to abuse. For *Liebesvereinigung* in ritual see Dieterich, *op. cit.*, p. 122, Reitzenstein, *Poimandres*, pp. 221, *Hell. Wundererzähl.*, pp. 53, 137, 142, *Hell. Myst. Rel.*, pp. 21, 110 and de Jong, *op. cit.*, pp. 84 foll. The last-named scholar rightly emphasises the need of caution and the dangers of over-crude interpretation of the facts.

the worshippers of Isis from Rome by Tiberius.[1]
" But if I add—it is what all know and will
admit as readily to be the fact—that in the temples
adulteries are arranged, that at the altars pimping
is practised, that often in the houses of the
temple-keepers and priests, under the sacrificial
fillets and the sacred hats and the purple robes,
amid the fumes of incense, deeds of licentiousness
are done." [2]   Tertullian's charge no doubt
could be substantiated, but it is the same author
who tells us that " He (the Devil), too, has
his virgins; he, too, has his proficients in
continence," and more than once warns his
Christian audience that in the matter of chastity
there are heathens who may sit in judgment upon
them.[3]   It is Augustine who probably fairly
represents the facts ; the moral teaching of the
mystery religions he admits ; it is, he thinks,
part of the devil's craft so to seduce men ; but
the practice of the heathen he condemns as
wholly loose.[4]   Here I think that there can be
no question that Christianity took a far stronger
line in condemning sexual vice.   It is a
matter upon which we have already touched in

1. The story is in Josephus, *Ant.* xviii, 3, 4, 5. It seems to be alluded to
by Suetonius, *Tiberius*, 36, Tacitus, *Annals*, ii, 85 and Juvenal, vi, 535.
Somewhat similar stories could be quoted, *e.g.*, [Aeschines], *Letters*, 10,
and I believe them to be founded on fact, though perhaps I expressed myself
too strongly as to the undoubted historicity of the Josephus story in *Folk-
Lore*, xxxv, p. 403, thereby doing Mr. Penzer an injustice. I believe it to
be historical, but there are good scholars who do not, see references in de
Jong, *op. cit.*, p. 82.

2. Tertullian, *Apol.* 15, for temples in Rome as places of assignation
see Juvenal, vi, 48, ix, 22. For the professional activities of persons attached
to the cult of Cybele see *Anth. Pal.*, vii, 222 and 223.

3. Tertullian, *de praescr. haer.*, 40, *de monog.*, 17, *de exhort. cast.*, 13.

4. Augustine, *de ciu. dei*, ii, 26.

connection with the teaching of the philosophers. Both philosophy and religion preached purity, but I do not think that pagans ever regarded sexual immorality with the same seriousness as Christian preachers, nor attributed to it the same importance.

Did not even Apollo himself return a gentle answer to the young priest of Heracles who had yielded to temptation and had broken his vow of chastity ? When in anxious remorse he enquired of the oracle whether his sin permitted of expiation, he received the reply, " All needful business doth the God allow." [1]

As regards the standard of sexual morality which was attained in practice by the average man, I think, therefore, that it is probable that Christians stood definitely upon a higher level than their pagan contemporaries. As regards general ethics I am less confident, though Christianity certainly stood no lower than paganism. But if the philosopher caught in adultery is no proof that philosophy encourages vice, and if the existence of bad Christians does not condemn Christianity, it may be well not to underrate the spiritual and ethical value of the pagan religious movement of our period by estimating it in terms of its scandals. Actually it provided examples of every degree in the range of spiritual experience, of the lowest certainly, but also of the noblest.

The general statement that the Samothracian mysteries claimed to make men " righteous " it

---

1. Plutarch, de Pyth. orac., 20,403F (Prickard, p. 100).

would, perhaps, be dangerous to stress too far. δίκαιος is almost a technical term, like " saved " in certain circles of emotional, popular evangelicalism. Probably it might mean much or little according to circumstances, and in its least spiritual interpretation will signify but little more than a state of magical excellence acquired by the due performance of required ritual actions.[1]

But if there are examples of belief in the magical efficacy of ritual purification, there are plenty of expressions even in the official ordinances and regulations of the mystery cults of the inadequacy of merely ritual purification and of the essential need of a pure heart.[2] We may indeed remind ourselves that it was precisely here that, mistakenly enough, both Julian and Celsus drew a comparison between pagan mysteries and Christianity, which was unfavourable to the latter. The welcome which was offered by Christianity to the sinner, to them appeared a betrayal of the standards of morality.[3]

---

1. Diodorus, v, 49, 6. γίνεσθαι φασὶ καὶ εὐσεβεστέρους καὶ δικαιοτέρους καὶ κατὰ πᾶν βελτίονας ἑαυτῶν τοὺς τῶν μυστηρίων κοινωνήσαντες. But this is an expansion of the doctrine represented in Schol Arist., *Peace*, 277, which betrays the root meaning of δίκαιος. δοκοῦσιν οἱ μεμυημένοι ταῦτα δίκαιοί τε εἶναι καὶ ἐκ δεινῶν σώζεσθαι. See Anrich, *Das antike Mysterienwesen*, p. 27.

2. Caste iubet lex adire ad deos, animo uidelicet, in quo sunt omnia. nec tollit castimoniam corporis, sed hoc oportet intelligi, quum multum animus corpori praestet obserueturque, ut casto corpore adeatur, multo esse in animis id seruandum magis nam illud uel aspersione aquae uel dierum numero tollitur ; animi labes nec diuturnitate euanescere nec amnibus ullis elui potest, Cicero, *de leg.* ii, 10, 24. Examples of the pagan interpretation of purity in a spiritual sense will be found collected in Fehrle, *Die kultische keuscheit im altertum*, pp. 50 foll., Wächter, *Reinheitsvorschriften im griechischen kult*, pp. 8 foll. See also Schmidt, *Veteres philosophi quomodo, iudicauerint de precibus.*

3. Julian, *Caesars*, 336, quoted below, p. 281, Origen, *c. Cels.* iii, 59.

Further, there were not wanting in the later paganism mystics who even spiritualised ritual completely away. The actual performance of ritual actions, in their view, is not necessary to bring man to God. This is the work, and can only be the work, of a spirit uplifted in pure ecstasy. [1]

---

1. For λογικὴ λατρεία and λογικὴ θυσία, in which " die Kulthandlung zusammenschrumpft oder wegfällt und das ganze Erlebnis in die erregte religiose Phantasie verlegt wird," see Reitzenstein, *Hell. Myst. Rel.*, pp. 21, 25, 106 foll.

LECTURE IX

MITHRAISM.

" As for Constantine, he could not discover among the
gods the model of his own career, but when he caught
sight of Pleasure who was not far off, he ran to her.
She received him tenderly and embraced him, then
after dressing him in raiment of many colours and
otherwise making him beautiful, she led him away to
Incontinence. There too he found Jesus, who had
taken up his abode with her and cried aloud to all
comers : ' He that is a seducer, he that is a murderer,
he that is sacrilegious and infamous, let him approach
without fear ! For with this water will I wash him and
straightway make him clean. And though he should
again be guilty of those same sins a second time, let him
but smite his breast and beat his head and I will make
him clean again.' To him Constantine came gladly.
. . . . ' As for thee,' Hermes said to me, ' I have
granted thee the knowledge of thy Father Mithras.
Do thou keep his commandments, and thus secure for
thyself a cable and a sure anchorage throughout thy
life, and when thou must depart from the world, thou
can'st with good hopes adopt him as thy guardian god '."

Julian, Cæsars, 336.

WE have now very briefly surveyed the general
character of the mystery religions and the religious
ideas which they attempted to express. I now
propose to summarise what is known about a
particular cult. For several reasons the choice
for this purpose fell upon Mithraism. The
history of the cult is intrinsically interesting and
instructive, and, it so happens, that the main
thread of its story is perhaps more easily separable

than that of other not less important religions.
For indeed the relative importance of Mithraism
has been exaggerated, partly because the magni-
ficent work of M. Cumont has made it the most
familiar among the oriental religions of the
Empire, partly perhaps because its high ethical
value and the peculiarity of the distribution
of what was essentially the soldiers' religion, has
appealed to the imagination; but mainly on
account of an *obiter dictum* of Renan. It is true
that the passage of Julian, which is quoted at
the head of this chapter, tends to make typical
antagonists of Christ and Mithras. Similarities
between Christian and Mithraic ritual led the
Christian Fathers to attack the Persian cult
with special venom, and in the pages of Tertullian
Mithras and his mysteries loom large. But for
all that, it may be doubted whether at any time
Mithraism was actually so important as, for
instance, the worship of the Great Mother, with
which it stood in close relation. Its real strength
lay along the frontiers, and quite other causes
than the rise of Christianity led to a decline in its
importance during the third century. To suggest,
with Renan, that there was ever any serious
probability of Western Civilisation becoming
Mithraist in the sense in which it became
Christian is almost ludicrously unhistorical.[1]

---

1. " On peut dire que si le christianisme eût été arrêté dans sa croissance
par quelque maladie mortelle, le monde eût été mithriaste," Renan, *Marc-
Aurèle, Histoire des origines du Christianisme*; 5th edition, 1885, vol. vii,
p. 579. Though I am inclined to think that M. Toutain presses his criticism
of Cumont a little further than the facts warrant (*Les Cultes Paiens* ii,
pp. 168-177), I am sensible in Cumont of a natural and very pardonable
tendency to overemphasise the relative importance of Mithraism.

The history of Mithraism reaches back into the earliest records of the Indo-European language. Documents which belong to the fourteenth century before Christ have been found in the Hittite capital of Boghaz Keui, in which the names of Mitra, Varuna, Indra, and the Heavenly Twins, the Nasatyas, are recorded. Further, the forms, in which the names are given, are not Iranian; and it almost certainly follows that, at the time when they were written, the Iranian and Indian stocks were not yet differentiated.[1] In the *Vedas*, Mithras is invoked as a divinity of light, subordinate to Ahura or Varuna. In the *Avesta* he is found as the spirit of light and fertilising warmth. Further we may notice that already Mithras possesses an ethical significance. His name coincides in form with a noun in Sanskrit which means " friend "; in the *Avesta* he is god, not only of light, but also of truth and of the oath or compact.

This double association with physical light and spiritual truth fitted Mithras for a place in Zoroastrianism, of which, as you will remember, dualism was a cardinal doctrine. The great Iranian prophet accounted for the problem of evil by supposing that the world was a battle-ground between the Good Principle, Ahura Mazda, and the Evil Principle, Ahriman. The powers of Good were identified with Light or Day in conflict with the powers of Evil, Darkness or Night, and Mithras, the spirit of light and truth, became naturally a celestial warrior on

---

1. See Giles, in *Cambridge Ancient History*, ii, p. 13.

the side of Ahura Mazda. This dualism remained throughout its history, fundamental to the doctrine of Mithraism.

The founders of the Persian empire seem to have been themselves followers of the Zoroastrian faith, but it was sound policy to show toleration to the various religious beliefs and customs of their conquered subjects. The hostile attitude of Cambyses to the national religion in Egypt was an exception. The attitude of the Achaemenids towards the religions of their subject peoples was in general that of tolerance, protection, and even patronage. There is little doubt, for example, that Darius, whose own profession of Zoroastrianism is again and again emphasised upon his monuments, was regarded at Babylon, just as Cyrus had been before him, as the legitimate successor of the old, divinely appointed Babylonian kings, and held his throne as the human representative of the Babylonian Marduk. The inevitable consequences of this religious policy within a single political, commercial, and cultural unit, which had been created out of a number of different but deeply rooted civilisations, were syncretistic. The various religions were put into a common melting pot ; they borrowed from each other, and their various conceptions of divinity were modified by supposed identifications of the gods of different peoples. In fact, the same kind of religious fusion took place in the Persian Empire as occurred in the Greek-speaking world after the death of Alexander.

In this fusion of religions the dominant

influence was naturally exercised by Babylon, which had for long been the leader of civilisation in the Middle East. It was from the Chaldaeans no doubt that the worship of Mithras first acquired its elaborate astral features. It would seem also that it was during this period and under such influences as we have indicated, that Mithras, already in the *Avesta* the god of fertilising warmth, became identified with the male consort of Anahita, the Mother Goddess of Nature. This association must at any rate have been firmly established by the time of Herodotus, for it is responsible for a curious mistake which he made. No doubt through a misunderstanding of his cicerone, the Greek historian (i, 131) confused Mithras with his consort and consequently makes him a goddess.

Solar monolatry is an admirable prop to the divinity of kings and well suits the political conditions of oriental despotism. Heaven will thus comfortably reflect and justify the existing order of things upon earth; the absolute power of the monarch will be regarded as the appointed counterpart of the royal power in the universe. As Breasted has said of Egyptian sun worship "in the ancient east monotheism was but imperialism in religion."[1] The predominance of forms of solar monolatry in the third century after Christ, which became more marked as the Empire became more openly an autocracy, tell the same tale. It is not surprising then to find

---

1. *Cambridge Ancient History*, ii, p. 111, Cf. Peet, *ibid.* pp. 203 foll. and Cook on the development of monolatry in the Amarna period in Palestine and Syria, *ibid.* p. 350.

that Artaxerxes adopted Mithraism as a royal cult. After the downfall of Persia, it remained an important religion in Asia Minor, and the continuous use of the name of the god in the formation of names, like Mithradates, bears testimony to his popularity. The Seleucid successors of Alexander paid worship to the god of light, truth and royalty, whose effulgence was equivalent to the Τύχη βασίλεως, which is but inadequately translated "the Fortune of the King."

This aspect of Mithraism as a royal cult is illustrated by the reliefs from the tomb of King Antiochus I Epiphanes of Commagene (69– 34 B.C.), which stood upon a spur of the Taurus overlooking the valley of the Euphrates. Here the king is represented with tiara and sceptre in the act of shaking the right hand of Mithras, whose Persian cap is surrounded by a rayed solar nimbus.

But though it thus retained its importance in the East, Mithraism does not appear to have passed into Greek lands. Mithras does not appear among the numerous gods of the Levant in Hellenistic Delos. There is one possible but not very probable reference to Mithraic usage in a proverb quoted by Herodas[1], but otherwise there is no reference to him in Greek writers before the Christian era. The only serious trace of Greek contact is, in fact, the art type of Mithras slaying the bull, which is patently derived from an original by some Greek artist

---

1. Herodas *Mimes*, iii, 93, see *Classical Review*, xxxvii, p. 105.

of the Pergamene school (second century B.C.), who must himself have drawn his inspiration from the statue of the bull-slaying Nike on the Acropolis at Athens.

Even in later times Mithraic remains are conspicuously absent from Greece. No doubt here the old established cults satisfied existing religious needs, in fact more than satisfied the needs of a Hellas so depopulated that its oracles were falling into decay.[1] Further, the clientèle of Mithras was predominantly military, and the Greeks of the Empire were merchants rather than soldiers. It is indeed a jest of Lucian's *Olympus* that the Persian god cannot talk Greek properly.[2] In too literal a sense this must not be pressed, for the official language of Mithraism was Greek, variegated only by a few survivals of old Persian words from its earlier liturgy, which by their sonorous incomprehensibility added the glamour of mysterious and antique awe.[3] But the adoption of Greek as its official language is not inconsistent with the absence of the cult in the Greek world, for the *koine* was, of course, the common speech of Asia Minor under the Seleucids.

The first notice of Mithraism in the West is its reputed advent to Italy with the pirate captives of Pompey in 67 B.C. But nothing more is heard of it until the latter half of the first century after Christ. It is possible, but by no means certain, that the soldiers of the Third

---

1. Plutarch, *de def. orac.*, 8, 414.
2. Lucian, *Deor. Conc.*, 9.
3. See Cumont, *Textes et Mon.*, i, pp. 238 and 313.

Legion, whose salute to the rising sun decided the issue at the second battle of Betriacum in 69 A.D., may have been worshippers of Mithras. In any case there were members of the sect among the Fifteenth Legion at Carnuntum on the Danube in 71 A.D., and under the Flavian emperors it became important. Wherever troops were permanently stationed in the Roman Empire, its monuments are to be found. It was introduced and propagated by the soldiers. Its character peculiarly fitted it to be a soldier's creed, and the principal Eastern recruiting grounds of the period—Pontus, Cappadocia, Commagene, and Anatolia in general—lay precisely in the area in which the cult was deeply rooted. By far the larger number of the dedicators of Mithraic monuments are soldiers ; the residue consists mainly of oriental slaves, customs-house clerks, or imperial officials.

For towards the end of the second century after Christ, Mithraism received the support of imperial patronage. Commodus was the first emperor to adopt it as an imperial cult. But the same affinities between solar monolatry and autocracy, which we have seen to be operative at an earlier period of the history of Mithraism, caused the official monolatry of the third century to take a solar form. The progressively autocratic imperialism of the time tended to find religious expreession in solar worship, a form of religion which could find justification and support in the current conception of the physical structure of the finite universe, which was part of the general mental background of the time.

This tendency is very plainly reflected, for instance, in the solar theories of Macrobius, and a similar presupposition that all pagan gods are to be considered as forms of the Sun, underlies the rather comical complaint of the Sun against the misrepresentations of pagan religion in Firmicus Maternus.[1]

Under such conditions Mithraism, as an important solar cult, naturally flourished; but during the third century its force began to wane. The distribution of the monuments suggests that except perhaps in Rome itself, it never took a real hold of the civilian population outside the areas in which troops were stationed. The loss of Dacia, which had been one of its strongholds, in the reign of Aurelian proved, no doubt, a severe blow. The imperial cults of the third century, partly owing to accident, tended to adopt the Syrian rather than the Persian form, the worship of Baal rather than the worship of Mithras. The latter was already a declining power when in the fourth century it was given its death-blow by the official adoption of Christianity?

It is profoundly to be regretted that we possess practically no literary evidence for the inner history of Mithraism, nor indeed of any of the pagan mystery religions of this period. A few random facts may be elicited from the *obiter*

---

1. Firmicus Maternus, *de er. prof. rel.*, viii. On the solar Attis and the solar gods with which he was identified, see Graillot, *op. cit.*, pp. 210 foll. Upon the predominance of solar cults in the third century see Wissowa, *R.K.R.*, pp. 304 foll. and for the development of their scientific and religious basis Cumont, La théologie solaire du paganisme romain, *Mém. Acad. des Inscr. et Belles-Lettres*, xii, 2, 1913, pp. 447-479.

dicta of Christian polemic, a good deal of information about the general character of the ideas to which they gave expression may be gleaned from the difficult study of Gnosticism in its pagan and Christian forms, from the writings of the Neo-Platonists, and from the careful examination of magical papyri. But, unfortunately, we do not possess a single detailed and consecutive contemporary account of any one of the mystery religions nor, what would be still more valuable, any of the liturgical books which were in use in any of the sects.

For it is generally agreed by scholars that Dieterich stated too high a claim for the Parisian papyrus, when he called it a Mithraic liturgy. His study of the document is one of the most important, as well as one of the most interesting, contributions to the history of the religious life of the period, and the papyrus itself undoubtedly contains Mithraic elements; but it is nevertheless not more than a syncretistic magical incantation, which conforms to the general type of its kind. For Mithraism, however, we are fortunate in possessing evidence of another kind. The numerous monuments which have survived and, thanks to the great work of Cumont, have been brought intelligibly together, enable us with some certainty to infer the main lines of its mythological and eschatological teaching.

Mithras is " the god from the rock " and is represented as having been born from a stone, perhaps a symbolical expression of the Sun rising behind the mountain. He contended with the Sun, got the better of him, and then swore

an oath of friendship. Henceforward they
became fast allies and their association furnished
the celestial type of loyalty and brotherhood.
The first creation of Ahura Mazda had been a
wild bull. This animal Mithras seized by the
horns and refused to relinquish his hold until
the animal was worn out ; he then took him by
the hind legs, slung him over his shoulders and
took him to a cave. This part of the story, no
doubt, goes back to some early rite of bull-
wrestling, which was certainly an early Anatolian
custom, and modified, perhaps secularised, forms
of which may be recognised in the acrobats of
the Minoan bull-ring and the *taurokathapsia* of
Thessaly.[1]

The bull, however, escaped from the cave,
and the Sun sent the raven, his messenger, to bid
Mithras to pursue and kill the bull in accordance
with the decree of Ahura Mazda. Accompanied
by his faithful dog, Mithras pursued and caught
the bull, pulled back its head, with his left hand
grasping its nostrils, and, with his right, plunged
a dagger in its throat A miracle followed.
From the blood of the slaughtered bull sprang
corn and animals. The Power of Evil in vain
despatched his emissaries, the scorpion, the ant
and the serpent to lap up the life-giving fluid,
which spread over the earth causing the
appearance of plants and animals.

This story is the subject of the relief of Mithras

---

1. The name *taurobolium*, though not the rite itself as practised in
historical times, implies the catching of a bull with a noose or lasso. For this
ceremony, which belongs to the worship of the Great Mother, see below,
p. 306.

slaying the bull, which stood in the apse of Mithraic chapels. In these monuments the life-giving potency of the bull's blood is sometimes symbolically represented by portraying the blood which flows from its neck in three streams in the conventionalised form of ears of barley. The animal's tail is sometimes similarly made to end in ears of corn.

A series of secondary pictures seem to refer to other efforts of the Powers of Evil to thwart the welfare of humanity. Ahriman tried, for instance, to dry up the world, but Mithras shot an arrow into the rock and thereby caused a spring of water to flow. There seems also to have been a story in which Mithras saved mankind from a flood. Finally at the end of his beneficent work upon earth Mithras took leave of his friend the Sun in a banquet, in commemoration of which his worshippers celebrated a sacramental meal.

Besides these episodes from the career of Mithras upon earth, the monuments often represent a number of symbolical accessory figures of which only the most important can find mention here. They are mainly allegorical personifications of astral symbolism, which are ultimately of Chaldaean origin. Thus the sun and moon, the planets, the signs of the zodiac, the seasons and the winds frequently appear. The elements are often represented, water by the vase, fire by the lion, and earth by the serpent. The main scene of the bull-slaying is usually flanked by two figures named Cautes and Cauto-pates. Of these, the first is holding his torch

upwards and has often the sign of the Bull which
indicates Spring; the other holds his torch
downwards and has the sign of the Scorpion,
which indicates Winter. They represent
respectively the rising sun, morning, spring and
the setting sun, evening and winter.

A curious figure, which recurs again and again,
is that of lion-headed Cronos. This composite
mystic monstrosity represents Aion, eternal Time
which is Destiny, the source and end of all things.
His lion's head represents Time which devours
all things; his wings denote the swift flight of
Time; he holds the sceptre and the thunderbolt
of power; and often the keys of heaven; [1] the
serpent, which is sometimes twined round his
body, may represent the sun's sinuous course
through the ecliptic, and the signs of the zodiac
are often figured upon his dress.

The myth of Mithras is a cosmogonical myth.
Mithras himself is a culture hero. He is between
gods and men, μεσίτης, an intermediary. Like
Prometheus, though thanks to dualism he is not
an opponent of the supreme deity, he is the
benefactor to whom men owe all good things.
His life was one of struggle, arduous but eventually
victorious, the struggle of Light against Darkness,
the struggle of Good against Evil in the universe
and in the heart of man.

In this great fight the powers of Good are
joined in close fellowship; for, though Helios

---

1. For Cronos-Aion as Himmelspfortner see Dieterich, *Mithrasliturgie*,
p. 66. Cf. the terra-cotta figurines which represent Cybele, Mater
Deum Salutaris, holding the key of heaven in her hand, Graillot, *op. cit.*,
p. 176.

and Mithras are sometimes amalgamated in a single deity Helios-Mithras, the monuments in general represent them as distinct persons joined in comradeship. Sometimes Helios appears to be thought of as a son of Mithras, and the visible sun is regarded as an intermediary between Mithras and mortals, just as Mithras is intermediary to the Supreme Divine Power.[1]

In Mithraism the soul was regarded as immortal, and its temporary sojourn in an earthly body was a period of trial. Upon the degree of purity and truth which was attained by the worshipper, and upon the part played by him in fighting upon the side of Good, depended the posthumous fate of his soul. In this mortal life Mithras stands by the side of the initiate as a divine helper. The band of his initiates are brothers bound in comradeship, as Helios and Mithras had been, in their sacred cause.

The background of Mithraic eschatology was provided by that theory of the relation of the soul to the universe, which we have seen to be a generally accepted view at the time, and which we meet with in Gnosticism and, with minor variations, in the magical papyri. The soul was thought to have descended at birth from the eternal home of light through the gate of Cancer, passing down through the seven planetary spheres

---

1. See above, p. 257. Mithras and Helios are both regarded as "fathers" of initiates. For the *unio mystica* of son and father in mystery religions see Dieterich, *Eine Mithrasliturgie*, pp. 67–68, 155–156. It occurred evidently in the theology of the cult of Sabazios. ταῦρος δράκοντος καὶ πατὴρ ταύρου δράκων
Firmicus Maternus, xxvi, 118, Clem. Alex., *Protrept.*, ii, 16, Arnobius, v, 21.

to earth. At each stage it became more heavily
weighted by accumulated impurity.[1] During
its time of trial upon earth came the opportunity
to acquire purity through moral struggle, that
is to say, by the conquest of passions and
appetites and the practice of courage, endurance,
fortitude, and truth; and also by means
of ritual and ritual knowledge, which was
progressively revealed in the successive stages of
initiation.

After death took place a judgment of the soul,
for the possession of which *devas* and angels
contended, and at which the arbiter was Mithras
the intermediary. If the good qualities out-
weighed the bad, the soul was enabled to rise
through the gate of Capricorn, passing in
reverse order through the planetary spheres
to Light and Eternal Bliss. At each upward
stage it shed like garments the impurities
which it had contracted upon its downward
passage.

With this return journey of the soul, Mithraists,
like the Gnostics and the magicians, were much
concerned. To secure a safe ascent to the
heights the watchers on the thresholds of the

---

1. The vices corresponding to the particular planets were sometimes
specified and the doctrine used to justify astrological practice. Docent
autem philosophi, anima descendens quid per singulos circulos perdat. unde
etiam mathematici fingunt, quod singulorum numinum potestatibus corpus
et anima nostra conexa sunt ea ratione, quia cum descendunt animae, trahunt
secum torporem Saturni, Martis iracundiam, libidinem Veneris, Mercurii
lucri cupiditatem, Jovis regni desiderium. quae res faciunt perturbationem
animabus, ne possint uti uigore suo et uiribus propriis, Servius, *Aen.*, vi, 714.
For discussion of this passage and of the possibly Egyptian origin of the five
planetary system (*i.e.*, the five "living stars" excluding the sun and moon)
see Reitzenstein, *Poimandres*, p. 53. For the gates of Cancer and Capricorn
see Porphyry, *de antr. nymph.* 11.

spheres ("the toll collectors," τελῶναι, as they were often technically called) must be intimidated, cajoled or deceived, into allowing it free passage.[1]

They may be compelled to do this by the magical or ritual knowledge of the initiate, through the protection of his identification with the Redeemer God, or by divinely effected concealment. But whether any or all of these means are employed, they are effective only through the grace of the guardian god, which enables the worshipper's soul to pass safely by the guardians of the planetary spheres and to escape the relentless clutches of Destiny.[2]

As an illustration, let me quote part of a gnostic document which is incorporated in the *Apocryphal Acts of Thomas*. "Let not the powers and the officers perceive me, and let them not have any thought concerning me; let not the publicans and exactors ply their calling upon me; let not the weak and evil

---

1. Thus of the Neo-Platonists Arnobius says, " quid illi sibi uolunt secretarum artium ritus, quibus adfamini nescio quas potestates, ut sint uobis placidae neque ad sedes remeantibus patrias obstacula impeditionis opponant. *adv. gent.* ii, 13. Further of magi (whether by this he means Mithraists or magicians seems to me ambiguous) neque quod magi spondent commendationicias habere se preces, quibus emollitae nescio quae potestates uias faciles praebeant ad coelum contendentibus subuolare, *ib.* ii, 62. It is, of course, this demonology which St. Paul has in mind. " For our wrestling is not against flesh and blood, but against the principalities, against the powers, against the world-rulers of this darkness, against the spiritual hosts of wickedness in the heavenly places." *Eph.* vi, 12. Cf. *Romans* viii, 38; *Ephesians*, i, 21, iii, 8; *Colossians*, i, 16, ii, 15.

2. The release from εἱρμαρμένη is discussed by Reitzenstein, *Poimandres*, pp. 77 foll. He quotes the Christian analogy from Clement, *Exc. ex Theodoto*, 78, μέχρι τοῦ βαπτίσματος οὖν ἡ εἱρμαρμένη, φασίν, ἀληθής, μετὰ δὲ τοῦτο οὐκέτι ἀληθεύουσιν οἱ ἀστρολόγοι.

cry out against me that am valiant and humble ; and when I am borne upward, let them not rise up to stand before me, by thy power, O Jesu, which surroundeth me as a crown ; for they do flee and hide themselves, they cannot look on thee. . . . Do thou then grant me, Lord, that I may pass in quietness and joy and peace, and pass over and stand before the judge ; and let not the devil (or slanderer) look upon me ; let his eyes be blinded by thy light, which thou hast made to dwell in me ; close thou up (muzzle) his mouth ; for he hath found naught against me." [1]

In spite of the obvious difficulty in carrying out any successful representation of this journey by mechanical means, it is nevertheless probable that it was in some way dramatically enacted by the neophyte. The problem of how such a drama could effectively be staged is analogous to that which we have already noticed (above p. 257) in connection with the descent to the threshold of Proserpine. To sceptics I can give no answer, but I am myself convinced that certain ritual actions were performed, perhaps in themselves crude and trivial enough, which did in fact work upon the emotional excitement of the neophyte and convey an experience of apocalyptic vision and of the soul's return, which may have been largely subjective, but was none the less

---

1. *Acts of Thomas* 148 foll, James, *Apocryphal New Testament*, p. 429. Compare, for a magical example, the passage in the Parisian papyrus, Dieterich, *M.L.*, p. 6, ll. 24 foll. After the necessary magical noises and spells have been uttered, καὶ τότε ὄψει τοὺς θεούς σοι εὐμενῶς ἐμβλέποντας καὶ μηκέτι ἐπί σε ὁρμωμένους, ἀλλὰ πορευομένους ἐπὶ τὴν ἰδίαν τάξιν τῶν πραγμάτων.

genuinely felt. Origen alludes to what seems to be the stage properties of this drama of the return of the soul when he describes the Mithraic ladders with eight gates, each of which was made of a different metal appropriate to a particular planet.[1] The seven grades of Mithraic initiates, for Dr. Phythian Adams has not convinced me that there were only six, seem certainly to correspond to the seven planets. In the sect of the Ophite heretics we find that the grades of initiates were called by animal names, which seem to correspond with the animal forms of the seven *archontics* or ruling powers of the planetary spheres.[2]

The chapels or Mithraea in which the worship of the cult was carried on, were technically called " caves," *spelaea*, and were constructed either in a natural cave or, for obvious reasons, more often in a subterranean building which was made to resemble a cave. This form was, no doubt, determined primarily by the myth of the god's sacrifice of the bull in the cave. In the most usual type of Mithraeum a portico led off the road into a vestibule, this led into a second sacristry, where probably the ritual dresses, etc., were kept ; beyond this again lay the shrine. The shrine consisted of an oblong subterranean vaulted chamber, the floor of which was sunk

---

1. Origen, *c. Cels.* vi, 22. We may compare Origen's own interpretation of Jacob's ladder as an allegory of the Platonic journey of the soul, *ibid.*, vi, 21.

2. The Ophite archontics are Michael the Lion, Suriel the Bull, Raphael the Serpent, Gabriel the Eagle, Thauthabaoth the Bear, Erataoth the Dog, Oroel the Ass, Origen, *c. Cels.*, vi, 30. Some of the Ophite initiates are called lions, others bulls, dragons, eagles, bears and dogs, *ibid.*, vi, 33. For the number of Mithraic grades see below p. 300.

below that of the sacristry and was reached
from it by descending a ladder. A long nave
ran down the middle of the building, in which
the officiants probably performed the ritual;
at each side were benches upon which the lower
grades of initiates were probably seated. The
vaulted roof represented the sky, and was often
adorned with representations of the starry
heavens. At the end of the building opposite
to the entrance was an apse, in which stood the
relief of Mithras slaying the bull. It would
appear that this was normally veiled with
curtains, and it is probable that an epiphany
of the god by the removal of the curtain,
not unlike the epiphany of Lucius after
initiation, formed a culminating point of the
ritual of service. The walls of the building
were covered with paintings and mosaics of
mystical design.

We have already noticed that it was characteristic of the mystery religions to be organised in
small and apparently independent communities.
Certainly, neither the Mithraic chapels nor their
congregations were very large. The latter formed
close associations, the members of which addressed
each other as *frater* or brother, and the head of
which was known as the *Pater Patrum* or *Pater
Patratus*. There were seven grades of initiation,
of which the lower three consisted of lay members,
ὑπηρετοῦντες or servitors, as contrasted with the
four higher grades of μετέχοντες or full partici-
pants. It is possible that there may have been
some slight variation in the names of the grades in
the East and in the West: in the West the

regular series, beginning at the lowest grade, is
Corax (raven) ; Cryphius (hidden one) ; Miles
(soldier) ; Leo (lion) ; Perses (Persian) ; Heliodromus (Runner of the Sun), or Helios, (Sun) ;
and Pater (Father).[1]   Each had its appropriate
mask and costume, as we can see in the rather
crude representation of a Mithraic sacramental
meal from Konjiča in Bosnia. The Pseudo-
Augustine tells us, further, that the initiates with
bird or animal names imitated the appropriate
cries.[2]

It requires but little imagination to realise
the feelings of awe, solemnity and religious
emotion which a Mithraic service in such
surroundings and with such accessories must have
evoked. The strange masks and robes of the
officiants, the weird decorations of the subterranean chamber, which were rendered the more
impressive by the flickering half-light of flaming
torches, the awe-inspiring character of the rites

---

1.   Dr. Phythian Adams, " The Problem of the Mithraic Grades," *Journal
of Roman Studies*, ii, pp. 50 foll., is sceptical as to the authenticity of the
grade of *miles*, and reduces the Mithraic grades to six. His able examination
of the monuments does not, however, convince me that Jerome's tradition
is to be rejected, and I cannot myself but believe that Tertullian knew of a
miles as a definite member of a grade. For possible differences of nomenclature in Eastern and Western Mithraism see below, p. 306. The name of
the sixth grade appears as Helios in the inscriptions of the Mithraeum of
the Piazza San Silvestro in Rome, see Phythian Adams, *op. cit.*, p. 55. With
the Heliodromus of Jerome compare the invocation of the Parisian Papyrus
Mimaut quoted by Reitzenstein, *Poimandres*, p. 147, επικαλουμαι σε·
δευρο μοι εκ των τεσσαρων ανεμων του κοσμου [ηλ]ιοδρομο[ν] μεγαν
θεον επακουσον μου εν παντι, ω σε παρακαλω πραγματι.

2.   *Quaest. uet et nov. test.* (a fourth century document), Migne, *Patr.
Lat.*, xxxiv, p. 2214. illud autem quale est quod in spelaeo uelatis oculis
illuduntur ? Evidently an allusion to some blindfolding of the initiates.
Alii autem sicut aues alas percutiunt uocem coracis imitantes, alii uero leonum
more fremunt. For animal noises see further Dieterich, *Eine Mithrasliturgie*, pp. 40 foll.

themselves, the nervous stimulant of the mystic draught of wine and the music with which the service was accompanied—all these must have worked the congregation into a high pitch of religious emotion, and have prepared them for the culminating experience of the revelation of the Saviour God and of communion with Him.

In addition to these esoteric services of communion and initiation, a regular routine of public worship was characteristic of the organised pagan religions of imperial times with their professional priesthoods. Here Mithraism was no exception. A perpetual fire, the earthly symbol of the eternal sun, was kept constantly burning. Daily worship was regularly performed at definite times. At dawn, at midday, and at dusk prayer was offered to the sun, the officiant turning to the East, South or West according to its position in the heavens. Each day of the week was associated with a particular planet, an association which the languages of Europe still maintain, and the 25th of December, the winter solstice, was celebrated as the birthday of the unconquered sun, a date which the Church found it politic to adopt for the Christian celebration of Christmas.

Mithraic initiation was progressive, that is to say, that in order to arrive at the status of full participation, a worshipper must first have passed through the three successive grades of lay membership; and in order to attain to the top grade of " Father " he must, in turn, have passed through the six lower ones.

At each stage a different symbolic ritual
and a further revelation of mystic knowledge
qualified the initiate for membership of the
order upon which he was now entering.
The lowest grades might be entered at
infancy.[1]

The idea of enrolment in the army of God,
the *militia dei*, was the common property of the
mystery religions and of Christianity.[2]   You will
find its technical terms in Livy's account of the
suppression of the Bacchanalian societies by the
Roman Senate, and we have noticed its appearance
in the initiation of Lucius in the mysteries of
Isis.   In such ceremonies in all these cults a
prominent feature was the *sacramentum* or military
oath of loyalty to the service of the god and to
the fellow members of the brotherhood which
was united in his common worship.   Very often
the oath included a formal renunciation of
specified sins, and an undertaking of a promise
of moral behaviour analogous to the formula
in *Didache* ii.   Mr. Nock has pointed out the
close parallel to Christian usage as observed by
Pliny (*Ep.* x, 96, 6), which is provided by the
regulations of a private cult, in Philadelphia, of
the first century B.C.[3]   To this we may add the

---

1. Initiation of young children was not peculiar to Mithraism.   Thus
the epitaph of the seven years old Aurelius Antonius proclaims him
ἱερεὺς τῶν τε θεῶν πάντων, πρῶτον Βοναδίης, εἶτα Μητρὸς θεῶν καὶ
Διονύσου καὶ Ἡγεμόνος, τούτοις ἐκτελέσας μυστήρια πάντοτε σεμνῶς.
C.I.G. 6206, Anrich, *op. cit.*, p. 55, where further examples are quoted.

2. See Cumont, *Mon. et Cult.* i, 317, *Rel. Orientales*, p. xv, Reitzenstein, *Hell. Myst. Rel.* pp. 71 foll.   Livy, xxxix, 8, 3, and above, p. 254.

3. Nock, *Classical Review*, xxxviii, pp. 58–9.   The inscription in question
was first discovered by Keil and Premerstein.   The text will be found in
Dittenberger, *Sylloge*, 3rd edition, No. 985.

oath of the Elchasaite sect at baptism, which is quoted by Hatch.[1] " I call these seven witnesses to witness that I will sin no more, I will commit adultery no more, I will not steal, I will not act unjustly, I will not covet, I will not hate, I will not despise, nor will I have pleasure in any evil." Another good example of a slightly different kind is the Hippocratic oath of the medical profession with its noble ethical profession, its practical realisation of the solidarity of the guild, and at least in its earlier forms its undertaking not to reveal the secrets of the profession to unqualified persons.

In this profession of moral conduct, Christian and pagan *sacramenta* show a resemblance ; a characteristic difference is that almost invariably the *sacramentum* of a pagan sect included an oath of secrecy and a promise not to reveal to the uninitiated the rites and knowledge which the neophyte is about to behold and learn. In the Apostolic Age, Christian ritual does not seem to have had this secret or mystical character. By the time of Tertullian, of course, the *arcana disciplina* is a feature of Christianity, and this is almost certainly an instance of the influence of the analogy of pagan mysteries upon the character of Christian ritual.[2]

---

1. From Hippolytus, ix, 10, Cf. the oath of the Essenes, *ibid.*, ix, 18. The Hippocratic oath has lately been discussed in detail by Mr. W. H. S. Jones, *The Doctor's Oath* (Camb. Univ. Press, 1924).

2. For the clause of secrecy in the pagan *sacramentum*, see above, p. 255. In appealing, for a different purpose, to the pagan analogy, Tertullian may be allowed to illustrate its influence. " If, then, Christians are not themselves publishers of their crime, it follows, of course, it must be strangers. And whence have they their knowledge, when it is also a universal custom in religious initiations to keep the profane aloof and to beware of witnesses." *Apol.*, 7.

Our knowledge of the initiatory rites of
Mithraism is inevitably fragmentary. We know
that in this, as in many contemporary cults, a
form of baptism represented the mystical washing
away of sin. The initiated in certain grades were
sealed upon the forehead with the mark of their
calling, probably with a brand. At the initiation
into the grade of Soldier, the neophyte was
offered a crown which he renounced with the
words " Mithras is my crown." The tongue
and the hands of a Lion were purified with
honey. Further, the general character of
the initiatory rites was that which the world
at large associates with Freemasonry, and
which, indeed, is common to all similar kinds
of religious ceremony in all stages of culture
down to the puberty ceremonies of savages.
They partook, that is to say, of real or
symbolic tests of courage and endurance
both physical and spiritual, and awe-inspiring
ritual actions and accessories were employed
to heighten the nervous tension of the
neophyte.

One of the principal Mithraic ceremonies was
the celebration of a communion service in
memory, it was thought, of the last meal of
which Helios and Mithra partook together
upon earth. The drinking of the mystical
haoma goes back to the ancient stratum of
pre-Zoroastrian Iranian religion ; in the West,
for obvious practical reasons of convenience,
wine, or, according to Justin (*Apol.* i, 66)
water, had taken the place of the *haoma*. The
cakes which we see upon the Konjiča relief

bear a curious resemblance to our hot-cross buns.

We have already noticed that at an early date Mithras had become associated in the East with Anahita, the Goddess of Nature, and was thought of as her divine consort. This association explains the close association of Mithraism with the Phrygian worship of Cybele, which was the form in which the Asiatic Mother Goddess had first come to Rome. There was, further, a general tendency for the oriental religions to seek the wing of Cybele, owing to her long-established official status in Rome. For the worship of this goddess in the form of the black meteorite from Pessinus, had been adopted by the Roman state towards the end of the Second Punic War, and was the only oriental religion which, under the Republic, enjoyed the status of an officially recognised cult. In any case the association was close, and it perhaps throws some light upon two matters which are not without interest.

Upon the whole the evidence seems to show that Mithraic initiation was reserved for men only, and that the cult of the Persian god offered no religious opportunities to women. It would appear, however, that feminine societies of *matres* and *sorores*, "mothers" and "sisters," corresponding to and in close association with the male Mithraic congregations of "fathers" and "brothers," were sometimes formed for the worship of Cybele. In this way, through affiliated communities the spiritual needs of the women folk of Mithraists could be provided for.[1]

The other matter is the practice of the *taurobolium* or baptism in bulls' blood, which is often, though erroneously, supposed to be a characteristically Mithraic rite, perhaps because of the prominent part which is played by the slaughter of the bull in Mithraic mythology and ritual. Actually the rite belonged to a primitive stratum of Anatolian religion. In Asia Minor it had not been confined to the worship of the Pessinuntian goddess, but with her it had come to the West. In any case the Roman Cybele by imperial times had come to embrace the other nature goddesses of Anatolia, which were regarded merely as particular forms of the one great Mater Deum Salutaris. To this cult Antoninus Pius and Faustina were

---

1. The evidence for female initiates in Mithraism proper consists of a passage in Porphyry (*de abst.*, iv, 16), where allusion is made to "hyaenas," or, as the text is usually corrected, to "lionesses." The passage also contains a reference to male Mithraic "eagles," for whom there appears to be no room in the seven grades which are attested for the West. But in this Porphyry seems to be confirmed by the occurrence of ἀετός on a Lycaonian inscription (Cumont, *Textes et Mon.* ii, No. 549, Dieterich, *Kleine Schriften*, pp. 265–6). It is possible, as Dieterich, I think, was the first to suggest, that there may have been some variation in the nomenclature of the grades in different parts of the Empire. In particular the Eastern practice may have been different from the West. This view Cumont seems to have endorsed in *Les mystères de Mithra*, pp. 155 and 182. He is further inclined to find confirmation for Porphyry's statement anent female initiates in a tomb-stone from Tripoli (quae lea iacet). It is, however, by no means certain that this "lioness" worshipped Mithras. A detailed criticism of the Mithraic interpretation of this inscription will be found in Adams, *J.R.S.*, ii, 1912, p. 62. It may be pointed out that the animal nomenclature of the Ophite grades suggests that similar animal names may have been employed in a larger number of mystical sects than we know of.

For the close relation between the cults of Mithras and Cybele and their complementary aspect, see Graillot, *op. cit.*, pp. 192 foll., and de Jong, *op. cit.*, p. 68.

particularly devoted, and it is from the reign of Antoninus onwards that the epigraphical evidence for the *taurobolium* mainly dates.

The last half of the word indicates that the original rite must have included the catching of the bull with a noose, a fact which suggests very early analogies of which the Minoan bullring is a possibly secularised form. This element, however, had completely disappeared in our period except for this etymological vestige of its earlier existence. The scene has been described by Prudentius (*Peristeph.* x, 1011–1050). The worshipper was placed in a kind of pit above which the bull was sacrificed and the blood was allowed to flow over him. The *uires* and the *bucranium* of the animal of sacrifice were subsequently buried ceremonially or dedicated to the Goddess.

The primary ideas at the bottom of this ritual appear to have been the magical prolonging of physical life by the absorption of the life-force of the sacred animal and also by the sacrifice of a surrogate, for the blending of two sentiments which in strict logic are inconsistent, is by no means infrequent in religious motive. The efficacy of the rite lasted for twenty years, a term which perhaps had its origin in a notion that a full generation consisted of forty years made up of two half-periods of twenty years, which seems to have been fairly general in the Mediterranean area.[1]

After the period of efficacy had elapsed the rite was renewable, and it is perhaps the general

---

[1]. See Clifford Moore, " The duration of the efficacy of the *taurobolium*," *Classical Philology*, xix, pp. 363-5.

view that the second baptism held good for eternity. In the difficult question which is raised by the phrase *in aeternum renatus* I should agree with Clifford Moore that it "represents rather the enthusiastic hopes of the devotee than any dogma." At least it must be noted that the common view, that the *taurobolium* once performed lasted for twenty years while its renewal a second time lasted for eternity, though often stated as an ascertained fact is in reality an hypothesis, which rests upon no ancient statement to that effect.

Naturally enough, the baptism of bull's blood came to be interpreted in a more spiritual sense than that of its originally magical purpose. The bath of bull's blood cleansed the initiate from sin ; its performance was regarded as the day of his spiritual birth (*natalicium*) ; he was reborn into eternity (*in aeternum renatus*).

This rite and that of the *criobolium*, which is a lesser form of the same procedure with the substitution of a ram for a bull as the animal of sacrifice, was performed in several different contexts. From the reign of Antoninus it was frequently undertaken "with intention" on behalf of the safety and welfare of the Roman Empire and the imperial house. In initiation to the lower grades of the mysteries of Cybele the *criobolium* was performed by the Archigallus on behalf of the assembled neophytes. At initiation into the higher grades the candidate himself had to undergo the major rite of the *taurobolium* in person. The practice of what may be called the private *taurobolium* as a personal

mystical sacrament became increasingly popular,
particularly with women to whom the idea,
which thus finds a repulsively crude and physical
expression, made a strong religious appeal.[1]
This idea is familiar enough in religious practice
or vocabulary all over the world, and that its
symbolic and verbal expression is not strange to
Christianity, we are reminded by Cowper's
well-known hymn.[2]

It is not impossible that a series of accidents have
caused the importance of Mithraism as compared
with the other pagan mystery cults to be over-
estimated. At the same time it cannot be
denied that its hold upon the armies was
conterminous with the frontiers of the Empire,
and that at the zenith of its fortunes it was a
serious rival. In some respects it was no
unworthy opponent of Christianity. Strongly
ethical in character, it inculcated the exercise of
the manly virtues in the unending struggle on
behalf of righteousness against the powers of
evil. It had the moral virtues of a soldier's
creed, and in them lay its true strength. Making
every allowance for the difficulty of achieving a

---

1. Upon the whole matter of *taurobolium* see Graillot, *op. cit.*, pp. 150–
188. List of texts referring to *taurobolium* on behalf of state and emperor,
p. 159; private *taurobolia*, pp. 167 foll; statistics of *taurobolia* performed by women, p. 173; minor initiation, p. 178; major initiation,
p. 171. See also Hepding, *Attis*, pp. 199-201. Hepding stresses the late,
secondary character of the practice as a private mystical sacrament. He
claims that the earliest known individual *tauroboliatus* is Elagabalus and the
earliest epigraphical record of the private rite *C.I.L.* vi, 497 of 305 A.D.

2. "There is a fountain filled with blood/ Drawn from Emmanuel's
veins," etc. Cf. Taurobolium quid uel cribolium scelerata te sanguinis
labe perfundit ? Lauentur itaque sordes istae quas colligis ; quaere fontes
ingenuos, quaere puros liquores, ut illic te post multas maculas cum spiritu
sancto Christi sanguis incandidet. Firmicus Maternus, xxvii–xxviii, 123.

sympathetic approach to the fragments of an alien mythology, the stories of Mithras cannot but strike us as, upon the whole, foolish and unsatisfactory spiritual food. Here, of course, the concentration of Christian doctrine around the character, life, and teaching of a concrete and historical personality gave to it a convincing reality which all its rivals lacked.

Again, as compared with other pagan religions, Mithraism was seriously at a disadvantage in its exclusion of women. Though the association with Cybele might provide, to some extent, for the needs of the wives and daughters of Mithraism, the Persian god had not the support of that ardent religiosity and fervent proselytism of devout women which had so large a share in pushing the fortunes of Isis and Cybele or in propagating the tenets of Christianity. Nor can we suppose that Mithraism, like Christianity or the cult of Cybele, reaped the benefits of that insidious household propaganda, to which Celsus takes so strong exception, and the conversion of the ladies and children by the slaves. Its strength lay rather in the practical morality of its teaching and in its emphasis upon ἐγκράτεια, self-control, which, as Mr. Cyril Bailey reminds me, is so much stronger than mere ἄσκησις or the observance of rules and penances, especially in its appeal to the soldier.

What struck the Fathers about Mithraic practice was the close and obvious similarity of many of its rites to those practised by Christians. The sacramental meal of bread and water (or wine), the use of baptism, the sealing of initiates, the promise of resurrection,[1] for such features as these they could account only by supposing that the devil had inspired a deliberate parody of divine ordinances.[2]

---

1. For resurrection in Mithraism, cf. Porphyry, *de antr. nymph.* 5, Cumont, *Textes et Mon.*, ii, p. 39, Πέρσαι τὴν εἰς κάτω κάθοδον τῶν ψυχῶν καὶ πάλιν ἔξοδον μυσταγωγοῦντες τελοῦσι τὸν μύστην ἐπονομάσαντες σπήλαιον τὸν τόπον.

2. ὅπερ καὶ ἐν τοῖς τοῦ Μίθρα μυστηρίοις παρέδωκαν γίνεσθαι μιμησάμενοι οἱ πονηροὶ δαίμονες· ὅτι γὰρ ἄρτος καὶ ποτήριον ὕδατος τίθεται ἐν ταῖς τοῦ μυομένου τελεταῖς μετ᾽ ἐπιλόγων τινῶν, ἢ ἐπίστασθε ἢ μαθεῖν δύνασθε. Justin Martyr, *Apol.* i, 66.

Sed quaeritur, a quo intellectus interpretetur eorum, quae ad haereses faciant. A diabolo scilicet, cuius sunt partes interuertendi ueritatem, qui ipsas quoque res sacramentorum diuinorum idolorum mysteriis aemulatur. Tingit et ipse quosdam, utique credentes et fideles suos; expositionem delictorum de lauacro promittit. Et si adhuc memini, Mithra signat illic in frontibus milites suos; celebrat et panis oblationem, et imaginem resurrectionis inducit, et sub gladio redimit coronam. Tertullian, *de praescr. haer.*, 40. Cf *de Bapt.* 5, *de corona*, 15.

LECTURE X

" Let us take note of the devices of the devil, who is wont
to ape some of God's things with no other design than
by the faithfulness of his servants, to put us to shame
and to condemn us."

Tertullian, *de Corona*, 15.

Habet ergo diabolus christos suos, et quia ipse antichristus
est ad infamiam nominis sui miseros homines scelerata
societate perducit.

Firmicus Maternus, *de err. prof. rel.*, xxii.

THE conclusion of the last lecture has drawn our
attention to striking similarities between Christian
and Mithraic ritual. Nor are such similarities
confined to Mithraism. For example, I have
quoted at the head of this lecture a similar
charge of diabolic parody which is brought by
Firmicus Maternus against the resurrection ritual
of Attis (Adonis ?), with its use of holy ointment
and its promise of salvation to the worshipper.
This controversy, indeed, as to the " borrowing "
of rites is a commonplace of Apologetic. To
attempt to deny the existence of these similarities
is quite idle.[1] The mere fact that the Fathers,
some of whom had themselves been initiates
before their conversion and were therefore

---

1. An enumeration of some of the most striking analogies will be found
in de Jong, *op. cit.*, pp. 32 foll.

accurately informed, felt that diabolic parody was a necessary explanation, is itself compelling evidence of the closeness of the analogy. But we are not, I think, likely to-day to feel able to accept the explanation which they offered.

Now, first of all, it is well to admit that some interaction between pagan and Christian religious influences there was, in the nature of things, bound to exist. It can hardly be denied that the influence of the pagan mysteries must be, in part at least, responsible for the very different attitude towards the celebration of the Lord's Supper and the rite of Baptism in the Apostolic Age and in the time of Tertullian respectively. Or, to take a point of detail, it is difficult not to believe that the custom of giving milk and honey to the newly baptised was not borrowed from pagan initiations, of which it was a common feature.[1] On the other hand, some apparent similarities of detail may be due to coincidence, for instance, the use of bread and wine in the Mithraic Communion Service, which has quite a different and very remote historical origin in the *haoma* sacrament of the Vedas. It is a legitimate and interesting matter for research, as it seems to me, to examine the resemblances between pagan and Christian ritual and to determine into which of these categories they fall. But the result of such enquiry, in my view, is irrelevant to any theological issue. It concerns the history of early Christian liturgy, not the problem of the value or truth of Christianity as a religion. For

---

1. Tertullian, *de Corona*, 3. Upon the whole topic see Usener, " Milch und Hönig," *Rheinisches Museum*, lvii, 1902, pp. 177 foll.

I cannot think that a faith that means anything
to a man is likely to be severely shaken by the
discovery that the practice of making the newly
baptised partake of milk and honey, which in
fact has been discontinued in Christian ritual,
was borrowed from pagan religion.

It is, indeed, our second category of what I
have loosely called coincidences, which are more
likely to give trouble, for most of the resemblances in more important matters will fall into
this class. For actual "borrowing," indeed,
one way or the other, we must inevitably maintain
a severe and critical standard of evidence before
admitting probability. We no longer think it
necessary, with the Fathers, to concern ourselves
seriously with the relative dates of Homer and
Moses, on the grounds that an idea which is
common to the two can only have originated
with one or other of them. But in taking that
line we admit, as indeed we must, something
more than coincidence, in the sense of purely
fortuitous accident. There is, in some degree,
a fundamental similarity of idea in the celebration
of a commemorative sacramental meal, whether it
be performed by Mithraic initiates or by Christians.

Something of my personal attitude towards
this question, I have already indicated. It
involves, it is true, the denial of any intrinsic
validity to religious ritual in itself. This is
possibly a view to which you will not all feel able
to assent, though candidly, if you do not, I do
not personally see where you can draw a line
short of the acceptance of magic.

My own view is that ritual is primarily a

vehicle of expression ; if you will, a specialised form of language. The more that I learn about it, the more I am impressed with the comparatively limited number of essential forms which it can take. I do not, of course, for a moment deny the ethical and religious value of the practice of ritual, any more than I should be prepared to question the ethical or religious value of prayer or, to push the analogy yet closer, of set forms of prayer. But it seems to me that too great intrinsic importance is attributed to ritual, and that the case of these alleged borrowings stands very much on the same footing as that of the undoubted use by St. Paul of a technical vocabulary, which belongs to the pagan religion and philosophy of his time.

There appear, in fact, to be certain basic ideas, which recur again and again in all religions and no doubt correspond to the psychological need which has urged mankind in all stages of culture to seek religious help. The methods of expressing these ideas are naturally dictated by human circumstance and, at any rate in their cruder forms, by physical circumstance. Religious advance indeed is marked by the spiritualisation both of the forms of the ideas themselves and of the ritual methods of expressing them, though the advance in these two departments is by no means *pari passu*. Indeed, thanks to the innate conservatism of mankind, which is peculiarly keenly insistent in the sphere of religion, progress in ritual is less continuous and less rapid than progress in idea. Reinterpretation in both departments is a more congenial instrument of change than radical alteration.

One or two examples may perhaps illustrate my meaning. Both in the Lower and in the Higher Culture you will find the existence of the notion that a process of physical cleansing is a ritual method of attaining magical or religious purity ; but, according to the stage of religious attainment, the emphasis will be laid either upon the ritual action of washing or baptism, or upon the moral purity of which ritual purity is regarded as but a physical symbol. Again, the ultimate aim of all religious exercise may be said in some sense or other to be the attainment of union with God. At the lower end of the scale of civilisation this may find expression in direct physical action of the crudest and most literal kind, as for example, in the actual eating of the sacred being by his worshippers in a communion meal, the type of sacrifice which the researches of that great scholar Robertson Smith did so much to illuminate. Such a crude form may survive into a comparatively lofty religion, and mysticism in particular is especially tolerant of crude survivals which, by their very bizarre savagery, provide a peculiar stimulus to esoteric interpretation. I am thinking, for instance, of such phenomena as the Dionysiac *sparagmos*, the rending of live animal representatives of the god and the devouring of their quivering flesh. Fundamentally the same idea, though its expression has been civilised and the action is not literal but symbolical, may be expressed in such communion meals as those of the Mithraic mystery. At the time when Christianity was

first preached this was indeed a common method
of religious expression, and was by no means
confined to Mithraism among pagan cults.[1]

Still more readily distinguishable, perhaps, are
the higher and lower forms of expressing complete
unity with God in terms of the sexual relations
of man. Crude forms of it are frequent in the
Lower Culture and will be found to occupy a
good many pages of *The Golden Bough*. The
more refined form where a man is formally
married to a goddess or a woman to a god, e.g.,
the annual ritual marriage at Athens of the wife
of the Archôn Basileus to Dionysos, is not all
uncommon at a relatively high stage of culture.
A liturgical fragment seems to indicate that the
ritual marriage of the initiate formed part of
one of the pagan mysteries,[2] and the Christian
use of metaphor inspired by the analogy of the
closest of human intimacies to express the

---

1. The crude idea of absorbing the divine substance directly by eating
survives, of course, in magic. Thus a Berlin magical papyrus reads καὶ
λαβὼν τὸ γάλα σὺν τῷ [μέλι]τι ἀπόπιε πρὶν ἀνατολῆς ἡλίου καὶ ἔσται
τι ἔνθεον ἐν τῇ σῇ καρδίᾳ. With this Anrich (*op. cit.*, p. 98) compares
the Marcosian celebration of the Lord's Supper, Hippolytus, vi, 39-40.
For sacramental meals in the worship of Attis see Firmicus Maternus, xviii,
102-3, Clem. Alex., *Protrept*, ii, 15, Dieterich, *Mithrasliturgie*, pp. 102
foll. ; of Cybele, Jupiter Dolichenus and Venus Caelestis, Graillot, *op. cit.*,
p. 180. An inscription from Tomi relating to the mysteries of the
Samothracian gods reads τὸ πέμμα σχίξας καὶ ἐγχέει τὸ ποτὸν τοῖς
μύσταις, *Arch. Epigr. Mith.*, 1882, p. 8, No. 14. In a sense a sacramental
meal may be said to have formed part of the Eleusinian mysteries, see
Farnell, *Cults*, iii, p. 195.

2. νυμφίε χαῖρε νέον φῶς, Firmicus Maternus, xix, 104, Dieterich,
op. cit., p. 122. It is possible that a form of ἱερὸς γάμος was celebrated in
the persons of the hierophant and priestess at Eleusis, Foucart, *Mystères*,
pp. 475, Farnell, *Cults*, iii, p. 176. Compare the formula ὑπὸ τὸν παστὸν
ὑπέδυον, (Clem. Alex., *Protrept.* ii, 15) and the νυμφών used in the mystic
rites of Demeter and Dionysus at Corinth (Paus., ii, 11), with the Valen-
tinians' celebration of a πνευματικὸς γάμος in a νυμφῶνα (Irenaeus, *Haer.*
i, 14, 2). Upon this see Anrich, *op. cit.*, p. 77.

relation of the soul to God or of the Church to Christ, will of course be familiar to you. In fact, the great objective of spiritual religious experience seems to be either more or less crudely envisaged according to the degree of the worshipper's spiritual attainments or education. Consequently I am not myself much more impressed nor surprised by the fact that the Christian religion found its expression in rites of a similar character to those employed by contemporary pagan cults[1] than by the use by Christian literature of the Latin and Greek languages or by Christian metaphysic of the imagery and vocabulary of Neo-Platonism. That it did, I have not a shadow of doubt.

In art again the debt of Christianity to pagan cults is certain. There can be little doubt, for example, that representations of Mithras shooting at the rock or Mithras mounting in the chariot of the Sun directly influenced Christian representations of Moses at Horeb or the ascent of Elijah.[2] Again the most interesting recent discovery of the pagan subterranean chapel at Rome has shown us the fully developed pagan prototype of the Christian basilica.[3]

---

1. It is a not unimportant difference that Christianity was fortunate in being a new religion. It had not the same *damnosa hereditas* as the pagan religions. The ritual forms which it shares with paganism, are the higher and not the lower forms of contemporary ritual expression.

2. See Cumont, *Les Mystères de Mithra*, pp. 237-8.

3. See the description by Mrs. Strong and Miss Jolliffe in *Journal of Hellenic Studies*, xliv, 1924, pp. 65-111. The sect to which the church belonged is quite uncertain. Cumont has suggested that it was the meeting place of the Neo-Pythagoreans; the most recent examination of the problem by Mr. Nock, in *Classical Review*, xxxviii, suggests that it belonged to an Orphic brotherhood. Bandinelli's theory that it was a mausoleum seems to me almost certainly wrong.

But even in more fundamental things than ritual or art there is at least an apparent resemblance. For the idea of a Saviour is widely shared by pagans, and in Gnosticism, pagan as well as Christian, the Saviour descends from the home of God bringing a knowledge of salvation to His worshippers, whose souls through His grace may safely mount to God. The germ of such a divine intermediary indeed lies in the Platonic *demiourgos* who forms the link between the world of "ideas" and the world of matter. An example of such a redeemer is Mithras, "demiourgos and lord of creation." [1]

This resemblance is a fact, but it requires definition. The Neo-Platonic Redeemer has quite a different origin to the Christian, and the similarities are superficial rather than essential. It is quite true, of course, that the Gnostic conception exercised a great influence upon Christian thought. It was precisely because the emphasis of Gnostic analogies bid fair to obscure for Christians the essential difference, the real uniqueness of the Redeemer Christ, that Gnosticism was so serious a danger. It was a fatal poison which must at all costs be expelled from the body of Christianity.

Upon this Gnostic Redeemer there is an excellent essay in Mr. Bevan's *Hellenism and Christianity*. He there points out the essential differences between the bringer of the *gnosis* of redemption, who is not in the same sense

---

1. Porphyry, *de ant.* 5, 6. δημιουργὸς ὢν καὶ γενέσεως δεσπότης

incarnate, is not an historical person but, like Mithras, is comparable rather to Prometheus than to Christ, and whose ascent and descent is, in essentials, but a reduplication of the Hellenistic ascent and descent of the soul. His, to my thinking, very just conclusion of the whole matter may be quoted. "The just craving of the anthropologist to establish connections must, however, it appears to me, have risen to a degree which destroys the finer instinct of discrimination, before he can suppose that by making any combination of elements taken from these, one could create the Christian idea of the Saviour. For if Divine self-sacrifice is the very point and meaning of the story as a whole, we do not prove much, even if we succeed in showing that details of the story are found separately elsewhere."[1]

But, perhaps, having brought our investigations so far, we are bound to ask ourselves the general question what is the real significance of these similarities between Christianity and contemporary pagan religions and philosophy? Or rather, to put it in another way, is it a fact that the progress of our knowledge of the pagan religions and philosophy constitutes a serious attack upon Christianity and, by stripping it of borrowed plumes, is likely to leave it empty of content? Approached by the road which we have followed, this, I may point out, is simply an historical not a theological question, and one which the enquirer may hardly shirk. The statutes of this University,

---

1. Bevan, *Hellenism and Christianity*, p. 106.

as you know, discourage the public expression of
any theological views within its walls, but here
I am not raising any questions as to value
but as to fact. Was there, or was there not,
something quite different which marked
Christianity out as unique among the religions
of the Roman Empire ?

Now first of all I notice, that both pagans and
Christians were themselves acutely conscious of
some radical difference between paganism and
Christianity. Whatever we may think of their
diagnosis of the difference, their view that a
difference existed is obviously important. Again
common sense suggests that, however largely
external material circumstances may have
contributed to produce the result, the mere fact
that Christianity survived and the pagan religions
did not, must indicate some real and essential
difference in their natures. Even if you like to
put it, that whereas pagan persecution failed to
crush Christianity, Christian persecution of
paganism succeeded, the moral remains the same.
Where, then, does the essential difference lie ?
I am inclined myself to find the answer in the
personality and teaching of the historical Jesus
of the first three Gospels. I should agree with
Wendland's blunt statement : " The preaching
of Christ has no relation whatever to Hellenism."[1]
It is quite true of course that His preaching often
agrees with that of Epictetus in the standard of
conduct inculcated but, as Origen noticed,[2] it

---

1. Wendland, *op. cit.*, p. 213.
2. Origen, *c. Cels.* vii, 63.

makes a difference *why* the same good actions are performed. Between the social ethics of Stoicism and Christianity there is a profound difference in the ultimate basis of motive. In the one case the appeal is ultimately to the self-respect of the good man, in the other to love and self-sacrifice. It is again the ideas of self-sacrifice and of redemption through voluntary suffering that absolutely divide the Christian from the Gnostic Redeemer.

About the Higher Criticism of the New Testament, I know very little, but I remember a view which used to crop up in the rather callow discussions of such matters in my undergraduate days, which for the sake of brevity I may express in its crudest form. Briefly so stated it amounted to the view that St. Paul was the real founder of Christianity. Quite on the contrary, I am sure that an unbiassed study of contemporary ethics and religion will throw into greater and greater relief the life of Jesus as depicted in the first three gospels as being the essential revolutionary event in the religious life of mankind. With this view St. Paul himself would have agreed. He had an almost uncanny genius for laying his finger upon the essential point, and this text of his seems to me to sum up in as few words as possible the essential difference between the old religions and the new, and between the social ethics of the higher paganism and those of Christianity. " And if I have the gift of prophecy, and know all mysteries and all knowledge ; and if I have all faith, so as to be able to remove mountains, but have not love, I am nothing. And if I bestow all my goods to feed the poor, and if I give my body to be burned but have not love, it profiteth me nothing." [1]

---

1. 1 Corinthians, xiii, 2-3.

LIST OF USEFUL BOOKS

GENERAL WORKS ON THE PERIOD

BOISSIER, G., *La fin du paganisme*, 4th edition, Paris, 1903.

DILL, SIR SAMUEL, *Roman society from Nero to Marcus Aurelius*, 2nd edition, London, 1905.

FRIEDLAENDER, L., *Roman life and manners under the early empire*, translated from the 7th edition by L. A. Magnus, London, 1908–13.

> (To this for convenience I have referred English readers. The 9th edition of *Darstellungen aus der sittengeschichte Roms, etc.*, was published in Leipzig, 1919.)

FRIEDLAENDER, L., Introduction and notes to *Petronii Cena Trimalchionis*, 2nd edition, Leipzig, 1906.

THORNDIKE, LYN, *The history of magic and experimental science during the first thirteen centuries of our era*, vol. i, New York, 1923.

> (This painstaking book has little value as a history of thought, but it contains extremely good summaries of the contents of the more foolish pagan and Christian literature of the period.)

WENDLAND, P., *Die hellenistisch-römische kultur in ihren beziehungen zu judentum und christentum*, 2nd and 3rd editions, Tübingen, 1912.

MATERIAL CONDITIONS

CHARLESWORTH, *Trade-routes and commerce of the Roman empire*, Cambridge, 1924.

JONES, H. STUART, "Administration" in *The legacy of Rome*, ed. C. Bailey, Oxford, 1924.

REID, J. S., *Municipalities of the Roman empire*, Cambridge, 1913.

PHILOSOPHY, SOPHISTIC, ASTROLOGY

ARNIM, HANS VON, *Leben und werke des Dio von Prusa*, Berlin, 1898.

BEVAN, E. R., *Stoics and sceptics*, Oxford, 1913.

BOULANGER, ANDRÉ, *Aelius Aristide et la sophistique dans la province d'Asie au IIᵉ. siècle de notre ère*, Paris, 1924.

CUMONT, FRANZ, *Astrology and religion among the Greeks and Romans*, New York and London, 1912.

MARTHA, CONSTANT, *Les moralistes sous l'empire romain*, 5th edition, Paris, 1886.

PAGANISM AND CHRISTIANITY

ANRICH, G., *Das antike mysterienwesen in seinem einfluss auf das christentum*, Göttingen, 1894.

GLOVER, T. R., *The conflict of religions in the early Roman empire*.

HARDY, E. G., " Christianity and the Roman Government," in *Studies in Roman history*, London, 1906.

HATCH, E., *The influence of Greek ideas and usages upon the Christian Church* (Hibbert Lectures, 1888) 8th edition, London, 1901.

MERRILL, E. T., *Essays in early Christian history*, London, 1924.

WOBBERMIN, G., *Religionsgeschichtliche studien zur frage der beeinflussung des urchristentums durch das antike mysterienwesen*, Berlin, 1896.

PAGAN RELIGION.

A.—*General Works*

BEVAN, E. R., *Hellenism and Christianity*, London, 1921.

CUMONT, F., *After life in Roman paganism*, New Haven, 1922.

CUMONT, F., *Les religions orientales dans le paganisme romain*, Paris, 1906 (English translation, Chicago, 1911).

DIETERICH, ALBRECHT, " Der untergang der antiken religion " in *Kleine Schriften*, Leipzig and Berlin, 1911, pp. 448-539.

FOUCART, P., *Des associations religieuses chez les Grecs*, Paris, 1873.

JONG, K. H. E. de, *Das antike mysterienwesen*, 2nd edition, Leiden, 1919.

MOORE, CLIFFORD, H., *The religious thought of the Greeks*, chapters vi-x, 2nd edition, Cambridge, Mass., 1925.

REITZENSTEIN, R., *Die hellenistischen mysterienreligionen*, 2nd edition, Leipzig and Berlin, 1920.

TOUTAIN, J., *Les cultes païens dans l'empire romain*, Paris, 1911.

B.—*Histories*

Aust, E., *Die religion der Römer*, Münster, 1899.
Wissowa, G., *Religion und kultus der Römer*, Iwan Müller's *Handbuch der klassischen altertumswissenschaft*, v, 4.

C.—*Particular Cults*

Cumont, F., *Textes et monuments figurés relatifs aux mystères de Mithra*, Brussels, 1896-9.
Cumont, F., *Les mystères de Mithra*, 3rd edition, Brussels, 1913 (English translation of second edition by McCormack, Chicago, 1910).
Foucart, P., *Les grands mystères d'Eleusis*, Paris, 1900. (The main theory of this book is untenable and much of the evidence in it is handled over-imaginatively. Farnell, *Cults of the Greek states*, vol. iii, which errs if anything in the opposite extreme, will supply a useful corrective on the facts.)
Graillot, *Le culte de Cybèle, Mère des Dieux, à Rome et dans l'empire romain*, Paris, 1912.
Hepding, H., *Attis : seine mythen und sein kult*, Giessen, 1903.
Lafaye, G., *Historie du culte des divinités d'Alexandrie, Serapis, Isis, Harpocrate et Anubis hors de l'Egypte*, Paris, 1884.
Maass, E., *Orpheus, untersuchungen zur griechischen, römischen, altchristlichen jenseitsdichtung und religion*, Munich, 1895.

D.—*Magic, etc.*

Abt, A., *Die apologie des Apuleius von Madaura und die antike zauberei*, Giessen, 1908.
Dieterich, A., *Abraxas*, Leipzig and Berlin, 1891.
Dieterich, A., *Eine Mithrasliturgie*, 2nd edition, Leipzig and Berlin, 1910.
Reitzenstein, R., *Hellenistische wundererzählungen*, Leipzig, 1906.
Reitzenstein, R., *Poimandres*, Leipzig, 1904.

LIST OF TRANSLATIONS

(L) Signifies Loeb Classical Library.
(O) Signifies the Oxford translations published by the
     Clarendon Press.
The works of the Fathers with whom we are immediately
     concerned have been translated by various hands in the
     Ante-Nicene Christian Library, edited by A. Roberts and
     J. Donaldson, and published by T. & T. Clark,
     Edinburgh.
Apocryphal New Testament, M. R. James, Oxford, 1924.
Apostolic Fathers, Kirsopp Lake, (L) two vols. This contains,
     vol. i, *Epistles of Clement, Ignatius, Polycarp, Didache,
     Barnabas*, vol. ii, *Hermas, Martyrdom of Polycarp, Letter
     to Diognetus*.
APULEIUS, *Apologia and Florida*, H. E. Butler, (O)
    Metamorphoses, H. E. Butler, (O), two vols.
     id. W. Adlington, (L), one vol.
AUGUSTINE, *Confessions*, W. Watts, (L), two vols.
Corpus Hermeticum. Hermetica. W. Scott (Oxford Press, 1925).
EPICTETUS, *Discourses and Manual*, P. E. Matheson, 2 vols. (O).
JULIAN, *Works*, W. C. Wright, 3 vols. (L).
JUVENAL and PERSIUS, *Satires*, G. G. Ramsay, (L).
LUCIAN, *Works*, H. W. & F. G. Fowler, 4 vols. (O).
MARCUS AURELIUS, *Meditations*, C. R. Haines, (L).
PERSIUS, see Juvenal.
PETRONIUS, M. Heseltine (L), one vol. with Seneca, *Apocolo-
     cyntosis* by Rouse.
  id. *Cena Trimalchionis*, German translation and notes
     by Friedlaender, 2nd ed., Leipzig, 1906.
PHILOSTRATUS, *Apollonius of Tyana*, J. S. Phillimore, (O), two
           vols.
  id.   *id.* F. C. Conybeare, (L).
  id. *Lives of Sophists*, W. C. Wright, (L), one vol.
          with Eunapius, *Lives of
               Philosophers*.

PLINY, *Natural History*, Bostock and Riley, six vols. (Bohn).

PLINY, *Letters*, Melmoth-Hutchinson (L).

PLUTARCH, The complete *Moralia* are to be found in the xviith century translation " by various hands," the revision of which by Goodwin in the xixth century has run through a number of editions. Unfortunately much of the rendering is loose, and in parts is rather paraphrase than translation.

The selection of Holland's *Moral Essays* in the *Everyman Library* is not very helpful for our purpose, nor is Plutarch, *Selected Essays*, vol. i, by Tucker (O).

On the other hand *Selected Essays* vol. ii by A. O. Prickard (O) contains a majority of the essays which are most important for our purpose, and is also a masterly translation of a text which is often difficult both in form and substance. Unfortunately it does not include the *Isis and Osiris*. For the convenience of English readers I have usually added the paginal reference to this translation when quoting from the treatises which it contains.

PORPHYRY, *Select Works*, Thomas Taylor, London, 1823. This contains the tracts on vegetarianism and on the Cave of the Nymphs. Appended is Taylor's own neo-Platonic treatise upon the wanderings of Ulysses.

SALLUSTIUS, *de diis et mundo*. The text may be found in Mullach, *Fragmenta Philosophorum*, iii; a translation is appended to Professor Murray's, *Four Stages of Greek Religion*, pp. 185-214 (*Five Stages*, etc., Oxford, 1925, pp. 239-267).

SENECA, *Epistulae Morales*, R. M. Gummere (L), to be completed in three volumes; two, containing Letters I-LXV and LXVI-XCII respectively, have hitherto appeared.

STATIUS, *Siluae*, D. A. Slater (O).

SUETONIUS, J. C. Rolfe (L), two vols.

INDEX.